the smart approach to®

# home
# DECORATING

### Third Edition

CRE**A**TIVE
HOMEOWNER®

the smart approach to®

# home
# DECORATING

## Third Edition

CREATIVE HOMEOWNER®, Upper Saddle River, New Jersey

**THE SMART APPROACH TO® HOME DECORATING (3RD EDITION)**

| | |
|---|---|
| SENIOR EDITOR | Kathie Robitz |
| SENIOR GRAPHIC DESIGN COORDINATOR | Glee Barre |
| GRAPHIC DESIGNER | Kathryn Wityk |
| ADDITIONAL PHOTO EDITING | Stan Sudol |
| PHOTO RESEARCHER | Robyn Poplasky |
| EDITORIAL ASSISTANT | Jennifer Calvert |
| INDEXER | Schroeder Indexing Services |
| COVER DESIGN | Kathryn Wityk |
| ILLUSTRATIONS | Vincent Alessi |
| ALL COVER PHOTOGRAPHY | Karyn Millet |

**CREATIVE HOMEOWNER**

| | |
|---|---|
| VICE PRESIDENT AND PUBLISHER | Timothy O. Bakke |
| PRODUCTION DIRECTOR | Kimberly H. Vivas |
| ART DIRECTOR | David Geer |
| MANAGING EDITOR | Fran J. Donegan |

Current Printing (last digit)
10 9 8 7 6 5 4 3

The Smart Approach to® Home Decorating, Third Edition
Library of Congress Control Number: 2006935502
ISBN-10: 1-578011-344-3
ISBN-13: 978-1-58011-344-1

CREATIVE HOMEOWNER®
A Division of Federal Marketing Corp.
24 Park Way
Upper Saddle River, NJ 07458
**www.creativehomeowner.com**

# acknowledgments

For the wealth of information and guidance they have provided, thank you to the American Society of Interior Designers (ASID), the International Society of Interior Designers (ISID), the International Furnishings and Design Association (IFDA), the National Kitchen & Bath Association (NKBA), the National Association of the Remodeling Industry (NARI), and the Color Association of the United States.

# contents

# introduction

Most people don't realize it, but there is an interior designer in them waiting to get out. The problem is that many people are afraid to take the steps that will give their creative persona its freedom. How often have you looked at a magazine or visited the home that was designed by a professional or decorated by someone who seems to have a flair for it, and been intimidated—convinced you could never get those kinds of results on your own? What those folks have that you may not is a knowledge of the basics of design. They know how to manipulate the architecture of a room and then go about adding colors, textures, patterns, lighting, and furniture to make the space truly unique. In *The Smart Approach to® Home Decorating,* you will learn those basics and more.

Because so much of what you do (or hesitate to do) to your home is a matter of confidence, *The Smart Approach to® Home Decorating* explains everything you need to know to make educated decisions about decorating projects. It starts with an easy explanation of space—how to analyze it and work with what you have. Simple instructions for creating your own floor plan, along with furniture templates at the back of the book, let you try out different layouts. A chapter on color, pattern, and texture gives you the inside information you will need to design flawless schemes with paint and fabric. And you'll learn how to select the perfect wall, window, and floor treatments to pull together one cohesive look. If you're debating about whether to buy new furniture or reuse existing pieces, you'll find the answer in the chapter on furniture. Besides describing furniture styles, it offers important advice for judging quality in a piece and when it pays to refinish rather than buy new items.

*The Smart Approach to® Home Decorating* also addresses the special concerns of kitchen and bath design. So that you can make these rooms efficient *and* handsome, you'll find space-planning guidelines from the National Kitchen & Bath Association, as well as a rundown on the latest in cabinetry, fixtures, fittings, and finishing materials. You may also have ques-

tions about decorating as it pertains to specific rooms of the house. The chapter on decorating room by room comes with tips from professional interior designers who offer their advice about foyers, living rooms, family rooms, dining rooms, bedrooms, kitchens, and baths—and how to make each one special. And because today's living extends beyond the front and back doors, *The Smart Approach to® Home Decorating* takes you outside with ideas for giving outdoor living spaces, such as patios, decks, and porches, the same consideration as indoor rooms. To help you with the overall process, Smart Steps in every chapter take you through each phase of the decorating process. There is also a portfolio of inspirational designs in each chapter.

As the renowned celebrity decorator Billy Baldwin once said, "The first rule of decorating is that you can break almost all the rules." *The Smart Approach to® Home Decorating* shows you how to make up your own rules with style and flair.

# 1

# design basics

P rofessional designers always begin a project by first analyzing the space with which they will be working. Things they look at include the size, shape, and intended use of the room. They also pay careful attention to any architectural features, such as molding, windows, and fireplaces, before considering colors, fabrics, and furniture. This chapter will help you think like a professional designer. You will learn about the conceptual nature of space and how to examine your own.

You'll also learn how to manipulate space to make it more functional and what tricks designers use to fool the eye when they are faced with decorating oddly shaped or ill-proportioned rooms. Finally, understanding the basic concepts of design, such as  scale and proportion, will sharpen your eye and help you create pleasing interiors.

The strong geometric lines of this modern home's architecture and industrial details play a large role in shaping the interior design.

Later in this chapter you'll learn how to take accurate measurements as well as how to sketch your ideas on paper just as professional interior designers do. Furniture templates, which you can find in the Appendix, will help you try out different ways to arrange your floor plan. But your first challenge as your own designer will be to become familiar with the basics of design.

# understanding your space

Most of the time homeowners decorate by intuition, and practice makes perfect—sometimes. There are no strict rules to follow; however, every serious student of design begins by learning several fundamental principals relating to space that are always useful when applied practically. These principles include scale, proportion, line, balance, harmony, and rhythm.

## Scale and Proportion

*Scale* and *proportion* work hand in hand. In decorating, scale simply refers to the size of something as it relates to the size of everything else, including people and the space itself. Proportion refers to the relationship of parts or objects to one another based on size—the size of the window is in proportion to the size of the room, for example. Good scale is achieved when all of the parts are proportionately correct relative to each other, as well as to the whole.

Although it is easy to see that something is too large or too small for its place, it takes a deliberate effort to achieve good proportion. Usually, it requires patience and experimentation with various objects and arrangements until something finally looks right, so just keep at it.

## Line

Next to consider is *line*. Simply put, line defines space. Two-dimensional space consists of flat surfaces, such as walls, floors,

and ceilings, which are formed by intersecting lines. Adding depth, or volume, to a flat surface creates three-dimensional space such as a room. However, lines do more than define physical space; they also suggest various qualities. For example:

▥ *Vertical lines* imply strength, dignity, and formality. A good example is a classical column, which always appears stately and strong.

▥ *Horizontal lines,* on the other hand, convey relaxation and security, such as a restful bed or a sturdy platform.

▥ *Diagonal lines,* such as a balustrade or a gable, express motion, transition, and change.

▥ *Curved lines,* like those of a winding path, denote freedom, softness, and sensuality.

As you start to select the furnishings to include in your room's design, look for ways to incorporate a variety of lines into the plan. Most modern rooms are rectilinear. To relieve the repetition of the squares and rectangles inherent in the architecture and make them more interesting, introduce a few curves or diagonals with furniture and accessories.

| RIGHT
**To soften the sometimes severe look of modern design, a designer has countered by introducing round shapes in some furnishings.**

# Balance

*Balance* is another important concept related to space. It refers to the equilibrium among forms in a room. All of the furnishings, large and small, should be distributed evenly throughout the space, not just to one side of the room, for example. With balance, relationships between objects seem natural and comfortable to the eye. For instance, two framed pictures of relatively equal size and weight look appropriate hanging side by side on a wall, whereas the pairing of two pictures of unequal size and weight seems awkward and out of balance. Balanced relationships between objects can be either *symmetrical* or *asymmetrical*.

CLOCKWISE (from above)
The asymmetrical assemblage of objects on a credenza, above, suggests an informal, contemporary sensibility. In a different home with more traditional leanings, an architect designed an oculus for the wall above a bank of windows in a breakfast room, above right. This feature, with classical roots, gracefully balances with the pitch of the ceiling. Finally, the staircase, right, epitomizes the sense of movement suggested by diagonal lines.

■ **Symmetry.** This refers to the same arrangement of parts, objects, or forms on both sides of an imagined or real center line. A good example of symmetry is the placement of a chair and sconce on each side of a fireplace. For the arrangement to be pleasing, however, the chairs must be of equal size, as must the sconces, and placement must be identical. Anything that is even slightly off will be distracting. Because symmetrical arrangements appear formal, they look appropriate in a traditional setting.

■ **Asymmetry.** This refers to the balance between objects of different sizes as the result of placement. For example, picture a grouping of tall, slender candlesticks on one side of a mantelpiece and a short, wide vase on the other. As long as the scale is correct, asymmetry can be every bit as pleasing as symmetry. Because asymmetrical arrangements are informal, they have contemporary sensibility, but they can also offset a too-rigidly formal look.

## Harmony and Rhythm

Two other concepts, *harmony* and *rhythm,* concern creating patterns in space. Harmony is achieved in design when all of the elements relate to one another. In other words, everything coordinates within one scheme or motif. Matching styles, colors, and patterns are good examples. Rhythm refers to repeated patterns. You'll read more about these two concepts in Chapter Two, "Color and Texture," on page 34. For now, keep in mind that harmony pulls a room together, while rhythm keeps interest going around to different areas of a room. The key to creating good harmony and rhythm is balance; always add at least one contrasting element to liven up things.

# creating a plan

Chances are there are some things you like about your existing space, as well as things you don't like. On the plus side, the windows may overlook a beautiful view, or the sunlight may stream into the room at the perfect hour of the day. However, there may be too many doorways and not enough solid walls for placing furniture, or the fireplace or some other large built-in feature, such as a bookcase, may be awkwardly situated. Maybe the room is too small for comfortable entertaining or too large to feel homey. Sometimes the space is oddly shaped; it may be long and narrow, for instance, or the ceilings may seem too high or too low.

Unless structural changes are an option, you'll have to work with the space you have rather than against it. In many cases, the negatives are not so much the structural aspects of the space but the scale of the objects chosen to fill it and how they have been arranged. Follow these Smart Steps to design functional as well as aesthetically pleasing space.

# smart steps
## where to begin

### Step 1 CREATE A NOTEBOOK

Use a loose-leaf binder to keep notes and any other information relating to your project, including your analysis of the existing space and your ideas and goals for it. Later on you can use it to hold paint chips, fabric and wallpaper samples, and pictures from magazines of rooms and furniture styles to which you may want to refer during this or a future decorating project. Begin by listing what you think are the best and worst features of the space. Call attention to important aspects, such as the orientation of the windows at various times of the day. Depending on when you typically use the space, you'll need to know whether it gets sunny in the morning (east-facing windows), at midday (south-facing windows), or in the late afternoon

(west-facing windows). Alternatively, the space may get very little natural light (north-facing windows). If you routinely take a nap in the family room before dinner, think twice about positioning the sofa across from windows with a western exposure, for example. Also, take note of the view. Big, beautiful windows lose much of their allure when there isn't something pleasant outdoors to admire.

Next, look at the layout in terms of permanent features, such as doors and doorways, windows, stairs, and closets. Are there too few? Too many? Does the location of any of them interfere with the layout? Are any shapes awkward? Consider adjacent spaces, too. Do they present problems concerning noise or privacy?

Jot down all of the different activities you expect the space to accommodate, along with any additional storage you may require.

Even if your budget is limited, make a list of all the possible solutions to your space problems. These might include enlarging the layout by building on or incorporat-

**RIGHT**
Positioning a bed so that it doesn't face a window may be necessary if you want to sleep in most mornings. If that's not possible, you can address the problem with light-blocking shades or curtain panels.

**OPPOSITE**
When you're planning a dining area—especially in tight spaces—it's important to think about clearances for comfortable seating, getting up from chairs, and passing and serving hot foods around the table.

ing adjacent existing space, or adding, eliminating, or moving a wall, doorway, or window. Of course, structural changes such as these can be costly and complicated and will require consultation with an architect or qualified remodeler. But the time for considering the possibility of making any one of them is during the early planning phases of your project, not after you've ordered new furniture based on the old layout.

## Step 2 WALK THE SPACE

Go into the room, walk around it, spend time in it. It's a good idea to carry a clipboard and paper so that you can record information to add to your notebook later. Is there an easy flow from one area to another, or are the aisles tight or cluttered? Observe the traffic pattern from all entrances into the room. Notice the direction in which the doors swing. Is the furniture arrangement comfortable and attractive? Is there a focal point—one substantial element, such as a fireplace or a large piece of furniture—that anchors the space? If the space is large, there should be more than one focal point. Are activity areas clearly defined, or do they spill into one another? What's your overall impression? Does the room feel cozy or cramped? Airy or cavernous? Are the furnishings the right

size? Remember, with space, everything is relative. The living room may not be too small; the sofa may be too big for the living room, for example. Sometimes it's the arrangement of furnishings that creates a problem. Pushing seating up against the walls isn't always the best placement. It's better to create small conversational groupings at opposite sides of a room if the space is large, or place one grouping in the center of a small space. Make sure you can move around these areas; traffic should never interrupt them. In later chapters, you'll learn how color, pattern, and light also affect your perception of space.

## Step 3 MEASURE UP

Invest in a good steel measuring tape, and take careful, accurate dimensions of the space. If you can, ask another family member or a friend to help; he or she can hold the end of the tape in one corner while you measure the entire length of a wall in a single step. This eliminates the possibility of the cumulative error that often occurs when measuring a wall in increments. If a window or doorway breaks up the space, measure from one corner of the wall to the outer edge of the opening, and then proceed from the outer edge to the next corner.

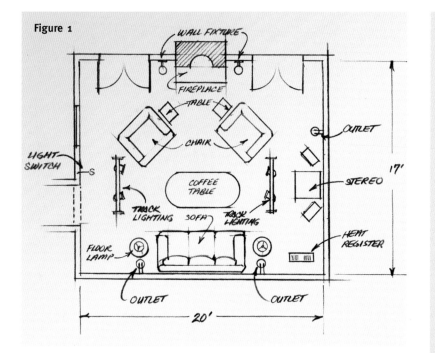

Figure 1

**ABOVE**
An informal sketch of the room you are decorating will help you to get a quick idea of what you can do with the space.

**BELOW**
Refine your plans with a formal drawing, which should provide an accurate scaled representation of the room's features and furniture.

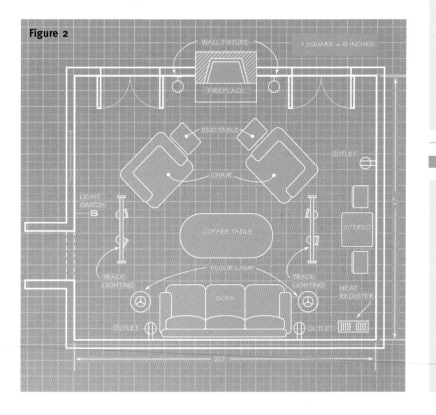

Figure 2

After obtaining the overall dimensions of the room, measure all the openings (doors and windows) and any other fixed features, such as a fireplace, staircase, closets, built-in book-cases, and cabinetry.

While you're at it, measure the existing fur-niture, too—even those pieces you may be thinking of replacing. With a few adjustments to the layout, you may decide to retain some of them. You can refer to these measurements when you're ready to add furniture pieces to your plan.

Another reason to measure all of the furni-ture pieces at this point is so that you can compare their heights with those of the fixed features in the room. Keep in mind that when you draw your sketch and floor plan later, they will reflect only the widths of these objects. For visual interest, you'll want a pleasing balance of tall and short elements in the final design.

## Step 4 MAKE AN INFORMAL SKETCH
As you walk through the space, make a free-hand drawing. Note all dimensions on the plan or in the margin, including the height of the ceiling. (See Figure 1, above left.) Pencil in electrical switches and outlets, cable input, phone jacks, radiators, heat registers, air ducts, and light fixtures, as well. Indicate adjoining rooms or areas on the sketch, too. You don't want to block access to any of them.

## Step 5 DRAW PLANS
Once you evaluate the existing space thor-oughly, get ready to draw the layout to scale on ¼-inch graph paper. Each square will repre-sent one foot. For example, if a wall measures 15 feet, the line you draw to indicate that wall will use 15 squares. To make straight lines and accurate corners, use a T-square; for the arch that symbolizes an open door, use a com-pass. If you don't have these tools on hand, be as careful as possible, and use any straight-edged instrument to draw your lines. You might invest in a handy ruler or yardstick.

## Figure 3

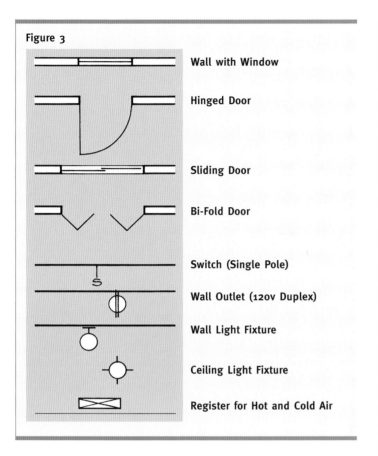

Wall with Window

Hinged Door

Sliding Door

Bi-Fold Door

Switch (Single Pole)

Wall Outlet (120v Duplex)

Wall Light Fixture

Ceiling Light Fixture

Register for Hot and Cold Air

On your drawing, indicate the measurements the same way a designer does: for 3 feet and 2 inches write 3'-2"; for 14 feet and 3¼ inches write 14'-3¼". Figure 3, on this page, shows the symbols to use for the room's major features. When your drawing is complete, you'll have a good idea about how much and what size furniture will fit into the space.

## Step 6 CREATE FURNITURE TEMPLATES

Next, make cutout templates of the furniture, using the same ¼-inch scale. Although you can refer to so-called standard sizes for furniture, be aware that there are variations. One manufacturer may make a 96-inch sofa, while another makes one that is 96½ inches. It's okay

**ABOVE**
If you want to be thorough, include the correct symbols on your plans. Figure 3 shows you how to indicate doors and windows, electrical fixtures, and registers for heat and air.

**RIGHT**
In tight corners, its important to get the most accurate measurements for furniture.

to estimate for your rough sketch, but you should be precise on your final drawing. Although a ½ inch here or there won't make any significant difference to your layout, it's best to use accurate measurements. For new furniture, refer to the manufacturer's spec sheet, which will include dimensions. Don't ever buy a piece of furniture you think looks like the right size. After paying for it and waiting weeks for its delivery, you don't want to find out your guess was wrong. If it's a custom order, you're stuck with it. Even with furniture you already own, don't assume standard size; measure it.

Use the standard furniture symbols in the Appendix to draw your templates. We've drawn each one to scale based on average dimensions, but you'll have to adjust the scale to your furniture's true size.

Cutouts to include in your template kit could be sofa beds, tables, chairs, freestanding bookcases, cupboards, or armoires, chests of drawers, and so on. If you are designing for the kitchen or bath, refer to those chapters and to the templates in the Appendix. Just remember that the appliances and fixtures in these two rooms cannot be moved as easily as pieces of furniture. There are technical considerations with regard to plumbing, electricity, and zoning regulations that affect placement. You may want to put your ideas on paper, but consult a kitchen or bath specialist or a licensed contractor before making actual changes.

ABOVE

In a living room—whatever the style—a balance of personal touches and company comforts always strikes a pleasing note.

# decorating room by room

With scaled templates in hand, you can move things around your scaled layout to see how to group pieces into different arrangements. Always note the traffic pattern in your floor plan when arranging furniture, however, and start by placing the largest, most important pieces first. For major aisles that will be used to move in and through the space, allow at least 3 feet if at all possible. Sometimes you can use furniture as a sort of boundary that prevents traffic through a work or conversation area—seating that is arranged around two or three sides of an area, for example. However, never place furniture in the middle of a major traffic lane.

If the shape of the space bothers you—it's too long, too narrow, too wide, too low, too tall—there are several simple tricks you can play on the eye to camouflage the problem visually. For example, if the room is:

▥ *Long,* divide the space by creating two separate, major groupings of furniture. Use area rugs to anchor each group in the divided space. You can also use square shapes, such as a square area rug, to "widen" the space.

▥ *Narrow,* arrange furniture on the diagonal. In the bedroom, for example, place the bed catty-cornered. In the living room, angle the sofa between two walls. Again, introduce more squares, such as a square coffee table.

▥ *Low,* add height with tall furnishings, such as bookcases, which will make the space feel grand. You might also consider tall lamps, such as torcheres, or window treatments that extend above the window frame and hang from the area just below the ceiling to the floor. Use as many vertical lines in the room as possible, even on wall and fabric treatments. Vertical-stripe wallpaper or curtains are good examples. (See Chapter 2, "Color and Pattern," on page 34.)

▥ *Tall,* lower the scale of the space by incorporating more horizontal lines in the room. Install molding one-half or three-quarters of the way up the walls to visually shorten them. Hang pictures lower on the wall. (See "Distinctive Touches," in Chapter 6, on page 132.)

**BELOW LEFT**
Tall bedposts illustrate how vertical lines can allude to height in a master bedroom situated under a pitched roof.

**BELOW RIGHT**
A tight grouping of furniture in a large living room feels cozy and keeps traffic out of the conversation area.

## Focal Points

There has to be one dramatic element in a room that draws your immediate attention. This is the focal point. If you are lucky, it may be a distinctive architectural element, such as a fireplace, a built-in cabinet, a staircase or entry door in a foyer, or a spectacular window. If the room does not have one, create a focal point with furnishings. This could be a beautifully dressed bed; a large central seating group; dramatic window treatments on an otherwise undistinguished window; a massive table, armoire, or cabinet; or wall art, particularly if it is highlighted. (For more information, see Chapter 3, "The Right Light," on page 56.) The focal point should be one of the first elements penciled onto your plan.

## Multipurpose Space

No matter how much space we have, most of us complain about needing more. One way to get it is to use a room or an area for more than one purpose. For example, the kitchen may also serve as a home office or family room; a hallway is another spot that can double as an office; even a living room can serve more than one function, whether that of a part-time dining room, guest room, or study. Seemingly impossible spaces can be adjusted to accommodate more than one function as well. Furniture that folds up when not in use is helpful. One excellent example is a drop-leaf dining table that can be stored unobtrusively against a wall in the living room, then opened up when necessary. If you entertain overnight

## smart tip  CLEARING OUT

If you are having trouble creating a pleasing arrangement of furniture in a room, it can help to remove all of the contents and start from scratch. This is a good idea if you have trouble picturing things on paper or if you aren't going to buy a lot of new furniture and just need a fresh start. If at all possible, strip the room down completely, removing all of the furnishings, including window treatments, rugs, wall art, and accessories. This way you can observe the true architectural nature of the space without distractions that influence your perceptions. For example, minus the trappings of curtains, you can see that two windows may be slightly different sizes or installed too close to a corner. Other things you may notice might be odd corners, uneven walls, radiators or heating registers that are conspicuously located, or any other quirky features that are unique to your home.

   Don't be in a rush to start filling up the room again. Live with it empty for a few days so that you can really get a sense of the space. Then slowly begin to bring things back inside, starting with the largest objects. You'll know immediately when you've crossed the line with something that doesn't belong. But you have to be willing to pull back and pare down.

**RIGHT**
In this studio apartment, a monochromatic neutral palette precludes any sense of clutter. A fireplace anchors the sitting area and serves as a focal point in the space.

guests occasionally but not often enough to reserve a special room for the purpose, buy a convertible sofa. Keep extra linens in an antique trunk that can also act as a coffee table, or purchase a large ottoman with a hinged top that opens up to roomy storage. In a dining room/office, use a folding screen to hide electronic office equipment when not in use, and house stationery and other supplies in the bottom half of the china cabinet. Another option, when the home office is shared space with another room in the house, is to purchase a computer armoire.

**RIGHT**
A small desk fits snugly in a corner. Like the other furnishings, it is painted a pale neutral color.

**ABOVE**
A full bed has been situated at an angle to take up the least amount of wall space, leaving room for a chest of drawers that faces the fireplace on the opposite side of the room.

You can also divide space with furniture. Remember: there is no rule that says all of it has to be arranged against a wall. Use tables or upholstered pieces to delineate separate functional areas of a room. Painting one wall a different color to visually separate one area from the other is another means of dividing space. If the front door opens directly into the living room, situate an open-shelving unit perpendicular to the door to create an entry area. If you've always wanted a quiet little getaway in your home but don't have the extra room, use a landing or the end of a hallway. A comfortable chair, a small table, and a lamp are all you need for a little peace and quiet with a good book or a CD player and headphones. What about a corner in the bedroom? Use your imagination and try out other ways to make the most out of every square inch of space in your home.

As much as you may want to enlarge the functional capabilities of space by dividing it up into separate zones, don't overdo it with a series of stuffy little warrens, either. To keep the overall appearance of the space free-flowing and balanced, you'll have to provide at least one visual link that moves the eye along. There are a few different ways to do this. One is to use the same palette throughout. You may want to vary the intensity of the color from area to area, but sticking to the same basic hue creates a cohesive backdrop for everything. Another option is to "stretch" space by using the same floor treatment, so that there is no separation as you move from one area to another.

## Furniture Placement by Room

There are recommended guidelines for clearances you should follow when arranging furniture. Just remember, they are not strict rules. You might try using them as starting points or to analyze an existing space. Then rework some things to suit your taste and lifestyle. The important thing is to make the room comfortable for the people who use it.

**LEFT**
Make use of vertical space. These built-in beds are nothing more than sturdy platforms and twin-size mattresses stacked in a corner and personalized with color.

**OPPOSITE**
Need a reader's corner or a spot for knitting? Position a comfortable chair out of the way, then add indirect lighting, soft cushions, and a throw for a catnap.

CIFIC MODERN
BY THE SEA
NIEMEYER HOUSES

LEFT
A comfortable mix of fur-
niture makes this living
room inviting. When a
crowd gathers, some
pieces can be rearranged
into several groupings.

BELOW
A generously propor-
tioned coffee table is
great for entertaining. Its
round shape is easy to
walk around even when
the room is crowded.

OPPOSITE
A family room can be
informal and attractive.
A built-in cabinet hand-
somely hides entertain-
ment equipment when its
not in use.

## ▥ Living Rooms and Family Rooms.

The kitchen may be the heart of a home, but the living room is where people can put their best foot forward. It's also the place, along with the family room, where many of us relax in front of the TV, listen to music, read, or just hang out. It's important, therefore, to have an attractive, comfortable arrangement of furniture in the living room, whether you use it only on occasion or everyday.

If you entertain often, rate the existing room's ability to accommodate large as well as small groups. Professionals recommend a distance of 4 to 10 feet between the sofa and chairs. Anything less is too cramped; anything more discourages easy conversation. For a comfortable amount of legroom, the coffee table should be positioned between 14 and 18 inches from the sofa.

When there's a large party, make sure there is space for guests to move around or break up into small groups. Most designers suggest one major seating area created by grouped upholstered pieces, plus several lightweight portable chairs located around the room. When company comes, these chairs can be moved around for socializing. Folding chairs are an inexpensive—and easily stored—option for entertaining, with a variety of styles and slipcovers available to suit your room.

office supplies, or files tucked away until you need them.

■ **Dining Rooms and Kitchen Eat-in Areas.** Certainly the table is the focus of any dining space, which could be a large, formal room, a niche in the kitchen, or even a spot in the corner of the living room. When analyzing your existing dining space, your first question should be, "Is seating around the table comfortable?" Good space planning calls for suitable room to get up, down, and around easily. A seated adult occupies a depth of about 20 inches, but needs 12 to 16 inches more to pull back the chair and rise. Placing chairs at angles to the wall can save a few inches, but you'll need either a round or square table for this strategy. Rectangular tables require 24 inches per person and 32 to 36 inches of clearance between the table and the wall. On the serving side, the table-to-wall distance should be at least 44 inches.

■ **Bedrooms.** It may be your adult retreat, where you get away from the kids, or it may be your teenager's domain, where adults are off limits; nevertheless the bedroom is primarily the place one sleeps, so it's only logical to begin designing this space by placing the bed. For your comfort, as well as for safety, there are minimum clearances recommended for the space around the bed. When two people share the room, there must be an aisle that is spacious enough for either party to get in and out of bed easily and without bumping into an open door or having to climb over another person.

Begin by measuring the floor space on each side of the bed. The minimum clearance between the edge of the bed and the wall should be 24 inches. In addition, allow at least 36 inches between the edge of the bed and any door that opens into the room. If you place two beds side by side, maintain at least 18 inches between them. This will accommodate a small night table and a pathway for the average adult to swing out of bed and walk between the beds comfortably.

Now that you understand how to analyze and design comfortable, safe, attractive space, you're ready for the next chapter: how to use a designer's most powerful decorating tool—color.

Do you watch TV in the room? If so, grab your measuring tape again. For optimal viewing, the distance between the TV monitor and the seating located opposite it should be three times the size of the screen. In other words, to comfortably watch TV on a 30-inch screen, you should sit 90 inches away from it.

Is there a focal point? All of the furnishings should take their cue from that important feature in terms of scale, proportion, and balance.

If you use the living room as a part-time home office, guest room, or dining area, look at how your existing arrangement is working now. Is the space organized in a way that keeps each function from interfering with another? Ideally, there should be a traffic lane that is at least 3 feet wide to move from one zone to another. If you don't have that much room, look for other ways to contain things. Your plan may have to include an armoire or chest that can keep items such as extra pillows and blankets,

# design workbook
## RELAXED ELEGANCE

## high drama

A vaulted ceiling ceates theatrical excitement in this converted outbuilding. Understated, but elegant furnishings refine the rustic charm of the space.

## counterpoise

Single French doors positioned on either side of the fireplace, a focal point, provide access to and views of the garden from the building's formal sitting area.

## light focus

In the kitchen just behind the dining table, top left, a chandelier has been centered above the island, anchoring the food preparation area stylishly.

## architectural detail

Pretty scrollwork dresses up an iron gate-inspired entry door, left. Like all rounded or curved lines, the curlicues soften the appearance of the heavy metal frame.

# design workbook
## VERSATILE ARRANGEMENT

### with the flow

This Southern California family room opens to an adjacent outdoor living area, so there must be an easy flow between the two spaces.

### in the mix

Furniture that can be moved between the two spaces suits the family's lifestyle. Groupings cater to various activities. (See also top left.)

### calls for attention

The fireplace, far left, angled and to the side of the wall-mounted TV, is a focal point in the large room. Artwork above the mantel draws attention.

### pattern & rhythm

A few exuberant prints, such as the chairs' upholstery fabric, keep the eye moving around the large, otherwise neutral-toned space.

# 2

# color & pattern

CREATING EXCITEMENT  INTRODUCING PATTERN
TEXTURE  YOUR COLOR SCHEME  DESIGN WORKBOOK

The color palette you choose will set the tone for your home decor. If you are a traditionalist decorating a formal living room, you may find yourself drawn to a subdued scheme. A kid's play room, on the other hand, may call for something lively. Of course, the size of a room and its light levels will also play a part in your choices. They not only affect color schemes but may influence your decisions regarding *pattern* and adding bits of *texture* to a room. Working with color, pattern enlivens an interior with movement, creating a measured flow between the elements in a room. It can also establish a theme or a particular decorative period. A third element, texture, is like a visual caesura, a pause that prevents a scheme from becoming boring. It, too, can suggest mood—rustic, luxurious, or sleek, for example. Here's how to competently use all three.

Cool, playful colors, subtly repeated throughout this large, modern space, tie together three distinct areas while adding a retro feel overall.

# creating excitement

**Intensity and Value.** Colors, or hues, may vary in their intensity—that is, the level of the color's purity or saturation. The primaries, secondaries, and tertiaries represent colors at their full intensity. There are several ways to lessen a color's intensity. You can lighten it with white to form a tint, darken it with black to create a shade, or add gray to arrive at a tone. In addition to changing the intensity of a color, these methods affect what is known as the color's value. Value is the lightness or darkness of the color. Tinting gives a color a lighter value, and shading, of course, makes it a darker value.

Color is the most versatile tool a designer can employ. It is both the easiest way to improve space and an effective way to alter it. It is the most exciting decorating element. Yet many of us find the power of color intimidating and, fearful of stepping into new territory, stick with neutrals. The palette for walls is often white or cream—colors that work fine as a backdrop for more richly hued furnishings but are less successful in rooms with neutral-colored pieces. Aside from the strength of color itself, the enormity of color choices available in paints, wallpapers, fabrics, and flooring options can also overwhelm us, making us retreat to the safety of white for the walls and neutrals throughout. So how do you break the monotony and establish an exciting color scheme? First you'll have to overcome your fear of color, then narrow your choices. An explanation of the color wheel is a good place to begin.

## How Color Works

Light reflected through a prism creates a rainbow, known as the color spectrum. Each band of color blends into the next, from red to violet. The longest band is red, then orange, yellow, green, blue, and violet. Modern color theory takes those bands from the spectrum and forms them into a circle, called the *color wheel,* to show the relationship of each color to one another.

The color wheel includes *primary colors* (red, blue, and yellow), *secondary colors* (green, orange, violet), and *tertiary colors* (red-blue, blue-red, and so on). Secondary colors are made by mixing two primaries together, such as blue and yellow to make green. A primary color, such as blue, and a secondary color, such as green, can be mixed to make a tertiary color—in this case, turquoise.

# color wheel combinations

The color wheel is the designer's most useful tool for pairing colors. Basically, it presents the spectrum of pigment hues as a circle. The primary colors (yellow, blue, and red) are combined in the remaining hues (orange, green, and purple). The following are the most-often used configurations for creating color schemes.

**Basic Color Wheel**          **Analogous**

**Complements**          **Split Complements**

**Triad**          **Tetrad**

## Putting the Color Wheel to Work

Now that you've got it in front of you, use the color wheel to help you envision certain color combinations. An analogous scheme involves neighboring colors that share an underlying hue.

*Complementary* colors lie opposite each other on the color wheel and often work well together. What, you ask? A red and green living room? Well, yes, in full intensity that might be hard to stomach, but consider a rosy pink room with sage green accents. The same complements in varying intensities can make attractive, soothing combinations. A *double complementary* color scheme involves an additional set of opposites, such as green-blue and red-orange.

Alternatively, you could go with a *monochromatic* scheme, which involves using one color in a variety of intensities. That way your room's color scheme is sure to be harmonious. When developing a monochromatic scheme, lean toward several tints or several shades, but avoid too many contrasting values—that is, combinations of tints and shades. This can make your scheme look uneven.

If you want a more complex palette of three or more colors, look at the *triads* formed by three equidistant colors, such as red/yellow/blue orgreen/purple/orange. A *split complement* is composed of three colors—one primary or intermediate and two colors on either side of its opposite. For example, instead of teaming purple with yellow, shift the mix to purple with orange-yellow and yellow-green. Lastly, four colors equally spaced around the wheel, such as yellow/green/purple/red, form a tetrad. If such combinations sound a bit like Technicolor, remember that colors intended for interiors are rarely undiluted. Thus yellow might be cream; blue-purple, a dark eggplant; and orange-red, a muted terra-cotta or whisper-pale peach. With less jargon, the color combinations fall into these two basic camps:

■ *harmonious,* or *analogous,* schemes, derived from nearby colors on the wheel—less than halfway around; and

■ *contrasting,* or *complementary,* schemes, involving directly opposite slices of the pie.

## The Psychology of Color

Few people get past kindergarten without acquiring a favorite color. Over the years tastes change and you may appreciate more than one hue, but most people can still name a preference when pressed. Picking out a few colors you like best—colors that make you feel happy—is as good a place as any to begin establishing your color scheme because it is largely an emotional decision. In narrowing down your choices and combining them with the preferences of those who will share the space, try to include both warm and cool colors. The warm hues—reds, yellows, oranges, peaches, and creams—are generally most effectively used in rooms where there will be a lot of activity because they make us feel livelier. Kitchens, office spaces, even bedrooms if you're a morning person, are all natural places for brighter, warmer, more uplifting hues. Cool colors tend to be more soothing and restful. You may want to reserve your blues, greens, and lilacs for the rooms where you go to unwind.

However, color responses are subjective and changeable. The pervasive use of green in schools and hospitals in decades past, for example, has prompted a visceral dislike of the color's "institutional" shades for many people. Some studies have suggested that red rooms may heighten blood pressure and yellow rooms make the occupants more argumentative.

Sharp contrasts or schemes that feature bold colors can be fun in rooms used only occasionally, but they can become tiresome on a daily basis. Of course, these are general guidelines. Some people never tire of a favorite color—even if it is repeated in every room of the house.

■ **Cultural Effects.** You may be less aware of how culture and era shape color responses. In America and much of Europe,

ABOVE
Artwork and a few other decorative accessories in this modern interior enliven the understated look with subtle but effective color accents.

blue is a perennial favorite color, while red ranks first in other locales, such as Spain and Japan. Western brides dress in joyful white—a mourning color in some Far Eastern societies. Even within one culture, the accustomed palette changes. In the Victorian era, early Impressionist paintings shocked viewers, who saw them as garishly bright. Yet to jaded eyes, the same paintings seem restfully pastel. Even closer to present times, you might chuckle or wince at colors and combinations from a decorating guide dated 1955 or 1969—colors that struck the readers of the day as perfectly keen or groovy. And a few decades hence, our own most stylish efforts may suffer a similar fate.

The pull of comfortable, traditional colors and the push for novel, fashionable choices have shaped the American palette since the nation's early days. But the home decorator can hold to one constant: human beings seek variety in their surroundings. Light colors seem upbeat, clean, and lively but turn cold and monotonous if unrelieved. Dark colors are plush and enclosing but in excess can turn gloomy. Midtones are attractively comfortable, but a room decked completely in midtones can be dull and monotonous. Bright, saturated hues are eye-catching accents but uncomfortably demanding in quantity. In short, one could do worse than to follow the old decorating maxim, "Something dark, something light, something dull, something bright."

## Altering Space with Color

As a designer, you can use warm colors and cool colors quite effectively to manipulate the way a room is perceived visually, as well as emotionally. For instance, you can cozy up a large room with warm colors. Because warm colors appear to advance, walls swathed in sunny hues seem closer together and make a room feel more intimate. Conversely, cool tones and neutrals appear to recede and can be used to open up a smaller space.

These color tricks can be employed more subtly as well. For example, suppose you've got your heart set on a cheery, predominantly yellow living room. But it's a smaller room and you'd also like to expand it visually as much as is possible. Do you have to switch your palette to blues and neutrals? Not necessarily. The less-intense version of a color will generally reduce its apparent tendency to advance or recede. Investigate the other intensities, the shades and tones of yellow, to see whether there's one that does the job.

Generally speaking, sharp contrasts have the same impact as a dark color, reducing perceived space. Monochromatic schemes enlarge space. Neutrals of similar value make walls retreat and can flow unobtrusively from room to room.

■ **Light and Color.** Lighting can change color dramatically as well. The quality of natural light changes through the course of the day, too. (See Chapter Three, "The Right Light," on page 56.) Make sure you consider this when choosing a color. Paint some test samples on the wall, and watch how the colors change depending on the position of the sun. Do they need to be adjusted? Rooms with a northern exposure will be filled with bluer, cooler light, which weakens warm colors but intensifies cool hues. Ones facing south will have a warmer, yellowish light. That light can have the opposite effect on colors. All in all, colors interact in complex ways, so these generalizations are not absolute, but they're good starting points for making initial judgements.

LEFT
A bold tangerine hue is a standout on the back wall of this recessed display area, drawing attention in contrast to off-white walls.

# introducing pattern

You can add pattern to a room in a variety of ways— wallpaper and fabric being the two most popular. Because pattern is largely a vehicle for color, the same rules that guide the selection of color effectively narrow the field when it comes to selecting a pattern or complement of patterns. The designer's old friend, scale, from Chapter One, is the other important consideration when picking patterns.

Large-scale patterns are like warm colors in that they appear to come toward you. They can create a lively and stimulating atmosphere and generally make a large space seem cozier. In a small space, handle a large-scale pattern with care or it can overpower the room. That doesn't mean rule it out completely, but perhaps use it sparingly. Small-scale patterns appear to recede, making small spaces seem larger. They can also be used effectively to camouflage odd angles or corners that you find in attic ceilings. Try a subtle, non-directional pattern for this kind of application. In a large room, the effect of a small pattern can be bland. From a distance, it may read as a single color. If you're using a small-scale pattern in a large space, pick one with vibrant colors.

**BELOW**
For a traditional-style interior, a designer chose a subtle print for the sofa, then added interest by accenting with deep crimson and floral-patterned pillows.

**OPPOSITE**
For a less formal and somewhat more youthful look, multicolored horizontal stripes in contrasting tones of red-orange and green-blue energize the otherwise subdued palette.

**How to Mix Patterns.** Mixing patterns can be intimidating, in part because it's subjective to experimentation, judgement, and "eye." Responding to this fear, manufacturers provide an abundance of coordinated wallcovering and fabric collections, available through wallpaper books and in-store design services. Such collections, selected by professionals, can save you a lot of legwork and still leave scope for your own input. If you prefer to mix your own patterns, try to match the scale of the pattern to that of the area over which it is to be used. The general rule is to use large prints on large-sized furnishings, medium prints on medium pieces, and small prints on accent pieces. A sofa, for instance, looks better than a dining room chair with a large-scale pattern. A delicate stencil makes a better border for a tabletop than on a wall. But these rules are not hard and fast.

Another trick for mixing patterns is to provide links of scale, motif, and color. The regularity of checks, stripes, textural looks, and geometrics, particularly if small-scale and low-contrast, tends to make them easy-to-mix "neutral" patterns. A small floral can play off a thin ticking stripe, while a cabbage-rose chintz may require a bolder stripe as a same-scale foil. You may choose to use the same or similar patterns in varying sizes or develop a theme by focusing on florals, geometrics, or ethnic prints.

The most effective link is shared colors or a similar level of intensity between the prints. A solid-color companion that pulls out a hue shared by two prints provides another connection. Exact matches are the backbone of manufacturers' coordinated collections. But to arrive at your own personal mix, you can interpret the principle loosely, and experiment to see which pattern combinations work for you.

OPPOSITE
The texture introduced into this dining room by rattan chairs has a relaxed, casual appeal. The material, which is a type of palm, is durable yet flexible, allowing it to be woven, here into a herringbone pattern, for example.

RIGHT
A heavily weathered clay pot reveals layers of paint colors. The texture of the chipped finish has a sensual quality and the uneven finish adds character to its design.

# texture

Texture doesn't have the obvious impact on a room that color and pattern wield. But how a material feels, as well as how it looks, does influence room design. Incorporating a variety of textures in a room adds to its richness in a way that's most comparable to the subtle inclusion of the line varieties discussed in Chapter One. A mix of textures plays upon the senses and adds another layer of complexity and sophistication to a design scheme. As with every aspect of decorating, mixing textures involves a balancing act. To give a room a distinctive character, you might let one texture predominate the room, but the right contrast can make the scheme more intriguing.

# Types of Texture

The easiest way to incorporate texture into a design is with fabric. Brocades and damasks, moirés and chenilles, tweeds and chintzes—all conjure up different looks and sensations. Fabrics, however, are just the beginning. Tactile interest can emanate from any material or surface that is coarse or smooth, hard or soft, matte or shiny. Coarse and matte surfaces, such as stone, rough-hewn wood, stucco, corduroy, or terra cotta, absorb light and sound. Glossy and smooth surfaces, which range from metal and glass to silk and enamel, reflect light.

■ **Spatial Effects.** To start adding texture into your design, assess your room's needs. Does it lack warmth? Or does it feel too closed in? Texture affects a room spatially. Coarse or matte surfaces will make a room seem smaller and cozier. A living room of only glossy surfaces can seem cold and impersonal without a velvet slipcover on the sofa to add warmth and contrast. Smooth and shiny surfaces do the reverse—they make a room look larger and brighter. A study that feels too stuffy, for instance, may benefit from the addition of a mirror or a glass-topped table. Light reflected off of either object will brighten the space.

ABOVE
Various types of textiles, such as the rug, bedding, and even the upholstery in this bedroom, offer different tactile and visual experiences that enrich the design.

■ **Pattern and Color.** Keep in mind that texture also affects pattern and color. With fabrics, texture can either soften or enhance a pattern. For instance, patterns are crisp on glazed chintz but are blurred on terrycloth. A coarsely textured surface tones down the intensity of a paint color, and gives the color subtle variations. High-gloss surfaces increase the intensity of a color. Think of how the gray color of a tweed jacket looks "heathered" and muted. On a silk shirt, however, the same gray color would look shimmery and more intense—a completely different effect. Every room has an existing element of texture—a stone fireplace, brass hardware, a gleaming hardwood floor, a stuccoed wall, or an iridescent tile border—that you may want to take into consideration when planning your design.

Relatively featureless rooms may be improved by adding contrasting textures. Wallpaper comes in a variety of textures—foils, flocks, embossed papers, and real fabric, to list a few. Paint can be applied in matte or gloss finishes and special painted effects, discussed in detail in Chapter Five, can add texture. Tile and other architectural embellishments, such as cornices and moldings, can also imbue a room with more tactile richness.

Window treatments are another natural outlet for texture. Fabric choices for draperies and curtains, as well as the fabrics and other materials available for blinds and shades, are enormous and varied. Texture can be enhanced by the way fabric is hung. Pleating, for example, creates a play of light and shadow. You can combine layers of fabric or fabric and blinds to show off different textures.

On the floor, carpets can be smooth, knobby, sculpted, or flecked for visual texture. Rugs, rush, coir, sisal, wood, or cork are warming texture options. Quarry tiles, ceramic tiles, marble, and slate make a room cooler. Varying the materials can make the effect more interesting. An Oriental rug over a varnished wood floor is a classic example.

**BELOW LEFT**
The wall's dark paint color and its matte finish allow the room's metallic elements to take the spotlight. For contrast, a light-colored shag rug offers a soft surface.

**BELOW RIGHT**
By comparison, a wall that's been painted, then lacquered with a high-sheen finish provides the drama in this room as the soft furnishings take a back seat while lending comfort.

# your color scheme

Y ou've analyzed your room, you've determined how you want it to function, and you'd like to make it restful and soothing. As luck would have it, blue is your favorite color. So now what? How do you get from there to choosing the "right" shade of blue, deciding where to use it, picking a coordinating print, selecting upholstery fabrics and window treatments, and then ensuring plenty of tactile richness to boot? Take it slowly, in steps—Smart Steps, that is.

## smart steps
### thoughtful choices

### Step 1 MAKE A SAMPLE BOARD

One way designers organize the colors, patterns, and textures that they plan to use in a room is to create a sample board. The white, foam-cored presentation board sold in art supply stores, measuring at least 8½ x 11 inches, is ideal for this purpose. Attach to the board with rubber cement (or tack to it with removable sticky material) any swatches of fabric, wallpaper patterns, or paint color chips you're considering. Keep the swatches and other items in the same proportion on the board as they would be in the room. For example, a paint sample that you're considering for the walls will be quite large, whereas an accent color will take up far less space. The fabric you plan to use on the sofa should take up more space on the board than one you're thinking about for a small window treatment or accent pillows.

As a general rule of thumb, designate about two thirds of your board for wall and ceiling treatments, and reserve the remaining third for samples of colors, patterns, and materials you plan to use on the floors and furnishings. Add and remove things as you experiment with different looks, colors, and prints, and be certain to review your choices in the room where you will be using them at different times of day, under both natural and artificial lighting conditions.

**TOP AND BOTTOM**
This rich-looking bedroom combines highly saturated colors with busy fabric prints. It's a highly sophisticated look that succeeds because the fabrics are linked by color and used proportionately.

# design materials

As you have likely gleaned from this discussion of color, pattern, and texture, designers rely on certain materials to carry various effects into a living space. Most design materials have specific functions and applications where they are preferable to other options in their category. In flooring materials, for example, ceramic tile may perform well in a kitchen setting but not as effectively in a living room. Within many categories, there are varying degrees of quality. Throughout this book, the appropriate applications of different materials and tips on how to judge the quality of some materials is addressed in pertinent chapters. In Chapter Four, for instance, you'll find an examination of flooring materials. Chapter Five contains an in-depth coverage of paints and wallpaper options. Here, because textiles are such integral players when it comes to delivering color, pattern, and texture, is a brief overview of some common decorating fabrics and their make-up.

- **Brocade:** Often weighty fabric woven of silk, cotton, wool, or a combination. A raised, floral design (called a jacquard) is its distinguishing feature. Typically used for upholstery and draperies.
- **Cambric:** A plain, tightly woven linen or cotton fabric with a sheen on one side. Curtain panels, pillows, and lightweight slipcovers can be successfully made from cambric.
- **Canvas:** A course, woven cotton material, available in heavy or lighter gauges. Canvas is strong and inexpensive. Will hold up for upholstery, slipcovers, or draperies.

- **Chintz:** Cotton fabric, often in floral or other all-over print, coated with a resin that gives it a sheen. Dry cleaning is necessary. Used for pillows, curtains, and some upholstery.
- **Cotton duck:** A cream-colored cotton that comes in various weights. Ideal for no-sew curtains. *See canvas.*
- **Crewel:** Plain woven, natural cotton fabric with wool embroidery. Traditionally used for upholstery and draperies.
- **Damask:** Another jacquard material made of cotton, silk, wool, or a combination with raised satin design. Widely used for draperies and upholstery.

- **Gingham:** Plain-weave cotton fabric woven in block or checked prints. Its crisp look makes it popular for trim, curtain panels, draperies, tablecloths, and bedspreads.
- **Lace:** Cotton or cotton-polyester blend material featuring open-work designs. Frequently used for curtains.
- **Linen:** An unusually strong fabric made from processed flax. Linen works best when used simply, such as tab-topped curtains.
- **Moiré:** A finish on a silk or acetate fabric intended to resemble watermarking. Washing removes the finish; dry-clean only. Depending on thickness, good for draperies and upholstery.
- **Muslin:** A course, plain weave cotton in white or cream. It is often sheer, and not as heavy as canvas is. Used for sheeting, curtains, and light slipcovers.

- **Organdy:** Light cotton washed in acid for a crisp finish. Used for trimming and curtains.
- **Satin:** A silk, linen, or cotton weave with a glossy surface and dull back, sometimes with a moiré finish. Satin isn't particularly durable, but fine for draperies and light-use upholstery.
- **Silk:** A soft, shiny fabric made from the fine fibers produced by silkworms. It is a sophisticated fabric that is favored for swags and formal drapery.
- **Taffeta:** Silk and acetate weave that appears shiny and maintains shape. Useful for trimmings and draperies.
- **Tapestry:** A heavy, woven cloth that imitates handmade tapestries. Often used for upholstery, accent pillows, and wall hangings.

- **Toile de Jouy:** An eighteenth-century cotton or linen fabric printed with pastoral scenes. First produced in the French town of Jouy. Used for curtains, upholstery, and accent pillows.
- **Velvet:** Made from cotton, viscose rayon, or polyester, velvet features a smooth, iridescent-looking pile. Velvet is available in different piles. Fine velvets are best when used for curtain panels; heavy velvets are appropriate for furniture upholstery.

## Step 2 DEVELOP YOUR PALETTE

Bringing to bear all you now know about color (how it affects mood, how it can seemingly expand or decrease space, what you like, and what your family likes), pick one. Frequently, you can establish your color based on elements already in the room that you don't plan to replace—an upholstered furnishing, a carpet, or even a favorite painting. Once you determine the main color, look at its complement or triad on the color wheel, and pick an accent or two. If you're painting your walls, go to the paint store and get sample chips of each of your colors in every intensity you can find. If you're planning to wallpaper, borrow the books with the kinds of patterns you like, and pore through them until you find something that works. Often you can pull your accent colors from the wallpaper pattern that you choose.

## Step 3 CONSIDER MIXING FABRIC PATTERNS

Most wallpaper makers offer fabrics to coordinate with their wallpaper patterns. Consider these, but also visit fabric stores to find other coordinating prints for upholstery and window treatments. Don't forget to check out ready-made slipcovers and window treatments, too. To experiment with mixing patterns, start simply. Geometric patterns often mix well together—stripes with checks or plaids or dots. It is always easier to mix patterns that contain one or more common colors. Two different patterns can be linked by color, fabric weight, texture, and degree of formality. You can mix patterns in different scales, but don't go overboard. Use a large pattern on a large element, such as a sofa, smaller prints for windows, and something smaller still for pillows. Same-size patterns fight for attention. As a

**ABOVE**
Cheerful yellow, in a soft golden shade, brings sunshine into this living room. The white fireplace wall and cabinet keep it from looking too hot in this airy space.

general rule, a good mix includes small-, medium-, and large-scale prints. Checks with stripes, dots with plaids, and florals with geometrics are all possibilities when coordinated tastefully. Designers develop a knack for picking eye-catching combinations—and through trial and error, you will, too. Look through magazines or wallpaper books for ideas. In any room where you're mixing patterns, it is important to give your eyes a place to rest. Be sure to add solid-color furnishings to the room as well.

**OPPOSITE TOP**
Pale cool blue accented with white has a restful quality that makes it a lovely choice for today's spa-inspired bathrooms.

**OPPOSITE BOTTOM LEFT**
Warm red has an energetic, animated quality. It sets a welcoming tone in this mudroom.

**OPPOSITE BOTTOM RIGHT**
Soft green appears unpretentious and relaxing in this guest room. It pairs beautifully with a blue-and-white print.

## Step 4 PICK ONE PRINT AND STICK WITH IT

If mixing does not appeal to you and you prefer to use one bold print, make sure the scale is large enough to carry the room. Paint the walls a saturated color picked out from the fabric. Use a second color for other large upholstered pieces or window treatments. Then pick the sharpest, brightest hue from the pattern for accents. Add variety with textiles—a rug, for example. Balance the pattern throughout the room.

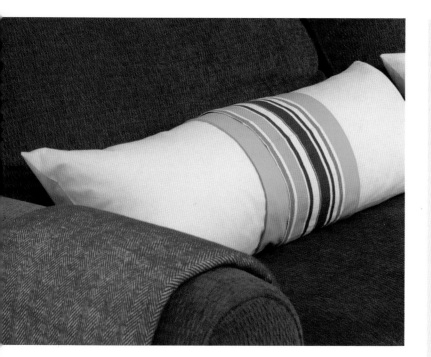

## Step 5 CUSTOMIZE YOUR PLAN

Color schemes aren't one-size-fits-all. The most successful ones are custom-tailored for a particular space. In your clear-eyed assessment of your needs, here are some aspects to consider:

■ Physical Space. Consider not just whether the room is large or small but how the dimensions drive the plans. In a big room, would you rather scale down for a more intimate mood or emphasize the room's lofty spaciousness? In tight quarters, will you pull out every space-enhancing trick or bring on rich, deep colors to create a cozy "jewel box"? Is the space disjointed by doorways, windows, and jogs, asking to be unified in a smooth sweep of color? Or is it a bland box that begs for detail? There may be elements you want to downplay. What are the room's finer features—the ready-made focal points?

Is the room located in a suburban ranch, a town

ABOVE
Soft-to-the-touch textiles, such as chenille or wool, bring comfort into a room.

OPPOSITE
A sophisticated monochromatic palette presents a formal attitude of understated grace in this dining room. Dried mophead hydrangea hint at blue and green as the only color accents.

house, a clean-lined apartment, a country house, or a beach bungalow? The color scheme may reflect a distinctive architectural period or regional character. You don't have to listen to the house's suggestions—an East Coast apartment can have a Southwest flavor or a country house some big-city slickness—but playing against type takes more design ingenuity. Also consider the prevailing climate. If you face chilly, rainy winters, consider the psychological warmth of sunshiny tints and deep textures. In hot regions, smooth surfaces and light backgrounds seem particularly fresh and cool.

■ Lifestyle Concerns. Will the room be a high-traffic space, requiring washable, forgiving surfaces and colors? A space reserved for company occasions might be jazzed up with glamorous, less-practical choices. What activities take place in the room—reading, crafts, watching TV, or conversation? Is it a family space? A family space may need a color scheme that won't show dirt. Do family members have any strong opinions on color that you'd like to accommodate? If so, consider incorporating a favored color by using it as an accent or even as the base color for the entire scheme.

Will you spend long hours in the room or brief periods? Rooms you pass through briefly can usually carry off more-dramatic colors and patterns than rooms where you linger.

■ Atmosphere. What sort of mood would you like the room to project? Elegant? Homey? The room's purpose often prompts the color choices. You might, for example, lean toward an invigorating tint for a home office. The atmosphere should also relate to the room's purpose. You may, for example, need a soothing color for a bedroom.

■ Natural Light. The room's orientation can influence the palette, depending on whether you're trying to tone down or maximize the available light. In a true sunroom, dark or bright textiles, which are prone to fading, might be reserved for easily changed accents. Before tailoring a room for sunshine, make sure the artificial lighting also flatters the selection. The next chapter, "The Right Light," will take you through the process of creating a lighting plan, plus it will show you how light affects color and how it sets the tone of a room.

# design workbook
## GOOD GRACIOUS

## classic style

Traditional colors and patterns come together in this gracious living room. Soft greens and creams and a mix of prints blend with elegant ease.

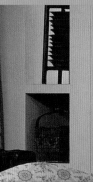

## rich variety

A plethora of fabric prints look harmonious with one another, linked as they are in scale and tone. The wall's green color is the important unifying element.

## warm ambiance

In the adjacent front hall, top left, red, green's opposite, adds contrasting drama. The warm color is welcoming to guests as they enter the house.

## distinctive details

Even the wood finishes and accessories, left, are in colors that are compatible with the room's soft furnishings—for example, the green glass hurricane lamps.

# design workbook
## A BOLD ADVENTURE

### high definition

Daring color choices pack a punch in a boxy modern—and architecturally bland—city apartment. Black and white tempers the palette.

### temperature rising

Interesting shapes and silhouette prints provide a pause in the spicey orange-red and gold hues on the bedroom wall and coverlet, top left.

### art underfoot

The rug, far left, with its daring oversize print, doesn't overpower the space, because the wall and furniture wear solid, albeit intensely saturated, colors.

### the white touch

The smart use of white on lamps and other small-scale items, left, allows the overall palette to stand out, as it should. Color, after all, is the star attraction in this home.

# 3

# the right light

A lighting plan plays a major role in any well-designed home. Not only is a well-lighted house safer and more functional, it also shows off colors, forms, and textures to their best advantage. A proper lighting plan should include the available natural light at different times of the day and the many different types of artificial light.

Whether you decide to devise a lighting scheme yourself or call in a lighting specialist, remember: good interior designers take advantage of the transformational power of light, and so can you. In this chapter, you'll learn how to use light to manipulate the perception of space, casting it up to make a low ceiling seem higher or washing the walls with it to make a small room appear spacious. You'll also learn how to use light in a painterly fashion to emphasize forms or objects.

The level of natural light a room receives changes with the time of day and the different seasons.

You'll also need to learn about the types of lighting, the different kinds of bulbs and fixtures, in addition to the terminology. This will help you with planning and will make you more effective when discussing ideas with experts and sales staff. For instance, many of us use the words "fixture" and "lamp" interchangeably, but when lighting professionals speak of "lamps" they are talking about "bulbs." Learn to speak the language.

Once you have prepared yourself, begin sketching out a lighting plan that can cover areas within one room and create a comfortable flow from one space to another.

Today, at the flick of a switch, you can illuminate your home inside—and out. You can program and store entire lighting schemes thanks to the latest technology. On command, create bright light for work, change the mood to cozy when you want to relax, or adjust it for TV viewing. Set your lights on timers for safety and security, or activate them by remote control.

For complicated situations, you may want to consult with a lighting design professional, or you may feel comfortable devising a plan yourself with the help of an electrician. In any case, it's wise to understand something of the basic science of light, how it is measured, and its effect on color. To make wise lighting choices from among the wide variety of types available, compare them on a level playing field. That's what lighting measurements can help you do.

# natural light

Any discussion about lighting your home has to begin with natural light. To the human eye, the desirable norm is sunlight. Part of its appeal is its variety. Consider the clear illumination on a cloudless mountaintop. Compare that with the diffused light on a misty morning or the intense brightness on a tropical beach. Then there's the changeability of sunlight between a cool rainy day, a clear winter afternoon, and a full summer blaze, or the contrast between the color of sunlight at noon and the way it appears as afternoon wears into evening.

**LEFT**
Glossy white-tile walls and polished-marble work surfaces reflect both natural light and the illumination from under-cabinet task lights and pendant fixtures.

**OPPOSITE TOP**
Recessed canisters provide good general lighting, while candles offer a warm glow.

**OPPOSITE BOTTOM**
A variety of fixtures, including pendants and floor and table lamps, add versatility to a home's lighting plan.

The amount and quality of natural light a room receives depends on the size of its windows and its orientation with regard to the sun. South-facing windows get the lion's share of direct sunlight for most of the day. East-facing rooms benefit from early mornings, while rooms that face west are sunny in the afternoon. Because its back is to the sun, a north-facing room receives only indirect natural light and tends to be cool and dim.

When you are renovating or redecorating a room, always look at the existing space and take the seasons, time of day, and orientation of the windows into consideration. Sometimes making a window bigger or adding another one doesn't make a room brighter. If the window's siting is toward the north, the room will just get colder. You can make a breakfast nook cheerier with a window that faces east, but don't try to take a late afternoon nap in a room with west-facing windows, unless you can control the light with shades, blinds, or lined curtains.

The natural light in the room will affect any tasks you perform as well. Never arrange a desk or worktable facing directly into bright sunlight. But be careful about having your back to a window. This can create shadows on your work surface. Ideally, follow the old axiom that recommends "light coming from over the left shoulder." By charting the light, and arranging your room and selecting window treatments accordingly, you can avoid problems.

# types of artificial light

A rtificial light picks up where natural light leaves off. It is the illumination that you provide, and unlike natural light, you can fine-tune it. In the daytime, artificial light augments natural light; after dark, it compensates for daylight completely. The key to devising a versatile plan that can change with each activity, as well as with the time of day or the weather, begins with knowing about the different types of artificial light. Here's a review:

## Ambient Light

Ambient, or general, light is illumination that fills an entire room. Its source is sometimes an overhead fixture, but the light itself does not appear to come from any one specific direction. Ambient light surrounds a room generally. An obvious example of

ambient light is ceiling-hung fluorescent strips in the average office environment. A covering over the strips hides the source and diffuses the light throughout the room.

A wall sconce is another good example of ambient light. The fixture washes light up the wall for an overall glow. The wall reflects the light, which diminishes the appearance of a single source. While you can tell the light is coming from the sconce, the overall glow is diffused.

The key to good ambient lighting is making it inconspicuous. Ambient light is merely the backdrop for the rest of the room, not the main feature. It changes with the surrounding environment—always providing light but never becoming obvious. For example, ambient lighting used during the day should blend in with the amount of natural light entering the room. At night, you should be able to diminish the light level so that it doesn't contrast jarringly against the darkness outside.

## Task Light

As its name implies, task lighting is purely functional. It illuminates a specific area for a particular job, such as chopping food on a kitchen counter, laboring over a woodworking project, or applying makeup.

Theatrical lighting around vanity mirrors is an excellent example of task lighting. It provides cross-illumination while avoiding the distorting shadows often seen with over-head lighting. Task lighting should always be included in any room where

specific functions take place, but its use should be optional. In other words, you can turn it on when you need it and keep it off at other times. Task lights should not be on the same switch with the fixture that provides general illumination. Using both types simultaneously creates a harsh, too-bright effect.

## Accent Light

Often overlooked but always the most dramatic, accent lighting draws attention to a particular element in the room, such as a handsome architectural feature or a work of art. Accent lighting makes a room come alive. It creates a mood. It shapes space. Lights recessed into a soffit above a handsome kitchen countertop cast a downward glow of illumination that offsets the counter without spilling light into the rest of the room. Cove lighting over a bathtub shimmers above the water and delineates a bathing area dramatically.

Without accent lighting, there may be light, but no focus, no character, no show business. With it, a design becomes exciting, theatrical, and rich.

## Decorative Light

While accent lighting draws attention to something specific, decorative lighting draws attention only to itself. The light can be kinetic, in the form of candles or flames in a fireplace, or static, such as fixed wall candelabra. It is there to grab attention. It is

OPPOSITE BOTTOM LEFT
A sconce mounted to the side of a bathroom mirror and aimed at an angle to the countertop provides the most flattering and glare-free task illumination.

OPPOSITE BOTTOM RIGHT
Cove lighting accents this large kitchen with warm illumination. Recessed canisters add suitable ambient light, while small task lights under the cabinets brighten the work surfaces.

LEFT
This hand-blown Italian-glass fixture is a work of art. To reduce glare from the glass tabletop, the homeowners dim the light at dinner time.

BELOW
The position of the fixture and the direction of the light makes this a comfortable place to read.

lighting for the pure sake of lighting.

Because decorative lighting is compelling, it can be a device to indirectly attract or distract. You can use it to draw the eye upward toward a cathedral ceiling, for example. By capturing your eye, decorative lighting forces your focus away from anything else. It doesn't highlight anything, as accent lighting does. And it doesn't provide a great deal of illumination, as ambient lighting does. It is the device that most lighting designers love to use, the final stroke in a complex multilayered plan.

Some types of decorative lighting include candles, chandeliers, neon sculptures or signs, a strip of miniature lights—any type of light that is deliberate and contrived. Include it to unify a room—to strike a balance among the various types of lighting, including natural light from the sun and moon.

## Contrast and Diffusion

Task lighting and accent lighting are examples of high-contrast lighting—they eliminate shadows and bring an object into sharp, crisp focus. Ambient lighting and decorative lighting are more diffused. They are softer, more forgiving lights that are comfortable and relaxing. Most rooms benefit from a combination of contrast lighting and diffused light, so incorporate both in your plan.

# recommended ranges of light levels

You can avoid eyestrain by having plenty of ambient light, thereby reducing the contrast to task lighting. Start by determining the level of light needed for the activity or task, and then relate it to the surroundings. (See "Determining Your Lighting Needs," on page 71 of this chapter.) Task lighting, lighting immediately nearby, and then the lowest lighting in the area (as in a room's corners) should range from no more than a ratio of four to one, preferably three to one near task lighting. You can compare watts and foot-candles cast by various light sources to determine the ratios or approximate them with your naked eye. The following table provides the recommended ranges of light levels for seeing activities in the home. The more intense the activity, the greater the light level should be.

| Activity | Easy or Short Duration | Critical or Prolonged |
|---|---|---|
| Dining | Low | Low |
| Entertaining | Low to high | Low to high |
| Grooming | Moderate | High |
| Craftwork * | Moderate | High |
| Kitchen/laundry chores | Low to moderate | High |
| Reading | Low to moderate | High |
| Studying | Moderate | High |
| TV viewing | Low to moderate | Low to moderate |
| Computer work | Moderate | High |
| Workbench * | Moderate | High |
| Tabletop games | Low to moderate | Moderate to high |
| Writing | Low to moderate | High |

* Benefits from supplementary directional light.

OPPOSITE
Noguchi lamps, with their soft paper shades, may provide a fair amount of indirect general light, depending on their size.

# selecting light levels

Design professionals have established a set of ideal lighting levels for performing the various activities and tasks that take place in any house. Your own personal preferences should lie within the minimum and maximum levels they have established. Some people favor more light; others prefer less. Good lighting begins with taking the recommended levels of light into account and tempering them with your preferences and those of people with whom you live. In common spaces, such as the family room, living room, and kitchen, it is better to err on the side of brightness. Adapt lighting in private areas, such as a study, bedroom, or workshop, to individual needs. Consult the Smart Tip "Recommended Ranges of Light Levels," on page 64, as a starting point in establishing your own levels. Once you've determined the level of light you require for each task or activity, relate this light to the surroundings. You can avoid eyestrain by including plenty of ambient light, thereby reducing its contrast to task lighting. Task lighting, the general lighting immediately nearby, and the lowest lighting in the area (as in a room's corners) should not contrast sharply. The light you use to read by, for example, should only

be two to three times as bright as the surrounding light in the room. Using a reading light in an otherwise dark room strains your eyes by forcing them to adjust frequently from light to darkness. The greatest range of light in any room should be a four-to-one ratio at most.

■ **Direct Glare.** Bare-bulb glare is obvious. You can avoid it by selecting the proper size shade, adjusting the angle of a fixture, or using a low-wattage bulb or one with frosting.

Lighting professionals caution against "glare bombs," fixtures that produce unavoidable, uncomfortable light. A common offender is the bathroom globe or strip light over the vanity; another is the exposed bulb in some ceiling fixtures; a third is an inferior fluorescent fixture that blasts you with bright direct light. In the first case, you might try replacing the bulbs with heavily frosted versions. If you plan to include track lights in your scheme, install baffles over the bulbs. They are devices that are designed to reduce spill light and glare. When you visit a lighting showroom, ask specifically to see bulbs and fixtures designed to reduce glare.

When you create a layout for your furniture arrangement, it's always wise to assess it for glare. For instance, if you situate the new family room sofa to face a game table, every time you flick on the suspended pendant light over the tabletop, you're creating glare for anyone seated on the sofa. Always check the field of vision from each seated, as well as each standing, position.

■ **Indirect Glare.** Any flat reflective surface can be the source of indirect glare. That includes shiny desktops, countertops, tables, mirrors and any other glass or metal surfaces, and TV and computer screens.

To determine reflected glare, simply place a mirror in front of or on top of any surface you suspect will reflect glare. The mirror will isolate reflected light glare. Place a temporary light where you plan to install a permanent source, and then do the glare check before making your final installation.

OPPOSITE
**For grooming, lighting at the vanity should allow you to see yourself as you would appear in shadow-free natural light.**

TOP RIGHT
**Using an opaque shade on a lamp is one way to soften strong direct light.**

BOTTOM RIGHT
**To light a dining table, test out lighting levels that make you comfortable, starting with 150 watts.**

# types of bulbs

J ust changing the types of bulbs, or lamps as professional lighting designers call them, in your existing household fixtures can make a major difference in the way the room looks, functions, and feels. Does this mean you should replace all of your fluorescent lamps with halogen fixtures and call off the rest of your remodeling plans? That might be exaggerating the power of the right light. But don't underestimate it, either.

Understanding the differences in lamps will help you select the right light sources for every area in your house. Most homes require the use of several different lamps. Light is like paint. You get different effects depending on the combinations you use. And color is nothing but the reflection of different types of light. When planning a lighting scheme, always consider the relationship between color and light.

## Standard Measurements for Color

Scales used universally in lighting assess the *color temperature* the lamp gives off and how light from the lamp affects the objects it is lighting. Chapter Two explored the concept of natural light and its effect on color. Now let's look at warm and cool artificial lights and how they affect color. The term color temperature describes the appearance of light in terms of the warmth or coolness of its color. Fluorescent lamps, which do not emit a continuous spectrum of light, are assigned a *correlated color temperature* (CCT) value. Lamps, which range in color from red to orange to yellow to blue to blue-white, are ranked according to the *Kelvin* (K) temperature scale. This rating will help you to select lamps that are closely matched, and you can vary the coolness or warmth of lighting for specific situations. Generally, light sources below 3,000K are considered warm, while those above 4,100K are considered cool. Midrange light sources fall between 3,200K and 3,600K.

*Color rendition* describes how a light source affects the perception of the color of an object it illuminates. The *Color Rendition Index* (CRI) is a way of measuring a lamp's ability to render true color (the color of an object in sunlight). The color rendering capabilities of lamps are rated from 1 to 100 with true color at 100. If you want different lamps to light an object the same way, match and compare temperature (or CCT) and CRI. Check the temperature first, then the CRI.

## Types of Bulbs

Most homes include a combination of warm and cool tones, so selecting bulbs that provide balanced lighting comfortably close to what appears normal to the eye is usually the most attractive choice. Experiment with various combinations of bulbs to create your own desired effect. Balance and layering are the two keys to success. Here is a brief description of the types of bulbs and their characteristics.

■ **Incandescent.** Like sunlight, incandescent bulbs emit continuous-spectrum light, or light that contains every color. Illumination from these bulbs, in fact, is even warmer than sunlight, making its effect very appealing in a room. It makes our skin tones look good, and even enhances our feeling of well-being. The drawbacks to incandescent bulbs are that they use a lot of electricity, are fragile, have a short lifespan, and produce a lot of heat.

**ABOVE LEFT**

A track system of small spotlights, which can be adjusted up or down and dimmed, brighten a dark corner that is dominated by a bank of open bookshelves.

**ABOVE RIGHT**

Cove lighting adds warmth to this all-neutral scheme. Low-voltage halogen spotlights draw attention to the fireplace and the displays that flank both sides.

**RIGHT**

A pendant that uses a single incandescent bulb may be the solution in a tight space, such as an entry hall, where you want to make a design statement but don't have room for a chandelier.

They come in a variety of shapes, sizes, and applications. (One type features a waterproof lens cover that makes it suitable for over a tub or inside a shower.) These bulbs usually are made of glass, and can be clear, diffuse, tinted, colored, or have a reflective coating inside.

■ **Fluorescent.** These energy-efficient bulbs cast a diffuse, shadowless light that makes them great for general illumination. The old standard fluorescents are very unflattering, however, making everything and everyone appear pale and bland. Newer fluorescent bulbs, called triphosphor fluorescent lamps, are warmer and render color that more closely resembles sunlight. Fluorescents are available both in the familiar tube versions and in newer, compact styles.

Because the life cycle of fluorescents is shortened when used for periods of less than three hours, place them in situations where the light will be left on for an extended period of time. For example, a fluorescent might not make sense in a storage area where light is only occasionally needed for a few minutes. On the other hand, installing a fluorescent fixture as your overhead kitchen light makes sense because it's likely to be on for hours at a time.

■ **Halogen.** This is actually a type of incandescent lamp that produces brighter, whiter light at a lower wattage and with greater energy efficiency. The disadvantages are a higher price tag and a higher heat output that requires a special shielding for fire prevention. Halogen lamps have a slightly different shape and thicker, heavier glass bulbs than incandescent bulbs. The low-voltage version of halogen bulbs produces a brighter light than a standard halogen, and is even more energy-efficient. Low-voltage halogens are typically used for creative accent lighting.

■ **Fiber Optics.** One of countless innovations gradually finding its way into the home, fiber-optic systems consist of one extremely bright lamp to transport light to one or more destinations through fiber-optic conduits. Used for accent lighting, fiber-optic lighting does not generate excessive heat, making it ideal for highlighting artwork.

ABOVE
"Old World" meets new world in these sconces. Their compact self-ballasted fluorescent bulbs produce light that resembles that of incandescent bulbs, but last five to fifteen times longer.

OPPOSITE
Small industrial-style fixtures, spaced evenly apart along a stairway, coodinate with this home's modern architecture.

## smart tip  DIMMER SWITCHES

You can dim lights just slightly to extend lamp life and save energy, and there will be very little perceptible change in light level. For instance, dimming the light to 50 percent will be perceived as though the light were only dimmed to 70 percent. Therefore, there is no dramatic dilation or constriction of the eye due to light level change.

# determining lighting needs

**W**hen a room isn't bright enough, most people just exchange low-watt bulbs for high-watt versions. Wattage, however, is simply a measurement of how much electricity a lamp consumes. The light output of a bulb is actually measured in lumens. If the bulbs you have been using aren't providing enough general light, substitute them with ones that have more lumens. The next time you shop for bulbs, read the packaging, which indicates the *lumens per watt* (lpw) produced by a bulb. The more lumens per watt, the more efficient the lamp. When looking for intensity produced by a lamp, refer to its *candlepower* (Cp). The more candela (units), the brighter the source.

But when planning a suitable light design, you must take other factors into consideration. Besides the amount of natural light the room receives, consider how you will use it—to rest, work, dine, entertain, or a combination of activities. Next, assess the reflectance levels in the room, or the amount of light that is reflected from a colored surface, such as a tile floor or a painted wall. Light colors are reflective; dark colors are absorbent. For example, white reflects 80 percent of the light in a room, while black reflects only 4 percent of it. Surface texture also makes a difference—mirrorlike surfaces can reflect as much as 90 percent. In practical terms, a room with satin or glossy white or pale walls requires less light than one with deep, jewel-toned walls.

Next, consider the size of the room. How high are the ceilings? High ceilings require brighter lights to dispel shadows. But you will have to tone down the level of brightness in a room with low ceilings because light tends to bounce off low ceilings and walls. How many windows and skylights are there? Do they face the sunny south, or is their exposure to the north, or somewhere in between?

Designers typically determine lighting needs by using suggested *foot-candle* (Fc) levels for different activities and areas. Foot-candles, which refer to the amount of light that falls on a surface, are used primarily for directional lamps. To determine the foot-candle power you will need to adequately light an area, divide the candlepower (Cp) of the bulb you intend to use by the distance (D) from the fixture to the surface squared (Fc=Cp÷D2).

There are no perfect stock formulas. But by looking at how each of these factors affects the others, you can make educated choices when developing your light plan. Keeping in mind the science and technology involved in lighting will help you assess your own requirements for the room. Ideally, you'll want to incorporate a variety of options for various activities, to create ambiance, and for decoration. Use the following Smart Steps to get started.

# smart steps
## where to start

### Step 1 EXAMINE YOUR ACTIVITIES

Above all, your lighting design should enhance the function of the room. Try preparing dinner with a new recipe or following a complicated sewing pattern without the right light. Make a list of all of the day and nighttime activities that may take place in a room, such as TV watching, studying, cooking, and crafts.

### Step 2 SKETCH AN INFORMAL PLAN

Refer to the floor plan you drew of the room or make a new sketch. (See Chapter One, "Design Basics," on page 12.) Circle the activity centers—work tables, reading chairs, TV viewing spots, and so forth. Not everything you expect to do will require the same level of light.

Note each activity center with a "G" for general or ambient light, "T" for task light, "A" for accent light, and "D" for decorative light. In some places on your plan, you may want to indicate more than one type of light. An easy chair may be used at times for reading and at other times for TV viewing, knitting, or even to rest, for example.

Place your general lighting first; then indicate where you'll need task lights. After you've noted every activity center for task lighting, decide where you want to install accent lighting. You might want some recessed fixtures over a countertop or piece of art. Maybe you want to highlight beautiful crown molding or hand-painted tile. If you want to use accent lighting but don't know where it should go, ask yourself what is the most interesting feature in the room. It may be something as simple as a wall-hung framed painting or print, a collection of first-edition books on a shelf, or a bay window with a beautiful view.

You don't have to place decorative lighting into your plan unless it is a wired fixture, such as a neon sculpture or a track system of low-voltage halogens. But if you know you'll be using candles in the room, it is a good idea to indicate them, too. That way you can plan a place that will hold them safely.

### Step 3 CHECK YOUR LOCAL CODE

Every municipality has its own codes regarding the placement of light and electricity around water. Before you purchase any light fixtures for the kitchen and bath, especially, check your local code with the building inspector or speak with your contractor.

### Step 4 VISIT LIGHTING SHOWROOMS

The best way to get ideas is to visit lighting showrooms and the lighting department in home centers. This will give you a chance to take an inventory of fixture types and styles currently on the market. Also, you can take advantage of the advice of lighting specialists employed at these stores. They can help you create the right plan and choose an appropriate style of lighting. Bring along your sketch and your list of activities, as well as the design materials you have compiled containing clippings, notes, sample plans, color charts, tile, paint, and fabric samples. The lighting designer can take it from there.

As you might already expect, some in-store advice is free. Ask about it. A few suggestions may be all you need to steer you in the right direction. Otherwise, you may want to consider an in-home consultation. Inquire about fees, which may be modest. Sometimes a small investment in professional advice pays off handsomely in the final result—and in the discount professional designers can offer on fixtures.

There are also systems that computerize a variety of lighting options. A lighting specialist can design an entire program that sets the lights throughout the room on a system devised for different moods and activities. Everything is preprogammed and controlled by one central panel. However, these "smart systems" can be high-priced.

**OPPOSITE**
This desk is in a rather dark corner, so a table lamp has been brought in to brighten the area. Positioned to the side of the desktop and with a translucent shade, the light source doesn't compete with the computer screen.

**LEFT**
In this family entertainment room, light has been addressed at various areas—at the bar with a "mod" retro fixture and in the sitting area with a table lamp.

# lighting fixtures

There's practically an endless number of fixture styles on the market to match every decor and catch everyone's imagination. The past few years have proved to be a lighting designer's dream as fixtures have become more decorative and lighting schemes more varied and eclectic. From nostalgic reproductions to architecturally inspired designs and contemporary styles, there are models to suit any look in the form of table and floor models, wall sconces, chandeliers, strip lights, recessed canister lights, track lights, ceiling fixtures, and novelty types. The copious selection of finishes in all of these styles offers lots of excitement, too. Look for everything from ceramic, glass, and colored enamels to brass, chrome, pewter, nickel, and copper; brushed, matted, or antiqued, as well as dramatic designs in wrought iron and verdigris. For more interest, select fixtures with a combination of finishes, such as a verdigris with antiqued brass or copper paired with wrought iron.

For a sophisticated look, combine more than one fixture type and avoid matched pairs, such as two identical table lamps at either end of a sofa. In a bathroom, a ceiling fixture that includes a ventilating fan is especially practical. For accenting in any room, pair uplighting fixtures, such as wall sconces, with downlighting types: recessed lights or a ceiling-mounted unit, for example. Install track lighting to wash an entire wall with illumination. Do this when you want to call attention to a beautiful wallcovering, a special paint technique, or a mural.

Finally, before you purchase a light fixture, ask to see it lit up in the store. That way you can be sure it produces the type of effect you desire.

LEFT
An etched opal-glass shade diffuses the light on this modern fixture. The housing has a brushed nickel finish that easily coordinates with other metals, such as bathroom and kitchen fittings.

RIGHT
A chandelier that comprises a cluster of Moravian Stars adds an Old World look to this dining room. Traditionally, the 25-pointed star has been a popular illuminated Advent decoration in Germany since the 1800s.

# the role of lighting in architecture

L ighted coves, soffits (or cornices), and valances make the most of architectural features in a room. Fixtures designed for this purpose create dramatic reflective light. Coves distribute light upward. Soffits distribute light downward. Valances distribute light both up and down. A shield, usually made of a piece of wood or plaster molding, hides the light itself. Baffles, louvers, or diffusers direct light and reduce glare. Consider incorporating one of these ideas into your design if you want to make a big splash with lighting.

**TOP LEFT**
Miniature spotlights in the ceiling call attention to the architectural lines and the glass wall in this modern house.

**BOTTOM LEFT**
Uplighting the top portion of this wall with sconces plays up the massive height of the ceiling here.

**BELOW**
Lighted coves bring drama to boring ceilings in large, open-plan spaces. (See the kitchen close up on page 62.)

Be creative when thinking about architectural lighting. Install it along the top or bottom of cabinets or inside the cove of a raised ceiling. Integrate a lighted valance with a vaulted ceiling or a curtain sweep; vertically light a wall niche; and highlight molding. Whatever you decide, first analyze your architectural lighting needs. Ask yourself these questions:

■ Is the reflected wall or ceiling smooth enough to be comfortable and attractive?

■ Can I alter the look of the lighting by tinting the surface upon which it reflects?

■ Can I increase efficiency by painting the interior of the valance, cove, or soffit white? (Remember, light-colored surfaces reflect light.)

■ Does the reflected light enhance the rest of the room's light or detract from it?

■ Is the ceiling high enough (at least 8 feet) to keep the light from spilling onto the walls? (The top of the cove should be at least 18 inches from the ceiling.)

Talk with your architect or contractor to see what kind of architectural effects are feasible in your design. Once you have established your lighting plan, proceed to the next step in your decorating adventure.

RIGHT
To counteract the cold effect of dark skylight shafts at night, the homeowners installed uplights, which brighten and accent these areas.

BELOW
In another area a few feet away from foyer pictured on the opposite page, built-in cabinets housing a wine collection and display feature both accent and task lights. The natural color rendition of the low-voltage halogen bulbs brings out the beauty and warmth of the caramel-colored marble and the wood floor.

# design workbook

## THE MANY LEVELS OF LIGHTING

## covering all bases

There are no dark corners in this large open living space, thanks to a well-balanced lighting plan.

## good general lighting

Pendants and recessed canister fixtures provide suitable overall illumination throughout the space.

## eye coordination

Using similar shapes and styles of shades helps to unify the appearance of the different lighting fixtures.

## comfort level

A reading lamp that provides a moderate level of light, top left, is positioned where it will not cause glare.

## taken to task

Illuminating work surfaces is a safety must in a kitchen, left. Note the under-cabinet fixtures and lights under the hood.

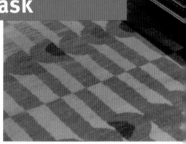

# design workbook
## ILLUMINATING A MASTER SUITE

## plan to relax

A soothing balance between the levels of natural and artificial light enhances this bedroom's calming look.

## stylish ambiance

This distinctive chandelier is a good source of overall light, and it adds a lot of style to the room.

## night light

Lamps near the bed are for more than reading— they are important for safety if you get up during the night.

## bright idea

Lamps on a console across from the bed, top left, add soft lighting near the entries to a closet and bath.

## in the right light

To cut down glare in a room with mirrored surfaces, the sconces next to the vanities, left, are shaded.

4

# style underfoot

WOOD FLOORING    LAMINATE FLOORING    RESILIENT VINYL FLOORS
CERAMIC DESIGNS    NATURAL STONE    CARPETING AND RUG
DESIGN WORKBOOK

Selecting a flooring material is one of the most important decisions you will make when decorating a room. The right material can enhance the color scheme and the overall look of the room, and flooring provides a unique tactile component to the design.

If you are are acting as your own designer, one of the first things you should do is learn about the various types of flooring—from wood to stone to vinyl—on today's market. The choices are myriad, and innovations in technology have widened the range of finishes.

Like a professional, be sure to consider the principles of color, texture, and pattern, relating them to your selection and to the rest of the elements in the room. (For more information, see Chapter Two, "Color and Texture," beginning on page 34.)

Carpet tiles, such as these, come in many colors, patterns, and textures, and let you customize an area rug or wall-to-wall carpeting.

If the room's wallpaper features a big, bold design, for instance, you'll want to tone things down with a solid-color floor or one with a small pattern. If the room is large, you can make it cozy with a number of area rugs that define intimate furniture groupings. A country-style living room might benefit from a textured tile that has rustic appeal or from braided rugs. A formal entry hall will make a stately impression with an intricate parquet border or a checkerboard marble floor.

# wood flooring

In bygone eras, a wood floor was simply one that was created by laying wide wood planks side by side. Later, as the milling of lumber improved, homeowners were able to choose narrower planks that look more refined than rustic. Parquet floors were created by woodcrafters with a flair for the dramatic and an appreciation of the artistic richness of wood grains set in nonlinear patterns.

Today's manufacturers have made it possible to have it all. The wood floor, factory- or custom-stained to suit a particular style or mood in a room, is still a traditional favorite. It's readily available in strips of 1 to 2¼ inches wide, or in country-style planks of 3 to 8 inches wide. The formal, sophisticated look of a parquet floor is unparalleled for richness of visual texture. Prefinished hardwood tile blocks are now manufactured in a variety of patterns, making parquet possible at a reasonable price.

## Types of Wood Flooring

Wood varieties available as a surface material are vast, and cost varies widely, depending on the type and grade of wood and on the choice of design (strips or parquet).

Softwoods, like pine and fir, are often used to make simple tongue-and-groove floorboards. These floors are less expensive than hardwoods but also less durable. Softwoods are not suitable for high-traffic areas, for rooms with heavy furniture (which can "dig" into the wood), or for kitchens or dining rooms, where chairs or other furniture will often be moved around. The hardwoods—maple, birch, oak, ash—are far less likely to mar with normal use. A hardwood floor is not indestructible; however, it will stand up to demanding use.

Both hardwoods and softwoods are graded according to their color, grain, and imperfections. The top of the line is known as clear, followed by select, No. 1 common, and No. 2 common. In addition to budget considerations, the decision whether to pay top dollar for clear wood or to economize with a lesser grade depends on use factors and on the design objectives. For example, if you plan to install a wood floor in a small room and then cover most of it with an area rug, the No. 2 common grade may be a good choice; lesser grades are also fine for informal rooms where a few defects just enhance a lived-in look. If your design calls for larger areas of rich wood grain that will be exposed, with scatter rugs used for color accents, a clear or select grade will make an attractive choice. Another factor to use in determin-

LEFT
**Bamboo is a relatively new flooring material that is built up from thin strips of fiber that can be laid vertically or horizontally, as pictured.**

OPPOSITE
**Engineered-wood flooring generally comes in 3- to 6⅛-in.-wide prefinished planks. This one has a cherry veneer that was stained a deep, warm amber.**

ing what grade to choose is the stain; imperfections are less noticeable with darker stains.

## Finishing Options

Color stains—reds, blues, and greens—may work in settings where a casual or rustic feeling is desired. This, however, is a departure from the traditional use of wood. Wood is not typically used to deliver color impact; instead it blends with and subtly enhances its surroundings. Natural wood stains range from light ash tones to deep, coffee-like colors. Generally, lighter stains make a room feel less formal, and darker, richer stains suggest a stately atmosphere. As with lighter colors, lighter stains create a feeling of openness and make a small room look larger; darker stains foster a more intimate feeling and can reduce the visual vastness of a large space.

Creative patterning of a wood floor can enrich a design. For example, create an Old World look by laying strips in a herringbone pattern. Decorative inlay with strips or parquet patterns can enhance richness and visual interest. Use inlays to "frame out" activity areas in large spaces that have multiple uses, such as living and dining areas.

## Installation

Unless you're particularly adept at measuring and cutting wood and have the time and skill that's necessary to properly finish the flooring surface, the installation, staining, and finishing of strip or plank floors can be a formidable project. Therefore, if the design plan calls for the laying of unfinished wood strips, factor the cost of hiring a skilled professional into your budget. Many manufacturers offer products with installation kits that make wood flooring a do-it-yourself option for those whose skills are good but don't necessarily approach a professional carpenter's level. Some make strips or planks already that are finished and sealed so that once the last nail is tapped into the flooring the project is complete. Most parquet tiles come finished and sealed as well.

## Maintenance

If a wood floor is appropriately installed and properly sealed with polyurethane, maintenance consists of vacuum cleaning or dust-mopping as needed. It's important to promptly vacuum up any gritty material that may be tracked in from outdoors, because sand and gravel can scratch or even gouge the surface. Waxing isn't necessary, although some who live with wood floors like the patina that results from periodic applications of wax.

**RIGHT**
It's hard to believe, but this "stone tile" floor is actually made of laminate, a material that costs less and is softer and warmer underfoot than the real thing.

**OPPOSITE**
Laminate is a great imitator of wood, too. A laminate wood look-alike floor comes in many styles. Be careful: a cheap version will quickly peel, crack, or chip, unlike a quality product, which can last many years.

# laminate flooring

Laminate flooring is the great pretender among flooring materials. When your creative side tells you to install wood but your practical side knows it just won't hold up in the traffic-heavy location you're considering it for, a wood floor look-alike might be just the thing. Faux wood and faux stone laminate floors provide you with the look you want tempered with physical wear and care properties that you and your

# resilient vinyl flooring

Like laminate, resilient flooring is also available in design-friendly sheet or tile form. Resilient floors can be made from a variety of materials, including linoleum, asphalt, cork, or rubber. However, the most commonly used material in manufacturing today's resilient floors for homes is vinyl plastic.

Price, durability, and easy maintenance make resilient flooring an attractive and popular choice. Do-it-yourself installation, an option even for those who are not particularly skilled or experienced, can mean further savings.

family can live with. Laminate is particularly suited to rooms where floors are likely to see heavy duty—kitchens, family rooms, hallways, and children's bedrooms and playrooms—anywhere stain and scratch resistance and easy clean-up count. Prolonged exposure to moisture will damage some laminate products, but many can now be used in wet areas. Manufacturers of laminate offer warranties against staining, scratching, cracking, and peeling for up to 25 years.

Laminate is made from paper impregnated with melamine, an organic resin, and bonded to a core of particleboard, fiberboard, or other wood byproducts. It can be laid over virtually any subflooring surface, including wood and concrete. It can also be applied on top of an existing wood, ceramic, or vinyl tile, as well as vinyl or other sheet flooring. You can even install it over certain types of carpeting, but check the manufacturer's guidelines before doing so.

## Installation and Care

The installation of laminate flooring is a reasonably quick and relatively easy do-it-yourself project. It requires sheets of a special foam underlayment followed by the careful placement, cutting, and gluing of the laminate. It's available in sheets that are ideal when your design calls for a uniform look, such as monotone stone, or a linear design that mimics strip or plank wood flooring. Laminate planks, squares, and blocks offer added design flexibility: with them, you can design your own tile patterns, lay strips of wood-look planks with alternating "stain" finishes, or border your floor with a contrasting color.

Proper care for this type of material includes routine vacuuming and an occasional damp-mopping.

## Sheet versus Tiles

Resilient flooring comes in an enormous array of colors and patterns, plus many of the flooring styles have a textured surface. With the tiles, you can combine color and pattern in limitless ways. Even the sheet form of resilient flooring can be customized with inlay strips.

Cushioned sheet vinyl offers the most resilience. It provides excellent stain resistance; it's comfortable and quiet underfoot and easy to maintain, with no-wax and never-wax finishes often available. These features make the floor especially attractive for areas with lots of kid traffic. Beware though: only the more expensive grades show an acceptable degree of resistance to nicking and denting. In rooms where furniture is often moved around, this could be a problem. Although the range of colors, patterns, and surface textures is wide, sheet flooring is not as flexible as vinyl tile when it comes to customizing your look.

Regular sheet vinyl is less expensive than the cushioned types, but it carries the same disadvantages and is slightly less resilient. Except for the availability of no-wax finishes, a vinyl tile floor is as stain resistant and as easy to maintain as the sheet-vinyl products. Increased design possibilities are the trade-off.

Here, as with other flooring materials, one possible way out of the choice maze is to take the unconventional step of mixing flooring materials. For example, use a durable cushioned sheet vinyl in more trafficked areas, but frame it with a pretty vinyl tile or laminate border.

# ceramic designs

**OPPOSITE**
Wood and stone aren't the only natural materials that laminate can imitate: it mimics brick in this sunroom.

**BOTTOM LEFT**
The cushioned sheet vinyl used on this bathroom floor is comfortable, but more importantly, it is slip resistant—a necessary factor in choosing any type of flooring for wet areas.

**BOTTOM RIGHT**
Like laminate, vinyl flooring can offer the look of a costlier natural material. Here, vinyl tiles with the appearance of stone complement the wood cabinetry, adding rich tones to the room.

eramic tile—actually fired clay—is an excellent choice for areas subject to a lot of traffic and in rooms where resistance to moisture and stains is needed. These features, combined with easy cleanup, have made ceramic tile a centuries-old tradition for flooring, walls, and ceilings in bathrooms and kitchens. Color, texture, and pattern choices available today make ceramic tile the most versatile flooring option in terms of design possibilities.

## Tile Options

Some handcrafted ceramic tiles are very costly, but today's manufacturers have created a market full of design, style, and price options. It's possible to create an elegant ceramic floor design even on a relatively tight budget. You can control costs further with do-it-yourself installation. Tiling tools are not very expensive, and many tile retailers will rent them—some will even make the trickier cuts for you. The adhesives, mortars, and grouts available today are easier to use than ever before.

Tiles come in a variety of sizes, beginning with 1-inch-square mosaic tiles up to large 16 x 16-inch squares. Other shapes, such as triangles, diamonds, and rectangles, are also available. Tile textures range from shiny to matte-finished and from glass-smooth to ripple-surfaced. Tiles are available either *glazed* or *unglazed*. Glazed tiles have a hard, often colored, surface that is applied during the firing process; the resulting finish can range from glossy to matte. Unglazed tiles, such as terracotta or quarry tiles, have a matte finish, are porous, and need to be sealed to prevent staining.

In creating a flooring design, consider whether the other elements in the room allow for an intricate pattern or work better with one light color as the dominant feature. Once you make that basic determination, create the design directly on a copy of your floor plan.

Consider using accent borders to create unique designs, such as a faux area rug, that visually separate sections of a room or separate one room from another. When added in a random pattern, embossed accent tiles add interest, variety, and elegance to an expanse of single-colored tiles.

Alas, no surfacing material is perfect. To assess whether ceramic tile is the right surface for your floor, take into consideration both the positive and negative points. Ceramic tile offers long-lasting beauty, design versatility, and simplicity of maintenance, but it also has some hard-to-live-with features. Tile is cold underfoot, noisy when someone walks across it in hard-soled shoes, and not at all resilient—always expect the worst when something breakable falls on a tile floor. If you have infants and toddlers around, it may be best to wait a few years for your tiled floor.

OPPOSITE
**Ceramic tile is a durable earthy material that is especially at home in the bathroom or kitchen.**

TOP RIGHT
**Stone tile is less expensive than a stone slab. Used here on the floor and fireplace surround, it is subtle and elegant.**

# natural stone

Like ceramic tile, stone and marble are classified as "non-resilients." Like tile, these materials offer richness of color, durability, moisture and stain resistance, and ease of maintenance. They also share with tile the drawbacks of being cold to the touch, noisy to walk on, and unforgivingly hard.

Stone and marble floors are clearly, unmistakably natural. As remarkably good as some faux surfaces look, no product manufactured today actually matches the rustic irregularity and random color variation of natural stone or the richness and depth of color in veined marble.

## Decision-Making Factors

With the kind of beauty and singularity you find in stone inevitably comes a high price tag. Whether it's polished marble, random-cut fieldstone, slate, brick, terrazzo, or limestone, the materials are expensive and the installation requires professional-level skills. Also, you may have to go through an interior designer for the flooring because some suppliers of stone and marble won't take small residential projects. Stone may pose a safety hazard on the floor, too, because it gets slick when wet. A fall on a stone floor can cause serious injury. Older persons and children are at particular risk. If you choose one of these materials, use slip-resistant rugs over it.

# carpeting and rugs

The terms carpet and rug are often used interchangeably, but they're not the same, in terms of both manufacture and design application. Carpeting is manufactured in rolls ranging from just over 2 feet wide to broadlooms that measure as much as 18 feet wide. Carpeting is usually laid wall-to-wall and can be installed over raw subflooring. Rugs are soft floor coverings that don't extend wall-to-wall and are used over another finished flooring surface. A mat is a small rug.

Differences in fiber composition, construction, color, texture, and cost make choosing a carpet or rug a complex job. Carpeting can be made of natural wool, synthetic fibers, or blends of wool and synthetics. Other natural fibers commonly used in area rugs, scatter rugs, and mats are cotton or plant materials known as cellulosics—hemp, jute, sisal, or grasses. Synthetic fibers are acrylics, nylon, olefin, and polyester.

## How It's Made

Carpet construction refers to the manner in which the yarn fiber meets the carpet backing, and carpeting may be manufactured by several construction techniques. Weaving, once the industry standard, is done on a loom. Weaving has given way to today's most commonly used technique, tufting, in which yarn is pushed through the backing from the underside, forming loops on the surface. Some tufted carpeting has a latex backing to prevent the tufts from pulling loose. Carpeting may also be needlepunched or needlebonded, techniques that involve the insertion of yarn into backing with hooked needles. A knitted carpet is created when needles are used to knit pile and backing together; a latex backing is usually added in this type of construction. Finally, carpeting may be flocked. Flocking employs static electricity to stand short fibers on end and uses an adhesive to bond the fibers to backing.

In general, woven carpet is the most durable; flocking, the least. The durability of other carpet types fall somewhere in between.

LEFT
**A custom stone-floor design was created for this entry hall using various shades, sizes, and shapes of the material.**

OPPOSITE
**Nothing beats carpeting for warmth and comfort when you roll out of bed in the morning.**

Type of fiber, the density and height of the pile, and the thickness and quality of the yarn contribute to a carpet's durability.

The texture of a carpet or rug is determined by a number of factors, including the height and type of pile. The term "pile" refers to the carpeting surface, created when the yarn is connected to the backing. When carpet construction creates yarn loops on the surface, the loops may be left intact (loop pile) or may be cut (cut pile); in some cases, a carpet may be a combination of cut and uncut loops (tip-sheared). To further complicate the picture, loops, cut pile, or both may be of uniform height or may be of varied heights. The resulting possibilities range from the informal, uniformly short-loop-pile carpeting, such as Berber, to the soft velvet of a uniformly cut, deep-pile carpet. The relatively informal look of a sculptured surface is created with multilevel loops.

## Advantages

Wall-to-wall carpeting adds softness and warmth to a room, both visually and physically. Carpeting also muffles room noise and, when installed on upper floors, reduces the amount of sound that is transmitted to rooms on lower floors of the house or adjacent ones.

With most types of carpeting, a padding underlayment enhances softness underfoot and increases the life of the carpet. Several types of padding—from rubber to a variety of natural fibers—exist, and some are coated with adhesive. The padding choice will depend on the type of carpet you buy; follow manufacturers' recommendations on what type to use. Cushion-backed carpet, made with the padding, is another option.

## Making Your Selection

Carpeting offers a huge variety of material, style, color, pattern, texture, and cost options. The simplest way to narrow down your choices is to decide on a cost and examine the options within your price range. That is not to endorse making a purchase strictly on price. Quality does matter when it comes to carpeting. The most durable carpeting (in terms of construction and fiber) is usually the most expensive. The converse is also true—the less

and Far East can be extremely expensive—essentially you're purchasing a work of art for your floor. A number of manufacturers make excellent reproductions, printing traditional Oriental rug patterns on factory-made rugs. Area rugs can also be made from smaller-than-room-sized pieces of carpeting; the section of carpeting must be bound at the edges to prevent unraveling and to create a finished look.

## Space Considerations

In decorating with area rugs, the general rule is to allow at least a foot of floor space on all four sides, creating a three-dimensional art piece consisting of the rug, furniture, and accessories, all set within that foot-wide frame. This rule, however, need not apply if your goal is to create special-use sections within a larger space. For example, a round hooked rug can be the perfect device for pulling together two comfortable wing chairs and a small coffee table, creating a conversation area within a large living room. In a large kitchen, an area rug slightly larger than your table and chairs can offset this eating space, separating it from the work space. A round or oval rug in a small rectangular or square space can allow you to "float" furniture away from the walls, visually enlarging an otherwise crowded-looking room.

Finally, carpet tiles, manufactured in squares of one or two feet, are an option if your decorating plans call for a softer tile pattern. Some types of carpet tiles must be glued to the subflooring, but loose-laid styles are also now available.

## Care

Carpeting and area rugs are easy to maintain—vacuum cleaning is all that is required for regular maintenance. Many small area rugs are machine-washable; others can be dry-cleaned. For both area rugs and carpeting, a wide range of spot-cleaning products are available for taking care of the occasional soiling problem. A periodic cleaning with a professional steam or shampoo machine will keep most good-quality carpets looking and smelling fresh throughout years of use.

expensive the carpet, the shorter its useful life. Ask yourself this question: "Do I really intend to stick with this carpet for the next 30 years?" Sure you need a durable carpet, but just how long is long enough? Think about it before you buy. Wool carpeting is the most durable and the most expensive; it also has the advantage of being naturally fire resistant. Carpeting made from synthetic fibers offers the greatest variety in terms of color, pattern, and texture, and in the short run is certainly more affordable. A good compromise choice would be a wool-synthetic blend, offering a reasonably wide variety of design options plus some enhanced durability without a pure-wool price tag.

Area rugs are an excellent device for creating small areas within a larger space, such as marking off an intimate conversation area in a living room. They are also a relatively inexpensive way to add accent colors and to help tie room designs together.

Some area rugs are inexpensive, manufactured floor coverings that come in a variety of sizes, colors, and patterns. Others are specialty items, such as the handmade dhurrie rugs from India, rya rugs from Scandinavia, and hooked, braided, and rag rugs made in a number of places through-out the world. Perhaps the most versatile in terms of decorating are the Orientals, which can blend extremely well with a variety of styles, from traditional to modern. Authentic, handmade Oriental rugs from the Near

Now that you've got the facts about each floor surface option, picking the right one for your design will be much less confusing. The following Smart Steps can make it downright simple.

# smart steps
## picking flooring material

### ■ Step 1 MAKE A "USE/ABUSE" ANALYSIS

Begin by asking yourself the most important question: How is this room used? Your answer should tell you just what kind of traffic the future floor surface will endure. With a relatively expensive investment like a floor, it's best not to guess. Instead, use this system to arrive at an accurate use/abuse analysis:

Imagine yourself in the room on a weekday morning through the entire day and determine who is likely to come through the room at those various times. Then do the same thing with a typical weekend. On a piece of paper, make columns headed "Who" and "Activities," and then list who in the family uses the room and what activities occur there. Do the kids play with toys on the floor? Do they do arts and crafts projects with paint, glue, and glitter? Does the family gather on Saturday afternoons and snack while watching a football game on television? Is it a formal living room where you entertain your friends and business clients? Is it a busy kitchen? Does the hallway extend from your front entrance or from a busier back door where the kids drop off their hockey skates?

The answers to these questions will help you to determine how durable and resilient a flooring surface needs to be, whether warmth and softness are requirements, and how much maintenance will be necessary to keep the surface clean and in good repair.

### ■ Step 2 DETERMINE DESIGN OBJECTIVES

Are you replacing just the flooring in the room? If so, your choices are limited by the style already established by other elements in the room. Your color choices can enhance the existing palette. If your project is a complete room makeover—including walls, furniture, and accessories—you have more flexibility, although your job is a bit more complex and involves more deci-

ABOVE
A classical motif, such as this Greek Key, can be fabricated in tile or stone, inlaid, or dyed or woven into a carpet to create a bold graphic border on a floor.

sions. Once you've determined your design objectives, compare your use/abuse analysis to the types of flooring that meet both your style and use needs. From the list of options that are left, you can narrow down your choices even more in terms of your budget.

### ■ Step 3 DRAW AND USE A FLOOR PLAN

After the use/abuse analysis and the list of design objectives have been completed, draw up a floor plan—a separate one for experimenting with your flooring ideas. Follow these guidelines: measure the length and width of the room, and plot it on graph paper, using a scale of 1 inch to 1 foot. If your room is larger than 8 x 10 feet, you can tape two pieces of 8½- x 11-inch graph paper together. Measure and mark the locations of entryways and any permanent features in the room, such as cabinets, fixtures, or appliances.

Make several photocopies of your floor plan. Reserve one copy as a template. Use the other copies for previewing pattern ideas for flooring that comes in tiles (ceramic, vinyl, or carpeting tiles). Buy multicolored pencils, and fill in your grid. You'll be able to determine not only how the pattern will look but also how many tiles of various colors you'll need to buy to complete the project.

## Step 4 COSTS PER SQUARE INCH

Chances are you have a budget in mind already, with an upper limit established. After you've completed the use/abuse analysis, determined your design objectives, and created a floor plan, the next step is figuring out how much of what kind of flooring material you can afford.

Most flooring is priced in terms of square feet. To determine how many square feet are in your room, round the measurements off to the next foot. Then simply mulitply the length by the width. For example, for a room measuring 10 feet 4 inches x 12 feet 6 inches, round the figures to 11 x 13 feet. Multiply 11 x 13 feet (that's 143 square feet). You will end up with extra flooring, but it is better to have more than less.

Some flooring—like carpeting—is priced in terms of square yards. To determine the number of square yards in your room, divide the number of square feet by nine. In our example, there are just under 16 square yards in 143 square feet.

Let's say you have a budget of $850 to purchase tile for your 10-foot 4-inch x 12-foot 6-inch room. For the sake of the illustration, let's assume your subflooring is adequate, you have the tools, and the cost of adhesive and grout for your room is about $75. That leaves you with $775. To determine how much you can spend per tile, divide the remainder by the number of square feet in the room. In our example, $775 divided by 143 square feet equals about $5.40 per square foot of tile. Now that your flooring has been decided, it's time to consider treatments for walls and windows.

ABOVE
A solid wood floor is costly to install, but it is quintessentially warm, decoratively speaking. Natural oak, which was used in this kitchen, has traditional country appeal. A durable clear polyurethane finish will protect it from water damage.

# design workbook
## SPECIAL TREATMENT

## medallions

A medallion can be a focal point on a large floor. It is typically round or oval, but it can also be octagonal, star-shaped or square.

## borders

Another way to bring attention to a handsome floor is with a border. Wood borders such as this one, top left, may come pre- or unfinished.

## faux effects

With stain and paint, it's possible to create out-standing effects. Different colors produce an inlaid effect, and paint was used to mimic marble.

## mixed media

Combing several types of tile, such as ceramic, stone, and glass, adds sophistication. For rustic appeal, handmade clay tiles and solid-wood planks form a winning duo, left.

# design workbook

## BEGUILE WITH TILE

## small tiles, big ideas

Ceramic tiles with a soft-matte finish resemble tumbled limestone. Their composition, done in several neutral colors, dresses an entry hall floor.

## pebbles rock!

Usually sold in interlocking sheets on a mesh backing, pebble tiles, top left, can be used on the floor for a natural look.

## layered effect

Combining large porcelain tiles with small stone or glass mosaic tiles in this way, far left, almost looks like an area rug is under the island.

## classic inspiration

Motifs with classical roots never fall from fashion. This rope twist mosaic accent border can be crafted by hand or purchased pre-assembled.

# walls and windows

THE WAY WITH WALLS   DECORATIVE PAINT TECHNIQUES
PAINTING WALLS AND TRIM   SELECTING WALLCOVERINGS AND BORDERS
WINDOW TREATMENTS   DESIGN WORKBOOK

Although they play an important role in interior design,

wall and window treatments are relatively easy to change. So if you are

looking for an easy, inexpensive way to freshen the look of any room,

think about painting the walls, adding a wainscot, or simply installing a

new window treatment. New wall finishes allow you to play with the over-

all design, and they offer the opportunity to introduce different color and

texture to the room. New window treatments can update a tired room

while allowing you to better control natural light and seal off drafts and

unwanted heat gain from outside.

When designing a room, it makes sense to consider

windows and walls together. In this chapter, you'll find

many doable ideas for them and see how these two

important architectural features relate to one another.

way it is perceived with regard to size and shape. (Refer to the first two chapters, "Design Basics," beginning on page 12 and "Color and Pattern," which starts on page 32, for more information.)

# the way with walls

The very size of a wall makes it an important element in your decor. A wall can stand as a dramatic statement on its own or serve unobtrusively as a backdrop, letting the furnishings take center stage. Paint and wallcovering are your two basic choices for finishing them, but there are myriad options and versatility within these two categories.

Generally, walls in contemporary interiors should be kept simple. Fussy wallpaper patterns won't work. Wallpaper designs that represent natural materials (especially textured ones) look best, as do walls painted in neutral hues or in faux renditions of stone.

Today's choices for decorating walls and windows are probably more varied than ever before. For windows, they run the gamut from neoclassical looks in swags and draperies to contemporary coverings such as pleated shades and Venetian blinds. For walls, there are infinite options, including painted effects, as well as wallcoverings in simple stripes and plaids or detailed florals and textures. Your ultimate decision will affect not only the finished appearance of the room in terms of its style but also the

However, feel free to dress up the walls of traditional and country-style interiors with lots of color, pattern, and pattern-on-pattern designs executed in wallcoverings or with paint. Florals, stripes, or heraldic patterns work well with traditional interiors; plaids, checks, and mini-prints look particularly appropriate in country-style settings. Stenciled borders and other unpretentious painted effects look equally at home. Use the following Smart Steps to help make your decision.

# smart steps
## surface value

### Step 1 ASSESS THE CONDITION OF THE WALLS

Before deciding whether to paint or use wallcovering, examine the condition of the surface. No matter which treatment you choose, make sure that the walls are smooth for the best result. What's the point of investing time and money in a new wall treatment if there are bumps or dents that will mar the new surface? Small holes can be fixed with joint compound and a light sanding. Large holes in wallboard or cracks in plaster will need more attention, perhaps from a professional. Minor imperfections can be ignored. Wallpaper will hide them, and some painted effects, such as faux stone or aged plaster, may actually look more authentic thanks to them.

If the existing treatment is wallpaper, remove it before painting or applying new wallpaper. Paneling presents other problems. If you take it down, you risk damaging the wallboard underneath it. However, you can paint over paneling as long as you lightly sand the surface first. You can also hang wallpaper over paneling, but you will have to install a special liner paper over the paneling to give it a smooth surface for the new application.

### Step 2 NARROW DOWN YOUR CHOICES

Sometimes it's easy to know what you want. But at other times, the freedom and variety of a multitude of options can quickly become a case of too much of a good thing. How often have you decided to just paint the walls white or beige until you're ready to decide what to do with them? How often have you left them that way? There's nothing wrong with painting walls white or beige, as long as it isn't done as a cop-out. So for the sake of cohesiveness, choose a wall treatment at the same time that you're making decisions about the rest of the room's furnishings. For inspiration, look at the pictures in this book, visit decorator showhouses, and read home-decorating magazines. If you're putting together a period-style room, go to the library and do some research about the colors and patterns that were popular during that era. Numerous well-known paint companies and wallpaper manufacturers offer products that have been inspired by or authentically reproduce historical colors or patterns. Ask your retailer about them. If you can't get samples, ask about the company's 800 number or Web site so you can order a brochure.

To narrow down the field even further, try out different options on your sample board. Get paint chips, swatches of wallpaper, or try out finishes, and then compare them with the fabrics and carpet you've chosen for the room. Live with them for a few days before making a final choice.

# decorative paint techniques

Solid-color painted walls will never go out of fashion, but these days the decision to paint can extend far beyond simply picking a hue. In addition to providing color, painted effects, such as sponging, stenciling, and *trompe l' oeil,* can add texture and dimension to an interior. These and other established techniques are enjoying a renaissance of popularity because they offer an easy and inexpensive way to add uniqueness and personality to a room, whether contemporary or traditional. Some of them are simple to do even if you're not particularly artistic. Others require an experienced hand. To give you an idea of what you can expect and whether you'll need to call in a professional, here is an overview of the most popular painted effects.

## Sponging, Ragging, and Combing

*Sponging,* which involves using a sponge to apply or remove wet paint, is probably the easiest and most versatile of all the decorative paint techniques. It produces a highly textured surface that has great visual depth, which helps to disguise imperfections in walls and hide fingerprints and soil in heavily trafficked areas such as hallways and children's rooms. First, select your paint colors or shades of the same hue—one for the wall background and one or more for sponging. The background color, often a light neutral shade, can be applied to the wall straight from the can, whether it's a latex or oil-based product, but the paint that you choose for the sponging has to be thinned first. Latex paints can be thinned with water to create a wash. Use paint thinner with an oil-based paint to make it a glaze. (The latex wash is often referred to as a glaze, too.) Commercial glazes are available and can be tinted to create the desired color. Sponges for sponge painting are available

**LEFT**
Walls with a ragged-on glaze finish have a smooth mottled appearance that resembles brushed suede in this small remodeled powder room. The finished effect depends on the type of cloth you use and the pressure you apply when working the glaze.

**BELOW**
The colors of the paint and glaze were blended using a soft cloth, while the media were still wet. Using other materials can create a variety of looks.

from paint stores and home-decorating centers. Wear rubber gloves when working the paint on or off the wall.

*Sponging on* entails dipping a moistened sponge into the wash or glaze, wringing it out, then dabbing it against the wall repeatedly until it runs out of color. This process is carried out over the entire surface. To sponge off, apply paint to a section of the wall (not too much, because the paint must remain wet to sponge off), and blot it with a sponge. Rinse the sponge in an appropriate solvent (water or paint thinner) when it becomes saturated with paint.

*Ragging on* and *ragging off* are similar processes to sponging on and sponging off, except the sponge is replaced with a clean, lint-free cloth. For this effect, have a lot of extra cloth on hand because the fabric is easily saturated and more difficult to rinse than a sponge.

With *combing* or *dragging,* the background color is revealed as a comb, brush, or other tool is dragged over a freshly applied layer of wash or glaze. (Appropriate tools are available at home-decorating centers.) For this technique, as with sponging off and ragging off, it is important to maintain a brisk work pace because the paint must be wet for the combed texture to take successfully.

**BELOW LEFT**
Some techniques are the answer for not-so-perfect surfaces because they hide imperfections, especially if you wish to create an aged look.

**BELOW RIGHT**
Dragging a brush through wet glaze created the wood-grain striations on these door panels.

# Stenciling and Stamping

*Stenciling* is simple, stylized, and charming. It has an honorable history going back as far as Pompeiian villas and Early American homes, and it is enjoying a widespread revival today. Stencils are frequently used as wall borders and accents in country-style interiors, as well as friezes in traditional decorating schemes such as Victorian. Craft and home-decorating stores have precut stencils in nearly every imaginable motif, plus brushes and appropriate paints. Precut stencils come with instructions for use. If commercial designs don't suit you, there are materials available for cutting your own.

The success of a stenciled design depends largely on your ability to keep the stencil straight. Precut stencils should have registration marks, but you will have to make them on any hand-cut stencils. Keeping the stencil flat against the surface is also key. You will need a separate brush for each color you're using. Also be careful not to overload the brush with paint. After blotting the brush on a paper towel, work the stencil in a light dabbing motion.

**ABOVE**
Stenciling the wall with fronds was an easy way to add the tropical look that the home-owners desired.

**LEFT**
A stamp was used to create the repeat pattern of stars on this surface. Metallic-gold paint was used for accenting.

**RIGHT**
For added sophistication, layer several techniques. Here, the wall was painted, then glazed and mottled. The stenciled border is the finishing detail.

Another quick and easy technique is *stamping,* which uses raised patterns for block-print painting. Random stamping is easy: just dip the stamp into a small amount of paint, and then press it onto the surface. Formal designs require plotting your motif on the surface beforehand.

## Glazing and Washing

A *glaze* is a paint or colorant mixed with a transparent glazing medium and diluted with thinner. A glaze produces a luminous translucent finish. A *wash* is a thinned-out latex or acrylic paint. It creates a flat, gauzy film of color. Both create a sense of added dimension to walls. Remember with thinned paint, the color or shade of the wall beneath the glaze or wash will show through. Choose colors for the wall, and wash or glaze with this effect in

mind. It is a good idea, with quicker-drying latex especially, to do an entire wall at one time so that paint dries evenly. To apply, use a paint roller, finishing the corners and edges with a brush.

## Marbling

Applied with a steady, practiced hand, an oil glaze or latex wash can also yield a beautiful faux-marble effect. Marbling is fabulous for adding classical details to a room, but it can also work well in contemporary kitchens and baths where natural materials abound. The technique for marbling is more advanced than the others discussed so far, however. The background and the effect are applied at the same time, and paint must be worked while the surface is still wet but not too wet. After adding the colors, blot them off gingerly using a clean rag. You can do the veining freehand using a feather and artist's oils or acrylics, depending on whether you're applying a glaze or a wash. You'll have to blot the veins, too. Make sure they are subtly blended before brushing a final glaze on top of the design. A bit of advice: if you don't have the patience to practice this technique until you've mastered it, hire a professional artist for the job.

## Graining

*Wood graining,* a technique suitable for wall panels, doors, and moldings, simulates a specific grain, such as mahogany or oak. It involves dragging with special graining brushes and detailing with rubber combs to make grains, knots, and whorls. The basic way to create the look of wood is to drag a dark brown wash or glaze over a yellow-painted background. Once the dragging is complete and before the paint dries, another tool called an over-grainer (available at home-decorating and craft stores) can be used to further manipulate the paint to look like wood grain. After the paint dries completely, it is sealed with a transparent surface coat that gives the "wood" its luster. Recreating the grain of a specific wood species is much more complicated and generally requires professional know-how. However, as with marbling, practice helps.

## Trompe l'Oeil

Increasingly popular with designers and homeowners alike is *trompe l'oeil* painting, used to make living spaces sophisticated or fun. Trompe l'oeil, or effects that "fool the eye," can be full-wall murals or simply small details. They can give the illusion of depth in a small space, for example, or create scenes such as a landscape or a sky that are so realistic that they appear to be what they depict. Unless you're a skilled artist, hire a professional for this job. The box above right explains how to find one.

RIGHT
You can carefully study the pattern of the grain in a particular type of wood to reproduce it faithfully, or you can take creative liberties. Dragging a comb through wet glaze on this bookcase created a handsome, if not authentic, wood-like pattern.

## smart tip FINDING ARTISTS

To find an artist who can give his or her clients a one-of-a-kind look that completes a decorating scheme, designers simply turn to their directories and pick up the phone. You may have to look a little harder, but not much. You can get a referral from a designer yourself, or check the source list at the back of any decorating magazine that features someone's work you may have admired. Designers who work at home centers or the staff at your favorite paint and wallpaper store may also have leads to recommend. And certainly, if you have admired a painted effect in someone else's house, ask how to contact the artist. Be sure to look at as many examples as possible of an artist's work before hiring him or her for your job. Any professional will be happy to show you a portfolio and supply references.

# Paint Products— Instant Effects

Homeowners who don't have artistic aspirations but do have the desire to add something special to painted surfaces can do so with paint products that yield special effects and easily applied textured surfaces. With all of these products come specific instructions that must be followed carefully. Some require spray applicators; others can be sprayed or rolled on directly from the can. If you're investing in one of these premium finishes, spend the extra money for high-quality tools, which can make a big difference in the final result. Because these paints cost more than standard products, you may want to use them sparingly or limit them to trimwork. Wherever you're applying an instant-effect paint, it's always a good idea to test the application on poster board before painting it on your walls. Help is available wherever these paints are sold. Instructional videos can make it easier to follow directions. A few of the looks you can create with a direct-application product include stone, metal, pearl, suede, denim, and a crazed or crackled finish.

ABOVE RIGHT
Elaborate trim and paneling provide a rich-looking framework for faux Moroccan-leather walls.

NEAR RIGHT
To achieve the look, Chinese red and black oil glazes—brushed over 75 percent of a dry, true-red base coat—must be blended by dabbing the wet surface with a cheesecloth.

FAR RIGHT
The final finish is a stunning surface of great depth that truly fools the eye.

ABOVE
A faux-stone wall is one way to dress up a plain entry hall.
Make a grid for the blocks with pencil or chalk lines.

Faux stone; finishes that simulate the shadowy, brushable nap of suede; and satiny pearl effects should be applied with a high volume, low-pressure sprayer. A professional painter might be able to get the desired look from this kind of paint by using a good, short-nap roller, but it is not the application method recommended by the manufacturer, especially for an inexperienced do-it-yourselfer.

Another faux-stone product comes as a two-process spray kit. First you apply the base coat, and after allowing it to dry, you finish it with a topcoat. When working with a sprayer, be sure to cover nearby areas to protect them from overspray. With a little practice, you can use a hand-held paint shield.

The aged effect called crackle, which resembles the dried, crazed quality of paint in old houses, can also be applied using a two-part method of paint and crackle medium. This is a popular technique to use on furniture or wood paneling.

Don't forget: when you're working with paint, always keep the room well ventilated.

ABOVE
A faux-stone wall is one way to dress up a plain entry hall.
Make a grid for the blocks with pencil or chalk lines.

## Kid Pleasers

Formulated and marketed for children's rooms, glow-in-the-dark paints and glittery topcoats are easy to apply. The glow paint is designed for highlighting designs such as stars, for example, that have been painted, stamped, or stenciled onto sections rather than for an entire wall application. To produce a really dramatic effect, you'll have to apply multiple coats of the paint. The glitter goes on over the base coat or the painted design with a roller. Even-handed rolling is important when using a glitter product. If you have to redo some spots with a second coat, the glitter will clump, and those areas will look uneven. As with any textured treatment, you'll have to lightly sand glitter-treated walls if you want a smooth surface when you repaint them later. Think about this before going ahead with this project.

# painting walls and trim

Even if you prefer to give your walls just a standard coat of paint (always a dependable decorating strategy), you've got a wide range of colors from which to choose; even neutral hues come in a variety of shades and tones. Professional designers typically bring samples of the fabric and carpet to the paint store to have a custom color mixed to match. These paints are more expensive but are worth it. Even two shades of white can clash. (See Chapter Two, "Color and Pattern," on page 32, for more advice.) You can also bring home sample color chips. Look at them with your furnishings in all types of light and at various times of the day. To pull your interior design together, select a color that you can pick up from the upholstery or drapery fabric, in either a matching or contrasting tone.

Generally, flat paints are best for walls and ceilings. These surfaces tend to mar easily, so you may not want to use flat paints for a surface that is prone to abuse or hand marks, such

## smart tip PAINT BASICS

Most interior paints are either alkyd-resin (oil-based) products or latex (water-based) varieties. Oil and water don't mix, and generally neither do the paints based on them. For multilayered effects, stick to one type or the other.

Alkyd paints are somewhat lustrous, translucent, and hard-wearing. But alkyds, and the solvents needed for cleaning up, are toxic and combustible, requiring good work-site ventilation and special disposal methods. Professional decorative painters often prefer slower-drying alkyds, which allow more time to achieve complex special effects. Alkyd paints are better suited to techniques such as combing and ragging, where glaze is brushed on in sections and then manipulated.

Latex paints, which now approach alkyd's durability and textural range, are nontoxic and quick-drying, and they clean up easily with soap and water. Most nonprofessionals find latex paint easier to deal with and capable of creating many popular decorative finishes. In general, latex paints are best suited to effects that are dabbed on over the base coat, as in sponging or stenciling. The short drying time can be an advantage because mistakes can be painted over and redone. Latex paint is usually the best choice for covering an entire wall, too, because the job can be completed from start to finish in just a few hours.

as a wall next to a staircase. For trim, a semigloss finish is the typical choice, although you may prefer a high-gloss enamel. Usually glossy paints are reserved for the kitchen and bathroom because they can stand up to the moisture and grime that accumulates in these rooms.

In addition to a variety of colors and shades from which to choose, top-of-the-line paints usually go on easier and require fewer coats. They also clean easier and will remain looking fresh longer. The money you spend on a better-quality paint saves the expense of more frequent repainting.

**LEFT**
The tone-on-tone stripes on the upper portion of this dining-room wall were painted with a narrow roller. The molding used to create wainscot "panels" wears a red marbled finish.

# selecting wallcoverings and borders

Wallpaper, fabric, tile, paneling, and mirrors are your choices in decorative wallcovering. *Mirrored glass* installed from floor to ceiling is a nifty device for creating the illusion of space in small quarters, but it is one that should be used sparingly. Solid *wood paneling* can look rich or rustic depending on the finish and trimwork. It also has insulating and sound-deadening properties. *Ceramic tile* is typically used in kitchens and bathrooms, but the vast number of decorative designs on today's market offer creative possibilities for

wall decor, including murals, in any room in the house. *Fabric* such as silk, linen, brocade, wool, and suede are delicate, elegant, and expensive. *Wallpaper,* on the other hand, can be affordable, stylish, and durable depending on what it's made of—paper, vinyl, or other natural or synthetic materials—and its finish. Myriad motifs, textures, and patterns add to its appeal.

## Decorating with Wallpaper

There's no getting around it: wallpaper is versatile, with an almost infinite number of styles, colors, patterns, and textures from which to choose. It's also a great mimic of fabric, natural materials, such as stone, wood, grass, or bamboo, and even painted effects. These lookalikes are cheaper to install than the real thing and are more durable and easier to care for. But what we call "wallpaper" may not be made of paper at all. (In fact, it rarely is, with the exception of some custom-made specialty designs.) Here's a rundown of more common types.

**Vinyl Coverings.** Vinyl is the most popular wallcovering because it can take a beating. Finger marks, grease, moisture, and water pose no threat to its long-lasting good looks and wear. There are three types for your consideration.

■ *Fabric-backed vinyl* has a vinyl top layer over fiberglass or cloth. It's tough, so you can scrub it when necessary. The material is heavy, and it usually doesn't come prepasted. Because it's porous, manufacturers recommend using a vinyl adhesive that contains a mildewcide, especially if you plan to use it in a room where there's a lot of moisture—a bathroom or kitchen, for example.

■ *Paper-backed vinyl* is lighter and typically prepasted, peelable, and washable. There are thousands of colors and patterns in its repertoire. Raised or expanded vinyls come with increased surface texture. These wallpaper products can simulate other materials, such as grass cloth, granite, textured painted effects, and decorative plaster work; their texture does a good job of concealing problems with irregular and cracked walls.

■ *Vinyl-coated paper* is inexpensive, but it doesn't have the durability of fabric- or paper-backed vinyl. Its thin protective coating tears easily and doesn't hold up to dirt and stains. Even natural oils from your hands can permanently mar it.

OPPOSITE
A pale, damask-pattern wallcovering mixes well with other blue-color prints in the room, including pinstriped linens and Asian ceramics.

LEFT
A vibrant toile has high impact in this powder room. Its earthy-gold background coordinates beautifully with the honey-color wood vanity.

on the design. Certain patterns may camouflage slight wall imperfections.

**Natural Coverings.** Grass cloth, hemp, and other natural weaves bring texture to a room. They are particularly suited to contemporary interiors. Some are very delicate and require application over liner paper. They can also fray and are not washable. These coverings should be professionally installed.

**Embossed Coverings.** *Lincrusta,* which is made of oils, resins, and wood pulp over canvas, is a heavy linoleum-like covering. Its embossed surface features stylized designs that simulate raised moldings made of wood, plaster, tile, or leather. *Anaglypta,* which is cheaper and lighter, is made of cotton-fiber pulp.

**Foil Coverings.** Like mirrors, foil wallpapers can make a room seem larger. But for these delicate coverings, the surface of the wall must be as smooth as glass because foil will magnify any of its imperfections. Installing liner paper before applying the foil can help. A painted effect over a plain foil can look dramatic. You might consider this as one idea for creating a focal point in a bland room. Avoid using foils in sunny rooms—their reflective surfaces can result in too much glare—but do consider them to bring cheer to a room that's dark. Foils are available with or without a prepasted backing. But because they are delicate and difficult to handle, professional installation is always recommended.

**Flocked Coverings.** Popularized in the eighteenth century, flocked coverings feature a raised, fuzzy pattern that resembles expensive cut velvet. They look at home with traditional or period interiors, but use them sparingly; they can be too ornate at times for contemporary tastes. Some flocked wallpapers are prepasted, and most are strippable. Their washability depends

Both types were first manufactured in the late nineteenth century and are once again popular. These rich-looking, durable coverings can be painted and repainted several times over the years. They also camouflage imperfect walls. You can use them for an entire wall application or halfway up the wall, chair-rail style. Anaglypta also comes as a border for friezes. You can find these papers in home centers today, but follow the installation directions carefully. Because of its weight, leave Lincrusta to a professional installer.

**Fiberglass Weaves.** Mainly commercial-grade products, fiberglass weaves are yet another option. Made of thickly woven strands of the material used for insulation, they are quite heavy. You can even apply them over concrete-block walls. What's even better, they won't rot, burn, or support mold or mildew, so they are excellent for areas exposed to moisture. The look of fiberglass weaves is varied and ranges from gauze-like patterns to designs that resemble vinyl wallcoverings. If you don't see them in your retail store, inquire about contacting a manufacturer directly.

Now that you've got the lowdown on the types of wall-coverings that are on today's market, here's what you need to do to select the right one for your project.

# smart steps
## wallpaper wisdom

### Step 1 FOLLOW DESIGN GUIDELINES

When you're shopping for wallpaper, consider the scale and proportion of the pattern in terms of the room you're decorating. Although a particular design in a sample book may attract your eye, think of how it will affect the perception of the size and shape of the room. There is no rule that says you can't use a large print in a small space; however, oversize designs can overpower tiny rooms. Of course, they can dramatize them as well. If your project is a formal dining room or an entry hall, go for boldness. But if it's the family room, you might want to be more conservative in your choice because you spend more time in this space and a large print may tire you. In terms of line, choose a pattern that can add the illusion of height in a room with a low ceiling. Vertical stripes would be excellent in this case. Install wallpaper halfway up the wall with a border paper at chair-rail height to visually lower tall ceilings. Think about balance. If all of the other features in the room tend to be oversize, a mini-print might look out of place. And don't forget harmony. Coordinate all patterns and colors with the other hues and fabrics in the room, as well as those in adjoining areas.

### Step 2 TRY IT OUT FOR SIZE

Don't ever guess about wallpaper. You may think it matches everything else, but as with paint, once you get it home and hold it up to the sofa or the curtains, you may realize you've made a mistake. Bring home

**ABOVE RIGHT**
Be unabashedly bold about wall pattern. Then go easy with solid-color accessories.

**RIGHT**
Combine wallpaper with paneling for a classic look. Crisp white paint on the wainscot makes the wallcovering stand out.

wallpaper samples and try them out on your sample board. Sometimes a retailer will let you take home the book for a few days. When you think you've found the right pattern, buy just one roll at first. Cut a few wall-length strips that you can tape to the wall and live with for a week. This will allow you to get a more realistic feeling for the effect the wallpaper will make on the overall room and at different times of the day in varying levels of light. It's worth the small investment in a single roll of wallpaper to make sure it's right for your project. If you don't like it, you really haven't lost much.

**ABOVE**
Look-alikes may be far more durable than the real thing. This vinyl wallcovering looks like a natural weave, but is tougher.

**ABOVE RIGHT**
Handsome hardware can be as decorative as the window treatment itself. Coordinate rod and curtain styles.

# window treatments

You can accomplish a number of things with a window treatment: control the amount of natural light permitted into the room; limit summer heat gain and winter heat loss; enhance a good view or conceal a bad one; provide privacy where necessary; camouflage architectural blunders, such as ill-proportioned or oddly placed windows, or (conversely) dress the window without obscuring its handsome features; or create a focal point for a room or underscore its decorating scheme. Typically interior designers will make recommendations about window decor during the planning stages of a project. It's not a good idea to wait until everything else is done. That isn't to say that you can't change a window treatment unless you make major alterations in the room. Of course you can; in fact, it's a good way to give a tired scheme a face lift. But if you are doing a major makeover, don't leave the windows as an afterthought. Here's how to get started.

## smart steps
### make no mistake

**Step 1** ASSESS THE WINDOW'S STYLE
Window style is the first thing to look at: compare it with the window treatment you're considering. What kind of architectural details does the window have or lack that you can modify or enhance? (See Chapter Six, "Distinctive Touches," page 132, for information on window styles and ornamental trim.) Always remember that

decorating and architectural styles are linked; not necessarily in the strictest sense, but there should be a relationship between the two. Heavy velvet panels paired with formal swags will appear out of place in a country parlor. In the same way, ruffled calico curtains strike the wrong note in a room that's streamlined and contemporary.

## Step 2 REMEMBER THE ROOM'S FUNCTION

A bedroom needs to feel cozy, so you'll want a window treatment that will keep out drafts at night but let in air and light in the morning. A bathroom requires something that can stand up to moisture and is easily washed. The same can be said for a kitchen, which in addition to moisture must suffer the assaults of the cooking grease and the grime that sticks to it.

## Step 3 NOTE THE ROOM'S ORIENTATION

Review the section on natural light in Chapter Three, "The Right Light," and consider the time of day that you use the room and its orientation in terms of the sun. This will tell whether you need to control natural light at the time of day you're most likely to use the room. It will also help you decide whether or not the window treatment should play a role in insulating the space—particularly if the window faces north, which means it receives no direct sunlight.

**LEFT**
Roman shades like these are a perfectly acceptable way to dress a bay of windows, especially if you prefer a simple, tailored treatment that is easily adjusted for light control and privacy.

**BELOW**
Layered fabric treatments can be expensive, but they can dress up a plain window. Linings and interlinings are important for shape and to protect against fading, especially in a sunny room.

## Step 4 CONSIDER WINDOW SIZE

Particularly in older homes, windows are often too small, even for modest-sized rooms. Sometimes that's just because the technologically advanced glazings we have today weren't available when the house was built, so the architect or builder kept the window small to avoid problems with heat loss. But you can create a more harmonious balance between window size and the room with the right treatment and installation. For a short window, install the rod above the trim or just below the ceiling line. Hang extra-long panels, and let them puddle on the floor just enough to make the windows appear grand. For a window that isn't wide enough for the wall, extend the window treatment beyond the frame on each side.

Some windows have the opposite problem—they're so large that they overwhelm everything else. In this case, you can tone down the scale by keeping the look simple. If a window is too tall, don't use long panels. Break the length up by dressing the top of the window with a valance or swag that's different from the rest of the design. When windows in a room are different sizes, deemphasize the difference with curtains that are all the same length. Don't pile on several layers, and avoid heavily patterned fabrics.

## Step 5 LOOK IN, LOOK OUT

What do you see through your windows—both from the inside and out? Whatever is seen through the windows becomes part of the decor. Likewise, remember that whatever you leave exposed to the world outside is on public view. In this crowded society, few people have the privilege of a great view with no neighbors. For most windows, you'll need something that you can open and close easily. A combination of heavy panels and sheers or shades, blinds, or shutters can be one solution to the problem.

ABOVE RIGHT
Because the bed is against the wall, an adjustable balloon shade is a smart choice for the location.

RIGHT
Curtain panels that can be easily opened or closed are practical in a bedroom.

## Step 6 ESTIMATE YOUR BUDGET

How much or how little you have to spend on this project will determine whether you will order custom window treatments, buy ready-made versions, or make them yourself (something that requires skill and patience). The first option typically includes professional installation. Complex designs often require special skills because the window treatments are actually constructed on the window itself. This also means that the installer will have to remove them for cleaning and reinstall them. Ready-made window treatments are offered in several standard sizes to fit standard-size windows. See the box, "Smart Tip: Adding Professional Flair," below right, which will help you put designer touches to any window treatment no matter how much or how little you have to spend.

## Step 7 THINK ABOUT MAINTENANCE

It's expensive to have window treatments cleaned professionally and then reinstalled by an expert, so take these factors into account when making your plans. If you can't afford to spend a few hundred dollars on this periodically, rethink your choice.

BELOW LEFT
Sumptuous fabric draped from the ceiling to the floor calls attention to a bay of handsome windows.

BELOW
Fine fabrics, such as delicate silk, will require professional cleaning and may fade in the sun.

# smart tip

## ADDING PROFESSIONAL FLAIR

You can give your window treatment designs a professional look by using decorator tricks to customize readymades or dress your own home-sewn designs. These could include contrasting linings, tassels, cording, ribbons, or couture trimmings such as buttons, coins, or bows applied to edges. Another trick is to sew a fine wire into the hem of curtains or valances to create a pliable edge that you can shape yourself. Small weights that you can sew into the hem of drapery panels or jabots will make them hang better. For more inspiration look at fashion magazines and visit showrooms.

# Full Formal Window Treatments

A full formal treatment often involves two or three layers. One layer, called the *casement curtain,* is installed inside the window trim area. Typically it's a sheer, solid, or lace panel that lays straight or is gathered at the top. *Overdraperies,* often referred to simply as draperies, make up the second layer. Generally, they cover the window and the trim and, space permitting, extend beyond it either to the sides or above the window.

The words "draperies" and "curtains" can mean the same thing, but some people make a distinction between the two. Generally, draperies are pleated and hang from hooks that attach to tracks in a traverse rod, which allows them to be drawn (closed) with a cord. Curtains hang on rods from rings, tabs, or ties; they're drawn by hand. Formal draperies and curtains should be lined to give them body. An insulated interlining that reduces cold penetration and muffles sound is also a good idea. When installed, they should brush the floor. Draperies that can be drawn may eliminate the need for a shade or blinds because well-lined draperies reduce sun glare efficiently.

The third, and optional, layer of a full formal window treatment is a *valance,* sometimes called a *pelmet,* which runs horizontally across the top of the window and covers the drapery or curtain heading. To some eyes, the window treatment is

**OPPOSITE**
A luxurious heavyweight fabric and elegant fringe trimmings enhance the sophistication of this formal treatment.

**ABOVE RIGHT**
A more contemporary-style approach has been taken in this bedroom where simple lines define the architecture and the furnishings, including the formal, but unfussy floor-length draperies.

**RIGHT**
Sheer cafe-length curtains, formal panels, and matching swag-and-jabot valances comprise this custom-made design. The fabric is a floral chintz that suits the English-country interior.

unfinished without this last element, but this is strictly a matter of taste.

A simple or soft valance made of fabric may hang on a separate rod, or it may be attached to the drapery or curtain. It may be composed of the same fabric as the drapery or a coordinating one. There are various styles including a swag or cascade, a pinch-pleated version, a tab-top, or a free-form valance that can be created by draping scarves or fabrics over a rod. The fabric can be the same as the drapery fabric or one that coordinates with it. Ornate soft valances often feature vertical gathers that make horizontal pleats for *ruched, ballooned,* or *festooned* effects. Many valances are trimmed or shaped into points or scallops at the bottom. Ruffles, fringe, tassels, and piping all add dressy details to the edges.

A hard valance, also called a *cornice* or a *lambrequin,* is usually made of wood and covered with fabric or upholstery. It is permanently fastened to the wall with screws. Box shapes and scalloped edges are the most common. Because they can't be removed easily for cleaning, the fabric covering valances should lay flat against the board backing or upholstery filler for easy vacuuming.

Fabrics that lend themselves to formal window treatments include luminous silks and damasks, weighty velvet, wool, tapestry, and brocade. (See Chapter Two, "Color and Pattern," on page 32, for more information.)

## Informal Window Treatments

Casual window treatments may consist of one or two layers or nothing at all. If location and privacy considerations permit, a beautiful window looks attractive without the dressing—especially when there's also something pleasant to see outside. Sometimes simple casement curtains installed on handsome decorative rods or just a valance looks attractive in informal

rooms. If only the lower half of the window needs covering, café-style curtains offer privacy without blocking light.

Swag-and-tail arrangements can look refined yet informal. Swags are often confused with valances because, like valances, they cross the window horizontally at the top. Unlike valances, however, the tails (or *jabots*) cascade down the sides of the window. Swags may sit over draperies in lieu of a valance, or they may be used alone. Decorative details like *rosettes* (clusters of fabric that have been gathered or pleated to look like a rose) can be used to attach swags to the window frame instead of the traditional rod. This is a good way to create a no-sew swag with just a bit of fabric gathered and fastened at each corner and left to swoop across the top of the window in the center. You can do this with inexpensive fabric remnants, sheers, or even sheeting to create an informal window dress-up for pennies. Special hardware is available that makes creating rosettes easy, too.

Fabrics that lend themselves to an informal look include anything cotton, such as chintz, ticking, toile, linen, gingham, and muslin. Unlike the fabric of formal draperies and curtains, most of these are washable. Just be sure to preshrink fabric if you are making the curtains yourself.

If minimal treatments pose a problem with light control or privacy, you can easily pair them with shades, blinds, or louvered shutters that roll out of sight when not needed.

**BELOW LEFT**
A tabbed valance hanging from an attractive rod can stand alone as a minimal, but attractive treatment on a window.

**BELOW**
This tailed balloon shade is also pretty by itself, but like a valance, it can be part of a multilayered design.

# Shades, Blinds, and Louvered Shutters

*Shades* are generally considered soft window treatments. They are made of a single piece of fabric or vinyl attached to a roller and operated with a cord or via a spring mechanism. Ones made of fabric can be flat, pleated, or gathered. Shades are versatile, too; they can block out the light entirely or simply filter it. Use them alone on a window for a casual look, or pair them with curtains for something formal. Popular variations include:

■ **Roman shades.** When pulled up, roman shades feature sleek, flat, horizontal pleats. They are well-suited to contemporary-style interiors.

■ **Balloon shades.** When pulled up, the gathered fabric forms billowing festoons or fans. An eighteenth-century design, balloon shades suit period and traditional-style rooms.

■ **Pleated fabric shades.** Lightweight pleated shades stack so tightly when rolled up, they almost disappear under a curtain. They come in a variety of colors and fabrics.

■ **Cellular shades.** The pleated-fabric construction of cellular shades resembles a honeycomb. They are available in a wide range of styles, colors, and faux finishes.

Whether made of metal or vinyl, *blinds* effectively block the sun and the outdoors in general when they are closed. Today's many styles include myriad colors, textured fabric finishes, and wood, and the choice of vertical slats or horizontal slats in standard, mini, or micro widths. Contrasting tapes are available to create interesting decorative details. Verticals are strictly suited for contemporary rooms, but the others look at home anywhere. Pair blinds with another treatment or let them stand alone.

Wooden louvered *shutters* always lend a tony appearance to any interior. Open them for air; close them for privacy. Stained wood finishes complement country or traditional-style rooms. Some shutter types come with a fabric panel that can be coordinated with other furnishings. "Plantation" shutters, which feature wide louvers, painted white or off-white, complement contemporary settings.

# design workbook

## PAINTED-ON GLAMOUR

### carried away

This living room recalls summer days spent in a luxuroius Italian villa on the Amalfi coast thanks to the custom-painted muraled walls.

### into the woods

In this dramatic master bedroom, top left, deep, dark woods are accented by painted murals that depict lush trees and greenery.

### country vines

Stencils were used on the area just below this ceiling, far left, to create a pretty vine. Shading and highlighting were added with a brush.

### random pattern

An artist used a negative stencil technique to decorate this wall, left, by applying fern fronds to the surface; painting around and then removing them to reveal their shapes.

# design workbook
## COORDINATING WINDOWS

### functional form

Proper shading from sliding Shoji screens on the windows with a southern exposure keeps this living room light but not overly bright.

### stylish versatility

On the opposite, north-facing side of the room, top left, insulated curtain panels can be drawn closed to seal out cool night air.

### translucent beauty

Translucent sliding panels, far left, let in filtered sunlight so that the room is never dark, while light control and privacy are easily managed.

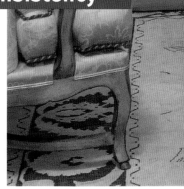

### design consistency

In the adjacent dining room, left, which can be viewed from the living area, red-striped curtains coordinate with accent pillows and additional upholstered furnishings.

# 6

# distinctive touches

ELEMENTS OF DESIGN   SPECIAL DETAILS   DESIGN WORKBOOK

I f your home is lacking personality, there are a number of things that you can do to improve it. For example, architectural elements can enhance the structural bare bones of a room. By exchanging a pair of flush, windowless doors for French doors, a dark dining room can be changed into a sunny, well-lit space; by adding an ornamental ceiling medallion and a cornice, a plain ceiling can become a showpiece. Decorative accessories are key, as well. A display of pottery turns built-in shelving into a noteworthy feature; a staggered arrangement of black-and-white photography adds interest to a stairway. Early in the decorating process, decide whether your space lacks architectural features, such as moldings. Maybe a fireplace needs updating with a new mantel. Even if it's a new way to arrange objects, you'll find the right ideas here.

Grouping different types of items for a display can be tricky but effective. This all-white theme is simple yet dramatic at the same time.

# elements of design

A t the initial planning stage described in Chapter One, when you analyze structural features, the room under scrutiny may not have any architectural or decorative details. Unless it's been altered over time, a period house, such as a Colonial or Victorian, may be rich with ornamentation. Today, however, many houses replicate the facades of those period buildings but eliminate the architectural elements inside. If you are faced with a nondescript room, you can introduce those features with store-bought trim or architectural salvage. The result can be an elegant foundation upon which to layer your carefully chosen design.

You can create a sense of style and history by changing door or window styles; replacing stair rails, balusters, and newel posts; or adding fireplace mantels. A window or fireplace can easily become the new focal point of a room. Other, more subtle touches, such as molding, ceiling medallions, and hardware, give a room a well-heeled resonance.

## Doors

If an uninteresting interior door does nothing for a traditional or period room's design, you might consider replacing it with a door style that provides greater visual interest.

Most doors are made of either wood, metal, glass, or a combination of these three. The two most common types of wood doors are flush and panel. *Flush* wood doors have a smooth surface; these doors may have solid or hollow-core construction and are preferred for

TOP RIGHT
Architectural trimwork, framed art, and accessories lend special distinction to this entry foyer.

RIGHT
Unique-looking louver doors made from a lightweight material complement this home's modern architecture.

contemporary settings. *Panel* doors consist of stiles (vertical members) and rails (horizontal members) with panels inserted between them. This type of door is favored for traditional interiors. An older and less common type is a *plank* door. It is composed of vertical boards (usually four or more) anchored together by two horizontal members and one diagonal member, which form a "Z" on the back of the door. Plank doors are suitable for country or rustic designs. In terms of styles for wood doors, there is a wide range, including double, pocket, Dutch (divided), louvered, and folding (accordion) types.

Metal doors, constructed of hollow steel with a solid-fiber infill, are rarely used for interiors in private homes, unless there is a need for protection from fire. Aside from flush-metal doors, some styles come with glass panels or louvers that may work for contemporary rooms.

Although frameless door styles exist, glass doors are usually framed in wood or metal, such as French doors or sliding glass doors. The glass itself offers a variety of decorative options. Glass can be etched, beveled, curved (slumped), and cut, as well as composed of stained or leaded glass or iridescent art glass.

**BELOW**
For architectural continuity, the arched tops of these French doors echo the shape of the home's interior doorways and are in keeping with the European-inspired design.

# Windows

Replacing ordinary windows with decorative bow, bay, arch-top, or even casement windows is another change that pays off big in terms of style. Before you choose a replacement window, consider how it will look from the exterior as well as the interior of your house; the new windows should be compatible with the architecture.

Residential windows come in wood, vinyl, or aluminum. *Wood* is the old standard; it can be painted or stained to match any decor, but it requires constant upkeep because weather exposure can cause deterioration. *Aluminum-* and *vinyl-clad wood* windows are two other choices; both are rot-proof and provide good insulation. A vinyl window is a sensible, low-maintenance option because it does not require painting or protective coatings, it resists corrosion and denting, and it offers excellent insulation. The color selection—white, gray, beige, and brown—is limited, however. Vinyl windows are available with wood cladding on the interior. *Aluminum* windows are easy to install but offer poor insulation qualities. They can be left unfinished (a metallic color) or coated with paint, enamel, or lacquer; wood cladding is also available.

Next, consider the basic types of windows and how they function. *Fixed* windows cannot be opened and are often used in combination with *operable* windows. *Double-hung* windows are the most common of the operable types; they have two sash that move up and down, which means that only half of the window can be open at any one time. *Casement* windows are hinged vertically to swing in or out in a door-like manner; they are operated by a crank. *Awning* windows are hinged horizontally to swing in or out. *Jalousie* windows have horizontally placed, narrow strips of glass that are opened louverlike by a crank. *Sliding* windows have top and bottom tracks on which the sash move sideways.

These practical considerations are important for your comfort, but you should also explore the various architectural styles of windows to match one with your decor. A group of three windows with an arch over the center unit is the classical makeup of a *Palladian* window. Some variations have three arches (one large, two small) or one fanlight-style arch over the three windows. This window tends to visually dominate a room, so it is good as a focal point.

A *picture* window is made up of one large fixed window flanked by two casements or double-hung units. As the name describes, picture windows are for framing dramatic views.

Like Palladian and picture windows, *bay* windows are also composed of three parts. The difference is that the windows are set at an angle to each other, creating an alcove. A curved version of this window is called either a *bow* window or a *circular bay.* A large bay window adds about 4 feet of extra space to a room, where you can situate a chair or a small dining table.

*Clerestory* windows are made of a strip of small, horizontal panes set high on a wall, near the ceiling. These windows are a good solution in spaces where you want natural light but need privacy.

**BELOW**
A comfortable built-in window seat and a pair of double-hung windows with muntined sashes lend charm to a more traditional-style home.

**OPPOSITE**
Thanks to energy-efficient glass, today's homes have larger windows that bring more of the outdoors inside. In this contemporary residence, casement windows suit the overall look of the home's classically modern lines.

There is also a variety of special small window shapes that are almost strictly decorative. These windows can be used independently or in combination with the standard types. An *elliptical* or *arched* window is often placed above double-hung or fixed windows, but it is also used alone in situations where a larger unit won't fit, such as in a dormer or a small bathroom. An *oval* (or *cameo*) window and a circular window are used in much the same way; both are sometimes located on narrow staircase landings to add light. For a more modern shape, a *triangular* window or a *trapezoidal* window is often paired with a large fixed window.

## Stairs

A staircase is also a good opportunity for embellishment, particularly because it is often the focal point of a space. Decorative newels, balusters, and railings are common stock millwork items. They're available in a variety of turned profiles, as well as standard sizes. With them, a staircase that was once only functional can become an attractive part of the room.

Other specialized brackets, with carved flourishes and fretwork-like designs, can further enhance a staircase. If you view a staircase from the side, the long leg of these L-shaped pieces fits beneath the edge of a tread, with the shorter leg extending the length of the riser. The bracket is simply nailed to the carriage the same way that you attach ordinary trim.

RIGHT
**Even spare modern structures have architectural details. The industrial metal railings, here, draw attention to the geometric lines in this open plan without closing off the various levels.**

Another way to dress up an open stair is to paint it in contrasting hues. The newel post, railing, and treads can be painted in a dark color, while the balusters, trim, and carriage echo the color of the walls in the room. Installing ceramic tiles on the risers can also add color and pattern to stairs.

## Mantels

A fireplace is invariably the focal point of any room in which it's located. There is good reason why it's one of the most desirable features in any home, new or old. It adds warmth—visually or literally—and it's striking in looks.

You may have an existing fireplace that needs to be dressed up because of a missing mantel, or you may want to add a new fireplace to your home. Either way, learn before you go shopping for a mantel and other fireplace parts so that you get exactly what you want. Here's a quick review of the basics:

▩ A *mantel* can be just a horizontal shelf above the fireplace opening or ornamental framing around the top and sides of the opening.

▩ An *overmantel* is a decorative treatment above the mantel that often incorporates a picture, mirror, or some shelving. Many Victorian mantels had overmantels with mirrors flanked by shelves that displayed knickknacks, for example.

▩ A *lintel* is a wood or stone beam that supports the top of the fireplace.

▩ The *jambs* are vertical supports along the sides of the fireplace, holding up the mantel.

▩ A *chimneypiece* is made up of the fireplace opening, mantel, and the overmantel.

■ A *hearth* is the floor that extends from the fireplace into the room. It is usually covered in a fire-resistant material, such as tile or brick.

■ A *flue* is the pipe or opening through which smoke from the fireplace is released.

■ Because the *chimney breast* contains the flue, it projects into the room. It is usually made of a fire-resistant material, such as stone, brick, or concrete.

Next, consider what type of fireplace will suit your decor best. The pared-down simplicity of a contemporary interior may call for a mantel-less (flush) fireplace, such as a stucco-finished wall around the opening, or an unadorned mantel. For traditional rooms, there is an unlimited choice of reproduction and salvaged mantels in period styles, including Colonial, Federal, Gothic, and Victorian. Mantels are usually made of marble, stone, wood, cast iron, or copper. A brick mantel is constructed as part of the entire fireplace; a wood mantel shelf is used for cobblestone and adobe fireplaces.

When choosing a mantel, keep certain clearances in mind. Make sure that woodwork, trim, and other combustible materials are at least 6 inches away from the fireplace opening. (This is the reason you'll often notice decorative tiles between the fireplace opening and a wooden mantel.) If a wooden mantel projects 1½ inches, it should be at least 12 inches from the fireplace opening.

When buying a mantel from an architectural salvage source, have your measurements ready before you go. You don't want to guess whether this expensive—not to mention heavy—item will fit. Also, salvaged mantels are one-of-a-kind. The one you want may no longer be there if you wait for another day.

If you buy a salvaged wood mantel, you may want to strip off the paint. Proceed carefully, particularly if it is ornamented. Much of the detailing on period mantels (and some current types, too) is made not from wood but from composition ornament (called "compo" for short), a pliable material that is molded into intricate designs, such as urns, swags, and rosettes, and that is painted or stained. Paint strippers may dissolve compo, so it is a good idea to work around these ornamented areas.

## Molding and Trim

Decorative trim gives a room a finished appearance. Installation is fairly easy, and materials are reasonably priced. An enormous variety of stock and specialty trim exists in a wide range of materials, such as wood, plaster, and fiberglass.

From the ceiling to the floor, shaped trim called molding is used on most parts of the wall. The cornice is placed at the top, where the wall meets the ceiling. Moldings for cornices come in two main types: dramatic *crown molding* that is frequently combined with other molding styles for an opulent look or the simpler *cove molding* that eliminates the ceiling line but doesn't stand out. The *frieze* is a wide band, sometimes ornamented with swags, that runs under the cornice but above the picture rail. As the name suggests, the *picture rail* is used to hang artwork. A *chair rail* (or dado cap) is placed on a wall, around the room, 30 to 35 inches from the floor and is often used in conjunction with a *wainscot* or *dado* (waist-high paneling) on the lower portion of

the wall. *Base moldings* give the floor line a higher profile and can be as elaborate or simple as you like. Window and door trim, called *casing,* is necessary to seal the gap between the jambs and wall. But again, it can be quite plain or more decorative, depending on taste.

Most of the molding profiles in use today have been around for centuries. Although the classical names for molding profiles may be off-putting, be assured that their forms are as familiar to most of us as is a panel door. Some of the common profiles are *cavetto* or *cove,* a concave quarter-circle; *ovolo,* a convex quarter-round; *scotia,* a concave semicircle; *torus,* a convex semicircle; *ogee* (also called *cyma recta* and *cyma reversa),* an S-shaped form; *beaded,* a smaller, convex rounded form; and *fillet,* a flat, narrow strip separating other moldings. These profiles can be used to frame walls and openings without being intrusive on the design; they add a three-dimensional quality that most rooms need.

CLOCKWISE FROM LEFT
Elaborate ornamental molding and trim adds richness to this home's interior, left. Lighting that is hidden behind the crown molding enhances the decorative effect. In a bedroom, bottom right, salvaged items add style. For example, an old mantel forms the headboard and a vintage window with hooks makes an artful display on the wall. Reclaimed metalwork, bottom left, looks unique in an entry foyer.

More-ornate moldings command more attention when incorporated into a design and should suit the overall decor. Some of the classic motifs that adorn moldings are: *acanthus,* a lobed leaf ornament; *anthemion,* the stylized flower and leaf of the honeysuckle; *dentil,* a series of ornamental notches; *egg-and-dart,* an oval-shaped detail that alternates with an arrow or tongue form; *guilloche,* a series of circular interlaced bands; and *paterae,* a cup-shaped ornament.

## Hardware and Grilles

Another place to look when scouting areas for embellishment is to the doors, large and small, that may provide a backdrop for decorative hardware. Door levers, knobs, and cabinetry pulls can be highly ornamental and a cost-effective way to deliver style. Metalwork such as heat registers, grilles, and grates are all available in decorative designs as well.

Don't overlook salvaged antique doors, windows, and hardware. Check the Internet for resources.

# special details

O nce the basic room and all of its elements are in place, that's your cue to make the space truly your own. The decorative objects you choose to accent your rooms reflect your personality and can give your design an individuality as unique as your own.

Basically, decorative objects fall into two categories: art and accessories. Art can be paintings, framed prints or photos, sculpture, pieces of architectural salvage that are used as *objets d' art,* and even textiles. Accessories tend to be small objects that are introduced into a room for either a practical reason or an aesthetic one (or for a combination of these purposes). A delicately patterned soup tureen flanked by silver candlesticks makes a beautiful centerpiece on a dining room table, for example.

Art and accessories shouldn't always be treated as an after-thought in the design scheme. A large piece of art can influence your room's decor, as may collections. Consider these elements as you are designing the room. Accessories may play a back-ground role, however, and can be worked in during the last phase of the design process.

**CLOCKWISE FROM ABOVE**
Accessorizing is one way to add personality to your home. Here are several examples. A large, carved folding screen, above, adds a dramatic element to a corner. An oil painting is the focal point over the sofa in this living room, opposite. A tabletop arrange-ment of favorite objects, below, adds a personal touch to any space. A themed grouping, such as these figural relief wall plagues, left, let you show off a special collection.

Whether you are hanging a group of prints or displaying a pottery collection, the configurations are either symmetrical or asymmetrical. *Symmetry* is an arrangement that is a mirror image on either side of a central (unseen) line. Picture a sofa table with a pair of brass lamps and matching porcelain figurines flanking a flower-filled vase, for example. You can achieve *visual* symmetry with objects that don't match perfectly but are approximately the same size, height, or color. Now imagine the same sofa table, but with porcelain figurines that are the same size, shape, and color but different images. The arrangement would still look balanced. *Asymmetry* is the opposite of symmetry. Using visual weight as a guide, unlike elements are grouped together to achieve an informal balance. An intricate wire birdcage can be placed with a small display plate on a stand and adjacent to three topiaries in various sizes, for instance. Each element in the arrangement is a counterpoint to the other: the wide birdcage plays against the tall topiaries and the round plate. (For more guidance on symmetry and asymmetry, see Chapter One, "Design Basics," beginning on page 12.)

## Art

Historically, every inch of wall space was filled with art, creating visual chaos. Today the thinking is different. Art is shown to its greatest effect in uncluttered surroundings. A large modern painting has more impact if left alone on a wall, for instance. Small- or medium-size artworks or drawings are more impressive when placed together on a wall.

If you are displaying drawings or photography, make sure that the frame is large enough to accommodate a mat. The frame should be 1 to 3 inches larger in dimension than the picture. For an up-to-date look, the trend is to make the mat at least 6 inches larger than a photograph or an illustration; this can be an effective way to draw attention to a small piece of art or photography.

When choosing matting, try picking up accent colors from your decor. If you feel your accents don't work with the art, look at your room's main hues. If all else fails, pick a neutral color that you like from the work itself to serve as the mat's color.

Frames should coordinate with but not necessarily duplicate any other frames used in the room. Unless you're making a statement with the juxtaposition, the frame style should also reflect the overall look of the room.

When buying a frame, examine the quality of the material from which it is constructed. Does it feel flimsy? Make sure that there aren't any gaps at the joints (the mitered corners of the frame). What is the condition of the finish? There shouldn't be any flaking or discoloration of metal frames; the finish on wood should be smooth and blemish free.

It takes some trial and error to create a pleasing wall arrangement. Here's how to do it.

# smart steps
## artful wall displays

### Step 1 EXPERIMENT WITH THE ELEMENTS
Before you hammer a nail into the wall, place all of the art on the floor, and try out different arrangements. A vertical grouping will make a room seem higher; a horizontal one will make the room seem wider. Don't get stuck in a rut: you don't have to arrange everything in a row. A triangular shape might work for an end wall in a room with a cathedral ceiling; a rectangle or oval in an area above a mantel or sofa. Check out the other geometric placement possibilities for art on page 146.

### Step 2 FIND THE RIGHT WALL LOCATION
Art should sit 6 to 9 inches above a sofa or at eye level when you are seated. Too high, and it will look like it's floating; too low, and it will interfere with headroom. When working with more than one picture, start by marking and measuring the spot for the center print. Then hang the middle row vertically, and follow with the rest.

### Step 3 CHECK THE PROPORTIONS
A framed piece that is too small will look insignificant over a large piece of furniture. The frame should be approximately two-thirds the size of the piece over which it hangs. If you still want to use the small piece, pair it with another that is approximately the same size.

### Step 4 BALANCE OUT THE ARRANGEMENT
In groupings where frames vary in size, try to keep the weightier pieces on the bottom, or place two smaller elements next to it. A large piece will anchor the grouping and keep the arrangement from seeming top-heavy or from trailing off.

OPPOSITE
Framed prints on either side of this antique hutch help to fill out the wall in a large room.

LEFT
A small demi-lune table is properly proportioned for displaying the sculpture here.

# art arrangements

Don't get locked into arranging framed pieces in rows. Try imagining a circle for prints hung in an entry. Or let the shape of your walls influence the arrangement, such as a triangle for a gable wall. Even if you stay within the framework of a rectangle, pictures and objects in various sizes will keep the grouping from looking too rigid. Just make sure to balance the visual weight of the arrangement (below and top right). A grid pattern works when you have different size mats; the orderly rows unify the pieces (bottom right).

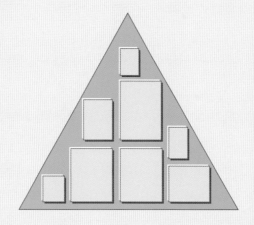

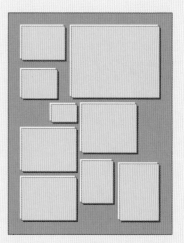

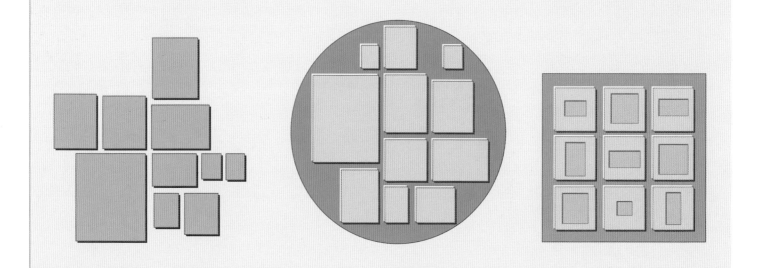

## Step 5 CREATE UNITY

**A mixture of art that doesn't have a common theme or color can be unified by using matching frames or mats. Conversely, art with a common theme or color, such as black-and-white photography, will work well as an arrangement even if the frames don't match.**

## Textiles as Art

Don't overlook the beauty and versatility of textiles when choosing your decorating accessories. Quilts, tapestries, appliqués, and printed cloths such as batik can stand alone on a wall, adding texture and color to the room. Textiles can be mounted on a wall in a number of ways. Smaller cloths can be conventionally framed and sandwiched between glass. Because it is difficult to keep fabric straight and balanced within the frame, you might consider turning the job over to a professional framer.

Larger cloths or rugs can be tacked directly to a wood furring strip, or 1x2, that has been nailed into the wall studs. As an alternative, you can attach the fabric to a wooden or cast-iron dowel with decorative finials (the type used for draperies). To attach the fabric to the dowel without damaging it, create a pocket by looping the top piece over the dowel and stitching it together.

# Accessories

With decorative accessories, there is no right or wrong in the pieces you choose. Use favorite found objects, collectibles, and tabletop items such as candlesticks, vases, and pottery. While there are no hard and fast rules about what will and won't work, there are certain guidelines that can help you determine where and how to display the items you select. Familiarizing yourself with them will make it easy to create attractive tabletop arrangements.

## smart steps
## tabletop finesse

### Step 1 GROUP SIMILAR OBJECTS

Choose items that share the same color, material, shape, or motif. For instance, even if the pieces aren't the same height and shape, a collection of blue-and-white delft pottery can make an impressive arrangement because the color ties the group together. Likewise, a row of Fiestaware pitchers, each in a different color, will work visually because of the repeating shape.

### Step 2 VARY ELEVATIONS

Any grouping benefits from including elements of different sizes. Pairs of objects that are all the same height can be monotonous. Instead of placing two topiaries with two candlesticks, try putting the topiaries with two picture frames. Small items, such as figurines or a decorative plate, can get lost in

an arrangement. Try raising them up with a small pedestal or a stand.

### Step 3 ADD DEPTH

Don't always place items in a straight line, which can look static. Instead, stagger the pieces from back to front. For example, if you have three objects, place them in a triangle. With a larger number of objects, experiment with overlapping triangles.

### Step 4 CHOOSE A FOCAL POINT

If the grouping is not coming together, arrange everything around one major object, such as a sculpture or a framed print.

### Step 5 DON'T OVERDO IT

A display of too many items looks like clutter. Choose accessories judiciously. Store extra items away, and freshen up your arrangements periodically with these pieces.

RIGHT
A pleasing display of Chinese porcelain pieces of various heights seems three-dimensional because they are staggered. The various sizes add interest while color unifies the group.

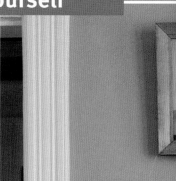

# design workbook

## MAKE IT PERSONAL

## express yourself

Original artwork with a common theme, volcanos, makes a big statement. Notice the even spacing between the framed pieces. (See also left.)

## check the scale

Instead of one large piece that might overwhelm a small room, a grouping of smaller pieces, top left, lends importance to a small wall.

## include nature

Fresh flowers or plants can bring color and sometimes pleasing scents into a room. You can rotate them with the seasons, too. (See also far left.)

## lend character

A tabletop collection may be one of the most personal displays in a home. The books and small items are things for the homeowner and guests to enjoy. (See also left.)

# design workbook

## SIMPLE ACCESSORIZING

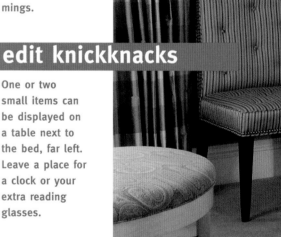

## limit distractions

In the bedroom, limit accessories to things that make the room special, not busy. Here, quiet colors and minimal decoration appears peaceful.

## add soft touches

Go for contrasting throw pillows, top left, to make the bed more luxurious. Pillows are small, so splurge on plush fabrics and trimmings.

## edit knickknacks

One or two small items can be displayed on a table next to the bed, far left. Leave a place for a clock or your extra reading glasses.

## select appropriate art

Use low-key art on the wall, left. Avoid paintings or prints that may over stimulate you visually. Keep to themes and colors that are restful.

# 7 furniture facts

TYPES OF HOME FURNITURE   MAKING CHOICES   FURNITURE STYLES
JUDGING QUALITY   RECYCLING YOUR FURNITURE   DESIGN WORKBOOK

Furniture plays a major part in your home's design. Does it have to be versatile and comply with a multitude of needs in your home? How much wear and tear do you expect it to handle? Are you planning to use it in a room intended for occasional entertaining or everyday use? Should it be casual or formal, built-in or movable?

What style suits your home? If you need help choosing, look at the architectural style of your house and take cues from there.

Also, think about cost. Nearly all furniture styles are available in low-end to high-priced versions. Paying top dollar doesn't mean you're buying the best—only durable materials and reliable construction can ensure that.

In this chapter you'll find out everything you need to know before buying furniture.

Contemporary-style furnishings and accent pieces reflect the owners' taste and the spare, clean lines of the architecture in this home.

# types of home furniture

Furniture has three basic functions: for seating, sleeping, and storage. Furniture can also efficiently divide space. Within a large room, you might want to create a cozy sitting area in front of a fireplace while storing entertainment equipment at the other end of the room. Or you may need to define living and dining areas within one room. A low-backed sofa can act as a room divider, as can a shelving unit or a sofa table. The key is not to block sources of natural light when dividing space with furniture.

## Seating

Furniture that functions as seating comes with a variety of options. It can roll, swivel, tilt or recline, stack, fold, or convert to another use such as a bed. Seating can also take numerous forms. Sofas, for instance, come in all shapes and sizes. There are three-seaters and two-seaters (sometimes called love seats). Other sofa terms are Chesterfield (overstuffed, tufted upholstery with padded arms), Lawson (arms lower than the back), and tuxedo (arms the same height as the back). Backs of sofas can be termed camel back, channel back, or tufted back, all of which are firm, spring-supported styles. Pillow backs are available as either attached or loose. Multi-pillow backs, or scatter backs, have more back pillows than seat cushions. Base treatments include skirts (with various pleating designs), upholstered legs, plinth (block) bases, and bun feet.

Chairs are categorized as upholstered or occasional. Popular upholstered chairs are termed club or wing. A barrel chair has a rounded back that extends in a smooth line with the arms. A club chair is square with arms lower than its back, and a wing chair has a high back with winglike extensions at head level. Occasional chairs are usually smaller than upholstered chairs. Characterized by wooden arms and legs that are combined with seats and backs that are sometimes upholstered, occasional chairs are often traditional in design.

Modular seating comes in any number of armless units, single-arm end modules, and corner pieces that can be arranged in various configurations to suit different spaces and needs. This type of seating is differerent from a sectional sofa, which consists of simply one corner unit and two end pieces.

**ABOVE**
Style is available in all price points today. But quality doesn't come cheaply. The best advice if you're on a budget? Buy the highest quality you can afford.

## Sleeping

Furniture for sleeping ranges from futon frames to platform beds and bedsteads with head- and foot-boards. Some bedsteads also include bedside stands, lamps, and built-in storage compartments. Convertible sofa beds offer extra sleeping accommodations for small spaces. Other options are the loft bed, which is on a raised platform and frees the space beneath for other uses; bunk beds; and trundle beds, which slide under another bed when not in use.

# Storage

Storage furniture is available to suit a wide range of needs. In the furniture industry, it is referred to as *casegoods* because of its boxlike structure (although tables also come under this category). It may include bookcases or any other type of open shelves, cabinets with hinged or sliding doors, cabinets that house audio or video equipment, breakfronts, chests, armoires, or desks. Casegoods come in many shapes and sizes and offer a place to display or protect collectibles and other valuables. Modular pieces can be used to create storage walls or room dividers. Storage walls are connected units that fit from floor to ceiling. They divide space while providing access to storage from both sides. Room dividers serve a similar purpose but do not extend to the ceiling or from wall to wall. They are most commonly used to divide living and dining areas.

Storage furniture for the bedroom consists of dressers, vanities, and chests. These pieces are categorized by the size of their contents. The smallest is a lingerie chest, followed by the drawer chest. The door chest is larger still, with drawers at the bottom and two doors at the top. The armoire, or wardrobe, is the largest chest available. A clothes rod inside defines it as a wardrobe.

Sometimes these pieces can serve multipurpose needs, so think about which ones you can get the most from, particularly if you are short on space. An armoire is an excellent example. It can be used in any room in the house. In the kitchen, it becomes a pantry; in the family room, it's an entertainment center; in the bedroom, it's a clothes closet; and in a spacious bath or in a hallway, it's a handy place to store linens and toiletries.

**BELOW**
When you're shopping for a dining-room cabinet, check for quality. Make sure the drawer slides and shelves are well supported. Open and close them to be sure they handle smoothly.

# how to choose

Once you've considered how you want to use the furniture in a room, you'll have to decide on a style that will coordinate with your decor. This is a matter of personal taste and your lifestyle. Even if you have a particular look in mind, you may want to take your time before making a final decision. Following these Smart Steps will help.

## smart steps
### style confidence

#### Step 1 EXAMINE EXISTING PIECES
What are your favorite pieces of furniture? What do you like about them? List the colors that most appeal to you. Do you have special items, such as artwork or family heirlooms, that you'd like to blend with new furnishings? List the pieces that you would like to keep and what ones you think you may want to replace, either now or in the future. If you're on a tight budget, plan furniture purchases for which you might be able to save in the meantime.

#### Step 2 CONSIDER YOUR FAMILY'S LIFESTYLE
Do you have young children or pets? Do you spend a lot of time at home, or are you always coming and going? Do you entertain frequently? How do you entertain, with a backyard barbecue or a formal sit-down dinner? Be smart: don't buy delicate upholstered pieces for the kids to flop on with the dog. Sometimes it makes sense to put your hankering for such things on the back burner and shop for something durable. Similarly, if you're an expert chef and love to serve meals on fine china by candlelight, splurge on your formal dining room's furniture.

## Step 3 PLAY UP ARCHITECTURAL STYLE

Find out when your house or apartment building was built. Research its architectural style using books on architectural history from the library, if necessary. Consider a period decorating style like Victorian or Colonial if it works well with the house style. Be sure to design around architectural details such as built-in cabinets or bookcases, which add character to your home. If you have hardwood floors laid with an interesting or contrasting pattern around the perimeter of the room, don't obscure them completely with the furnishings you choose. Detailing around your door and window frames and at the tops and bottoms of your walls can help you decide whether a room would look best as a formal or informal setting. Think about how some types of furnishings complement these details.

## Step 4 NARROW DOWN YOUR CHOICES

If you're still at a loss, look at magazine pictures of room settings. Clip out your favorites. After you've collected a few, look at them all together. If they all have things in common, *voilà:* you may have just found your favorite style. If you've clipped examples of different styles, group the similar rooms together, and pin up each grouping in separate areas on the wall. Keep them pinned up for several days, and look at them as you walk by. At the end of the week, can you say which group of pictures is your favorite?

OPPOSITE
A somewhat eclectic group of furnishings can be tied together by common colorways and finishes.

RIGHT
Special finishing details add elegance to upholstered pieces. Here, decorative upholstery nails call attention to the graceful silhouette of this chair.

# furniture styles

Three general furniture styles to consider are traditional, contemporary, and country. But that is a very broad statement. Within each of these categories are numerous different styles of furniture that you can usually mix and match.

**Traditional.** Traditional-style furniture takes its design cues from furniture made before 1900. Its shapes and motifs are references to classical architecture. Within this category you will find familiar period pieces, such as a Queen Anne chair or a Chippendale mirror. The original designs take their names from influential people of the times as well as from architectural styles, such as Baroque, Gothic, and Victorian. Traditional sofas and chairs are often upholstered with heavy, luxurious fabrics and elaborate trim. Most furniture of this style is tailored with kick-pleat skirting and rolled arms. You'll find button-tufting and nailhead trim as well as fringe, braid, and cord trim and other fine upholstery details on the cushions and frame. The wood finishes are usually dark and rich, such as mahogany.

**Contemporary.** Furniture styles from 1900 to the present are termed contemporary. These styles also reflect the Modern movement, including Arts & Crafts, Art Deco, and Art Nouveau. Contemporary furniture designs are streamlined and incorporate natural materials such as wood and stone with metal and glass. Upholstered sofas and chairs tend to be larger than traditional styles—you won't find buttons or skirts on these pieces.

**Country.** Like its European counterparts, American country-style furniture is casual and unpretentious. It often has a period flavor, but one that is rustic rather than genteel. Upholstered pieces might include ruffled skirts, pillows, and other homespun details. Tables and storage pieces are usually made of pine or oak, sometimes painted rather than stained.

You may choose to stay true to these design themes or create an eclectic mix of styles in your home. Think about softening the hard lines of contemporary furniture with a few country-style accents, such as handcrafted pillows or rugs. A few pieces of antique furniture can complement the architectural style of your home no matter which general decor you've chosen.

# judging quality

Even if you have a good idea of what types of furniture you're looking for as well as the general style that appeals to you, there is a maze of purchase options you'll have to negotiate. How do you know what you're getting for your money? What's the difference between the $800 sofa and the $1,200 one? How do you judge the quality of a table? These are important questions. To answer them, it will help to understand what's beneath the upholstery of a sofa and how a wood chair or table is put together.

TOP LEFT
A wooden table featuring plain legs has modern appeal. Plush cushions on the metal-frame benches provide comfortable seating.

LEFT
Armless upholstered chairs seem to take up less space than standard club chairs. This pair features detached seat cushions and loose pillow backs.

# Anatomy of a Sofa

Quality furniture is comfortable and durable. Four elements determine the integrity of upholstered furniture: the frame, the springs, the cushions, and the upholstery fabric.

▧ **Frames.** High-quality frames are made of seasoned hardwood, kiln-dried to resist warping. The frame is joined using dowels and corner blocks that are screwed and glued together. Legs should be extensions of the frame and not attached with screws. Center legs add additional support.

▧ **Springs.** The spring systems in upholstered furniture are either hand-tied coils or sagless (sinuous) constructions. Eight-way hand-tied springs are of the highest quality. These funnel-like coils are tied with twine to each of the eight adjacent coils and attached to a heavy-duty webbing underneath with steel

clips. This type of construction gives even comfort and prevents "bottoming out" of the seat no matter how heavy the sitter. Four- or six-way tied springs are not nearly as supportive. Good-quality webbing is tightly woven and may be reinforced by steel straps under each row of springs.

Sagless, or sinuous, springs are S-shaped, flat wavy bands of steel that are fastened to the front rail and run front to back a few inches apart. Sagless springs have a firmer feel than coil springs and are often used in contemporary pieces that are lower to the floor.

■ **Cushions.** The frame and springs are the foundation for the cushions. A good frame is padded with cotton or polydacron so that the upholstery fabric never touches the wood. Quality seat cushions and loose back cushions consist of a combination of down and other feathers wrapped around a polyurethane foam core—or loose down or feathers for back cushions. Test the quality of a cushion by lifting it. If it feels light, it may be made of poor materials. A 2- x 2-foot cushion should not weigh less than 2 pounds.

Back cushions are supported by springs or webbing. If back cushions are loose as opposed to attached, there are no springs. Webbing will supply the only support. This type of construction is less expensive than attached cushions and will feel less resilient than spring support. Pocketed springs are best for

## smart tip   TRADE TERMS

- *Collection:* A grouping of related furniture pieces from the same manufacturer. Furniture is usually displayed in collections.
- *Reproductions:* Copies of fine antiques made with materials and details similar to those of the originals.
- *Adaptations:* Furniture designs that are loosely based on originals. Tags may say "based on," "adapted from," or "in the style of."
- *Sectionals:* Upholstered seating pieces that are made in three or more sections that fit together in a particular configuration.
- *Modulars:* An unlimited number of pieces that are upholstered and may be used in many configurations.
- *COM:* Custom-ordered material; means the furniture is made to your specifications. For instance, manufacturers may offer you a choice of COM fabrics or let you supply your own.
- *Apartment-size furniture:* Furniture that has been scaled-down to fit in smaller spaces.
- *RTA:* Ready-to-assemble furniture; comes in pieces. Because you put it together, it costs less.

comfortable back cushions. You may also find some pieces with sinuous spring backs for less money.

■ **Upholstery.** You can often choose from a range of price levels, called *grades,* of fabric or coverings. These grades are assigned a letter from A to D, with A at the high end. Grading is determined by the quality of the materials, the amount of fabric needed for a good match of the pattern, and the source of the pattern design (with famous designers' patterns costing more). An important factor to consider when selecting upholstery fabric is durability. In general, tightly woven fabrics wear best. Fabrics with woven-in patterns wear better than printed fabrics. Various natural and synthetic fibers offer different looks and textures as well as cleanability and wearability performance.

Natural fibers include cotton, linen, wool, and silk. Cotton is soft to the touch and durable. However, its fibers will disintegrate under prolonged exposure to direct sunlight.

Cotton is also less stain resistant than synthetic fibers. Linen has a tailored, crisp feel and is one of the most durable fibers available. It is most often found in natural colors because it does not dye well. It, too, can be damaged by sunlight. Wool is extremely hardy, as well as abrasion and stain resistant, but should be mothproofed before use. Silk is a beautiful but fragile fabric. Soft and luxurious, it is difficult to clean and discolors when it is exposed to strong light.

Synthetic fibers have been developed as alternatives to natural fibers and are often blended with them. Polyester is strong and easy to clean. It withstands direct sunlight and is flame- and abrasion-resistant. Rough in texture, it is often blended with natural fibers to soften its touch. Olefin is used to create heavy, textured fabrics. It is a coarse and bulky fiber that is strong and stain resistant. However, it does not wear well under direct sunlight. Nylon is the strongest and most soil-resistant fiber. Recent developments in nylon give it the look and feel of wool. It, too, is sensitive to sunlight.

As an informed shopper, you will be able to make your purchase with confidence. Never judge the quality of an upholstered piece solely by the fabric you see on it. The fabric can be easily replaced, but the frame and support system cannot. Always go to a reputable furniture retailer when purchasing upholstered pieces. Because you can't see what's underneath the fabric, you'll have to ask questions about the construction. So it's important that the salesperson be knowledgeable and trustworthy. If you're still not satisfied, contact the manufacturer.

## smart tip  TRADE TERMS

Keep the following in mind if you want to trim off some of the cost of your purchases:

- *Frame design:* Curves, such as rounded arms, are more expensive to cover than straight lines.
- *Pattern design:* Large, complex patterns are harder to match than small, overall designs.
- *Details:* Trimmings, such as pleats, welts, braids, buttons, and fringe, all add to the final cost.

# The Signs of Good Construction

Furniture can be constructed of hardwood or softwood. Hardwoods come from deciduous trees, such as cherry, maple, oak, ash, pecan, teak, walnut, mahogany, and poplar. Hardwoods are often used in high-quality furniture because they are stronger than softwoods. Softwoods come from conifer trees, such as fir, pine, redwood, cedar, and cypress. Softwoods have to be well-seasoned and kiln-dried before use, or they will split and splinter easily.

Veneers are thin sheets of hardwood that are glued to a core of less expensive wood. They were once associated with poor-quality furniture, but today's wood veneers may sometimes be stronger than solid wood: wide boards of solid wood will warp and crack with changes in temperature and humidity, while veneer is much more stable in these conditions.

A "solid wood" label allows use of composition boards, such as plywood and particleboard, in areas of the furniture that will remain unseen. You will find these materials applied this way in medium-priced furniture. In budget-priced furniture, they may be used more extensively.

**Joining Methods.** Wood can be joined together with staples, nails, screws, joints, and glue. Several of these methods may be used in one piece of furniture. To evaluate quality, look for strong construction at the joints. Joints are where one part of a piece of furniture matches up with another. They are usually glued together or fastened with screws. Staples are used only on

the cheapest furniture and should not be used to join any piece that bears weight. Furniture joints can be made using one of the following joining methods.

▧ *Butt joints* simply join the flat sides of two pieces where they meet. They are weak joints and should be used only in places that are not subject to stress or weight, such as where a bureau top meets the frame.

▧ *Miter joints* are often used to join pieces at right angles. The ends of the two pieces are angled to fit together perfectly. These joints may be reinforced with dowels, nails, or screws.

▧ *Tongue-and-groove* joints are used to join two boards together side-by-side, as in a tabletop. A groove is cut into one side of a board and a tongue on the other. When placed side-by-side, the tongue of one board fits into the groove of the next and so on.

▧ *Dovetail joints* are used to join drawer sides. Notches cut into the ends of each piece should fit together tightly.

▧ *Double-dowel joints* use two dowels to peg joints together. These are sturdy joints used in casegood framing and to attach legs to side rails of chairs.

▧ *Mortise-and-tenon joinery* is the strongest method of joining pieces of wood at right angles. The end of one piece of wood is shaped to fit into a hole in the other.

▧ *Corner blocks* provide extra support for dowel joints. They can be held in place with either glue or wood screws. However, screws should not be used on everything just because they hold the joints rigidly. A good example is a chest of drawers. Glue blocks should be used to attach the top of the frame because wood panels can expand and contract, which causes the wood to split.

**LEFT TO RIGHT**
Real antiques are often perfect candidates for restoration because they have usually been well-crafted. But mass-produced reproductions, such as the scroll-arm divan, opposite, and the chest of drawers, left, can be distinctive and should be considered, if they are well made, in lieu of the real thing. Vintage drawer pulls, above, lend an authentic touch to a reclaimed piece.

# identifying your furniture

Poke your nose into almost anyone's basement, attic, or garage, and you'll likely find a hodgepodge of old furniture. Style clues to look for include the shapes of the arms, legs, and back, as well as any ornamentation and finish. Mixing similar styles is perfectly acceptable and may even add interest to a boring room. Just keep in mind that some combinations work; others don't. Here's a quick reference that can help you decide whether to take a particular piece of furniture out of storage and incorporate it into your home's decor.

◀ **Ball-and-Claw Leg:**
A cabriole—a furniture leg that curves and narrows down into an ornamental foot—distinguishes this style. It mixes well with other formal, eighteenth-century-inspired designs.

▼ **Spindle Leg:**
In a highly polished rich wood, spindle-legged furniture is at home with other traditional styles. Made from pine or oak and sometimes with a painted finish, it takes on a country-style personality.

▶ **Chippendale Leg:**
The later, less ornate version of Chippendale style pairs well with any eighteenth-century look, especially formal English-inspired furniture such as Queen Anne or Windsor.

▶ **Contemporary Leg:**
Streamlined contemporary pieces crafted in natural or man-made materials defy fads. Other styles that coordinate well with the look are simple Shaker and geometric Art Deco pieces.

◀ **French Provincial Leg:**
The French version of country style has graceful, curvaceous legs that make it a good match with almost any furniture that has European flair.

**ABOVE**
Tables of wood, glass, and metal cohabit with upholstered furnishings in this city apartment. The seating pieces wear unassuming plain white-cotton slipcovers and offer a perfectly unobtrusive backdrop for the mixing of various materials, textures, and styles.

**Finishes.** The final touch on a piece of wood furniture is its finish. Finishes can add color and protection through the use of stains, paints, or lacquers. A clear finish will allow the natural grain of the wood to show through. Wood stains will change the color of the wood. Finishes can make a piece of furniture look refined or rustic.

Distressing is a popular means of making new wood look old. The wood is literally battered before the finish is applied, aging it and enhancing its rustic charm. These finishes tend to hide any scratches or fingerprints the furniture may be exposed to, so they make good choices for use in active areas such as family rooms and for rustic, country-style decors.

Painted finishes are also popular for a nostalgic look. Unlike a distressed finish, however, paint tends to highlight flaws in the wood. This makes painted pieces more expensive than

**OPPOSITE**
A rattan-and-wicker cabinet inspired a South Seas theme in this room. It's a fine piece for storing additional linens, but heavy items may need stronger support.

**BELOW**
To maintain its good looks, furniture with a painted finish needs a protective top coat—preferably one that won't affect its color, such as nonyellowing polyurethane.

# smart tip CASEGOODS

Casegoods refers to any piece of furniture that is used for storage, such as a chest of drawers; tables are also part of this category. The furniture industry uses a variety of labels to denote the construction materials. The meanings of these labeling terms are regulated by the Federal Trade Commission.

- *Solid wood* (i.e., "solid oak" or "solid pine") means that the exposed surfaces are made of solid wood without any veneer or plywood. Other woods may be used on unexposed surfaces such as drawer sides and backs.
- *Genuine wood* means that all exposed parts of the furnture are constructed of a veneer of a type of wood over hardwood plywood.
- *Wood* means all of the parts of the furniture are made of some type of wood.
- *Man-made materials* refers to plastic laminate panels. The furniture may also include molded plastic that mimics wood panels, carving, or trim.

# smart tip

## QUALITY CHECKS

When shopping for wood furniture you'll find varying levels of quality and pricing. Use this checklist to judge what you're getting for your money.

### FRAMES
- Veneers and laminates should be securely joined to the base material.
- Joints bearing weight should be reinforced with corner blocks.
- Back panels should be screwed into the frame.
- Long shelves should have center supports.

### DRAWERS
- Drawers should fit well, glide easily, and have stops.
- Drawer bottoms should be held by grooves, not staples or nails.
- Drawer interiors should be smooth and sealed.
- Drawer corners should have dovetail joints.

### DOORS
- Cabinet doors should open and close smoothly.
- Hinges and other hardware should be strong and secure.

### FINISHES
- All finishes should feel smooth unless they are intentionally distressed or crackled.

**RIGHT**
An armoire is a versatile storage piece than can accommodate linens, a TV, or even a compact home office. When you're shopping, be sure that the one you choose was manufactured for the use you have in mind. An antique clothing armoire may be handsome, but it will not be suitable for your computer equipment.

**OPPOSITE**
This pine cabinet may or may not be antique. Nowadays, it's hard to tell whether a piece is wearing the patina of fine age or simply a recently applied distressed finish that imitates the appearance of a much older piece.

those with natural finishes because extra care must be taken at the factory to remove imperfections from the wood.

Finishes should always be strong enough to resist moisture. Inexpensive pieces may be simply coated with a layer of polyurethane. The finishing of high-quality furniture includes sanding, applying multiple coats of a clear finish with sanding between coats, waxing, and hand buffing. Compare the look and feel between inexpensive and expensive pieces. Always check that the surface is hard, smooth, and even. Watch for uneven colorations, bubbles, or cracks in the surface. If you're debating about whether or not to retain your existing furniture, examine the integrity of its structure and the condition of its finish. If you own genuine antiques that need repair, contact the American Institute for Conservation of Historic and Artistic Works, in Washington, D.C., to find a qualified restorer. Antiques are loosely defined as pieces more than 100 years old.

# recycling your furniture

Do you have a favorite old chair, or is there a wonderful piece you found at a flea market last month that you'd love to include in your new room? If so, slipcovering, refinishing, or reupholstering may be an alternative to shopping for brand-new furniture. Although re-covering won't necessarily save you money, it will save those family heirlooms and antique shop rarities. As long as the wood frame is well-constructed and in good condition with no dry rot, worm holes, or loose or broken joints, those pieces can be brought back to life using new fabric.

All hardware should be removed and the frame cleaned. If the seat platform of an upholstered piece is weak, the upholsterer should replace it and cover it with burlap. This should be hand-sewn to the springs in a diamond pattern to prevent it from slipping. A layer of horsehair gives resiliency to the seat and should be covered with cotton to prevent the horsehair from poking through. A fine upholsterer will then cover the cotton padding with muslin.

The vertical surfaces of the frame should always be covered with webbing, never cardboard, and then layered with bonded Dacron. Depending on the desired plumpness of the filling, an upholsterer may use polyester wrapped in either Dacron or down. Down is the most expensive option.

## smart steps
## to reupholster—or not

### Step 1 ASSESS SKILL LEVELS NEEDED

You can choose to do the work yourself or hire a professional. Depending on the shape it's in, wood furniture requires various levels of skill to restore or refinish it. Fitted slipcovers require careful measuring, good sewing skills, and many hours of labor. Reupholstering is a fine art that uses special techniques. You may be able to find classes in your area if you'd like to learn these skills.

Finding a professional upholsterer or furniture restorer is best done by word of mouth. Ask your coworkers and neighbors for references. Fabric stores that carry upholstery material might be able to refer you to someone, or look in the Yellow Pages of your local phone book under "Furniture" or "Furniture makers." Make an appointment to visit the person's shop. Ask to see examples of their work.

### Step 2 KNOW WHAT TO EXPECT

Make sure that the refinisher or upholsterer shows you what he or she plans to do with your piece beforehand and gives you an estimate for the work. First, the frame should be stripped and checked for any weaknesses. Repairs should be made to weak joints by redoweling, regluing, and rescrewing (never nailing) joints together.

ABOVE
Reupholstering can give a new look to a piece of furniture, but don't do it unless the piece is well made.

ABOVE
Quality, upholstery-grade fabric is the only thing suitable for making over seating pieces. Special stitching on the chairs here adds a distinctive custom detail.

## Step 3 SELECT THE FABRIC

Fabric considerations for reupholstering are comparable to selecting a new piece of furniture. For a formal look, consider a brocade, damask, or velvet. If your style is casual, a linen or chintz may be more suitable. (See "Upholstery," on page 160 of this chapter, and the box "Design Materials," on page 47 of Chapter Two, "Color and Pattern," for more information.) It's always a sensible idea to buy fabric that has been treated at the mill for stain resistance if it will get a lot of use, but it's not worth the extra money for a sprayed-on treatment that you can apply yourself.

Also, keep in mind that a talented reupholsterer can change the look of your furniture in subtle ways with fabric. For instance, a contemporary piece can be made more traditional by adding a skirt along the bottom. Neat pleats in the skirting will give the piece a tailored appearance, while ruffles will complement a country-style decor. When ordering fabric, think about extra material for coordinating window dressings and throw pillows.

## Step 4 CALCULATE YARDAGE

Some upholsterers will work with fabric you supply; others will sell it to you. Whether working with a professional or on your own, make sure you calculate the needed yardage carefully before buying the fabric. Here are some general guidelines for how much you will need for reupholstery. Slipcovers require slightly more fabric because they are not as fitted.

- Three-cushion sofa: No skirt, 10 yards; tailored skirt, 12 yards; pleated or gathered skirt, 14 yards
- Wing chair: No skirt, 5 yards; loose seat cushion, 5½ yards; skirted, 6½ yards
- Club chair: No skirt, 5 yards; skirted, 6½ yards

Lastly, avoid trendy looks. Buy classic, quality pieces that will last a lifetime. Remember, the new furniture that you buy today may have heirloom value tomorrow and may possibly become a treasure for the next generation to enjoy.

# design workbook
## SNUG, SMART, AND STYLISH

## thoughtful choices

Smart furniture choices make the most of this small house. Note the built-in TV and audio cabinet in the hall—saving space for living-room seating.

## scaled-down comfort

A small chair that fits in a corner, top left, and ottomans provide extra seating when company comes. Little tables can be moved around as needed.

## versatile seating

A long sofa, which doubles as a guest bed, fits neatly against one wall, leaving space in the center of the room for traffic to pass with ease. The short L at one end of the sofa (see also left) doesn't jut too far into the room, but it provides a bit more seating. The furniture's sleek design doesn't crowd the room visually.

# design workbook
## OPEN AND SOPHISTICATED

## pleasing arrangement

Furniture groupings make the best use of this open, multipurpose space. Twin sofas face each other in front of the fireplace— a perfect set up for conversation.

## the perfect accent

An oval coffee table is easy to walk around in a small area. The glass top was a smart choice—heavy wood can appear bulky in tight quarters.

## a console table

A long, narrow table behind the sofa, top, can display pottery or photos. But it's also useful as a place to put down a drink or a tray of hors d'oeurves.

## entertaining shape

A round pedestal dining table, left, was a smart decision. It seats more people than a comparable-size rectangle, and the glass-and-chrome design is informal and modern.

# 8

# room by room

Now it is time to get down to business. The preceding chapters have all dealt with some aspect of decorating from a general point of view. In this chapter, you will go room to room and see how professional designers applied the principles of good design to specific spaces. Not every issue raised will be relevant to your home, but certainly some will prompt you to consider aspects of design that you may not have thought about before. You may be suprised to learn that a small adjustment could solve a problem or change the entire look of a room.

The whole-house tour in this chapter begins in the foyer and proceeds through the hallway into the living room, family room, dining room, kitchen, bedroom, children's room, and bathroom. Remember, even if your style is different, the basics of good design are universal.

Light-filled and welcoming, this front-entry hall presents an inviting, casual style that reflects the informality of the rest of the house.

# foyer and hallway

First impressions count. Your foyer should be a reflection of your style and an introduction to the rest of your house. Although many people treat the foyer as a solely utilitarian space, filling it with umbrella stands, hall trees, and the like, it can also be an ideal spot to display cherished family photographs or interesting artwork. Touches like these make your entry warmer and more inviting.

Hallways should tie into the rooms they connect. "Do not forget to treat the walls," says Barbara Schlattman, ASID, of Barbara Schlattman Interiors in Houston, Texas. "That area 5 feet above the ground is especially important because that's what your eye sees." Faux paint finishes, art, and mirrors add visual appeal.

## Furnishings

Pick up a color or pattern from an adjoining room, and use it on the walls of your foyer or hallway. If you decide to use the same wallcoverings in the foyer and living room, change the molding or floor treatment to differentiate the two spaces. Ceramic tile is a popular choice for entryway floors because it stands up to harsh weather conditions and dirt that's tracked in. Large foyers might have a hardwood floor with a colorful area rug in the middle. If the space is long, break it up visually with two area rugs. Always consider safety when choosing a flooring material for your foyer. The surface shouldn't be slick, and rugs must lie securely, so use a rubber pad.

If space permits, designers may add a console table and an interesting wall mirror in a foyer for both aesthetic and practical reasons. This arrangement is also fitting on stair landings. The table provides the ideal spot to drop off the mail or keys. A mirror helps to visually expand what is often a small or narrow space. Most designers draw the line at mirrored walls, though. The foyer is a well-trafficked spot and mirrored walls will make it look too busy.

TOP LEFT
Notice that the color of the front door ties into the color palette of the front-hall rug.

LEFT
A table is handy as a drop-off for mail, keys, or even the cell phone. A small display adds a decorative touch here.

## Lighting

Hallways have to be well lit. Use one ceiling fixture in a small hallway or wall-mounted sconces in a larger one. Halls 75 to 150 square feet in size need only a single fixture, which should be at least 12 inches in diameter. A chandelier should be at least 18 inches in diameter. A small space (20 to 75 square feet) requires a fixture that is 8 inches or more in diameter. If you install a pendant lamp or chandelier, make sure it clears the top of any door that opens into the space. Recessed lamps should be on dimmers. "Although having enough lighting is important, you don't want a foyer to be glaringly bright, especially when coming in from a dark night," notes Melinda Sechrist, of Sechrist Designs in Washington, D.C.

## smart tip FOYERS

Pale paint colors may brighten a narrow hallway or entry, but keep in mind that constant traffic will take its toll on the walls. Consider using warmer colors that are less likely to show marks. A gloss-finish paint will wipe clean easier than a matte-finish product, too. If you prefer wallpaper to paint, use a simple pattern that will provide a spark of color, but will not overwhelm the space.

# living room

The living room is actually a multipurpose space in many instances, acting as an everyday gathering spot for family, a place to entertain guests, as well as the media room where the computer, television, and stereo system all find a home. The living room might also double as the kids' play area or a guest room in a crunch. So unless your living room is off-limits except for company or it's covered in plastic (remember those slipcovers?), it must be able to withstand plenty of wear and tear.

## Style and Color

The style of the living room should complement adjacent spaces. But often it's the style and palette chosen for the living room that sets the tone for the rest of the house. Go with a look that appeals to you and complements your lifestyle. For example, if your living room functions essentially as the family room, with kids, toys, pets, and typical everyday clutter, it will be difficult to maintain the "less is more" philosophy of the minimalist contemporary style. You can try it, but it will never look the way you want. On the other hand, an informal country room will allow you to add rustic trunks and ruffled baskets that can contain the clutter and are in keeping with the popular homespun style.

LEFT
A chandelier can be a glamorous substitute for recessed ceiling fixtures in an entry hall if the space is large enough for it. This one, an antique, features etched glass.

In houses with a family room, the living room may take on a full-time formal look. Keep in mind that formal doesn't mean stuffy and uncomfortable. You might go with richer woods and colors or more delicate patterns, such as small roses or stripes, but the upholstered seating should be inviting and the other furnishings usable. You want to create an enjoyable space for conversation that makes guests and family members feel relaxed.

When making your mind up about colors for your living room, choose hues that you wear and in which you look best. Stay away from trendy hues. Copy a trick designers like to use: repeat colors. For example, you might use a wonderful fabric on the sofa, then pick up one of the colors in its pattern for the window treatments or chair cushions. Accent solid-color sofas and love seats with vibrant throw pillows. If you're choosing white for the walls, select the paint shade carefully. Avoid stark white in traditional settings. Warm yellow-tinted versions lend a soft, tranquil feeling to rooms. Cool whites, those with blue tints, work better in contemporary settings.

Think twice about using light solid colors on the furniture in busy living rooms. An all-white sofa will look great the day that it arrives, but not for long if kids, guests, and you use it everyday.

ABOVE
Contrast piping and tufted upholstery adds distinction to the simple lines of these chairs.

RIGHT
An almost-all-neutral scheme on the walls, windows, and furniture lets the view take center stage.

OPPOSITE
The only pattern in the room is bold—a zebra-print rug that adds an exotic touch. The choice is a daring one that turns the floor into a dramatic focal point.

## smart tip LIVING ROOMS

You may not need new furniture for your living room—just a fresh perspective. Try removing or rearranging some pieces. For instance, pull the furniture away from the walls; create two or more conversation groups; or arrange some pieces, including sofas, on a diagonal to make a room seem wider. Also try paring down the amount of furnishings in the room. For example, two large upholstered chairs can make a cozy setting, but three can be overkill unless the room is large. If the upholstery looks tired, a throw can hide a worn spot, or, try a new toss pillows.

## Focal Point

"Every room benefits from a focal point. When you walk into a room, your eye bounces from place to place until it finds somewhere to rest—if nothing stands out, it keeps bouncing," says Dale Bruss, director of training and education for Decorating Den Interiors. "If you find that you feel a little uncomfortable in a room and you don't know why, the lack of a focal point might well be the reason. Accenting or creating one is the designer's job."

The focal point in many living rooms is the fireplace. If there is no fireplace, a large picture window can assume the role. However, a main area of focus can also be created with a dramatic piece of furniture, such as a bookcase or wall unit, a large coffee table, an eye-catching painting, or a sculpture.

## Furnishings

Give careful consideration to the furniture you choose for seating and storage. Always be practical. Choose pieces that can be easily moved around on special occasions when you may have to add chairs to accommodate guests or make room for the Christmas tree, for example. Seating should be comfortable and durable, especially when it takes daily use. Buy the best pieces you can afford. If you avoid trendy styles, good furniture will remain serviceable for many years. To judge the quality and construction of a piece, see Chapter Seven, "Furniture Facts," on page 152. If you have a family room, you will probably reserve the living room for company or special occasions, so you may be able to get away with less-expensive seating covered in fabric that is beautiful as well as durable.

Avoid furniture suites. Just because a sofa, love seat, chair, and coffee table are grouped together in a showroom does not mean that you have to buy them as a set. Furniture retailers create these groupings to sell products from the same line together, especially if you're unsure of your own design skills. But this kind of buying robs you of the fun and satisfaction of choosing furniture piece by piece. There's no reason a cherished antique or a family heirloom can't fit into your design, for example. Items like these add comfort and reflect your personality more than static sets. "Things that are too matching become very boring," says Sechrist. "Often, putting in an old piece makes the room much more interesting." You might reupholster an old chair in a floral fabric that coordinates with the new solid-color sofa or select a reproduction table in a similar style as the antiques in the room.

However, some old pieces may have to go when you're redecorating because they no longer suit the new design scheme. "If it's a piece you're not crazy about or one that clashes with your new design, even if it cost you a bundle at one time, out it goes. Try moving it to another room," suggests designer Cheryl Casey Ross, of Cross Interiors in Van Nuys, California.

When choosing furniture, keep an eye out for scale. Don't choose oversized furniture for a small living room, no matter how comfortable it is. Once you cram it into the space, in the only location it can possibly fit, you're stuck with it—in the same spot—for the duration. It's nice to rearrange a room occasionally and this will preclude that pleasure.

In living rooms that function also as family rooms, storage is a must for eliminating clutter. Select a cabinet for the video and sound equipment. Try to keep these devices behind closed doors when not in use. Add shelves to hold decorative accessories and books.

If your living room will double as a guest room, buy double-duty furnishings, such as a sofa bed or a love seat with a pullout bed. Some extra-large chairs also feature this option and are handy in smaller rooms. Another practical idea is to use an attractive trunk as a coffee or end table. That way, you can tuck sheets, blankets, and an alarm clock in the chest. Other options include storage ottomans or even a bench with a hinged top. Stay away from the large toy box you'll have to empty out every time your little one can't find the tiny figurine hidden at the bottom.

BELOW
**Folding doors above the fireplace open to reveal a flat-panel TV screen for viewing.**

OPPOSITE
**A tall mirror that has been propped against a wall is a trick designers use to add the illusion of more space.**

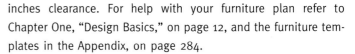

OPPOSITE
An antique console and an original oil painting fill out a wall behind a pair of chairs in this living room.

ABOVE
On the opposite side of the room, a sofa completes the seating arrangement in front of the fireplace.

RIGHT
When the coffee table is not called into use for entertaining, the homeowners use it to display treasured objects.

# Defining Space

"Furniture should be arranged conducive to how it will be used," says Barbara Schlattman. "So if an area is going to be used for conversation, create a U-shape or box shape with the seating." This arrangement is comfortable and allows people to face each other when they speak.

Designers also keep furniture away from the walls whenever possible. Float some pieces and create a cluster. In a large living room, create several groupings: one in a square configuration for conversation, another around the TV area, and a quiet corner for one or two people to enjoy a book. For easy passage around or through furniture clusters, leave a minimum of 28 inches clearance. For help with your furniture plan refer to Chapter One, "Design Basics," on page 12, and the furniture templates in the Appendix, on page 284.

When the living room plays more than one role, decorative screens can help divide separate areas and close off what you don't want to be seen, such as paperwork or clutter in a home office. Also, look for furniture that can house an entire office-worth of computer equipment or a media center behind doors. Use a different area rug to define separate spaces or wall-to-wall carpeting with contrasting carpet borders. Wallcoverings and wall colors can change throughout the space, but keep the change subtle to avoid creating visual chaos.

## Lighting

Concentrate on general lighting in addition to task and mood lighting. Ceiling fixtures or recessed canisters with dimmers are good for providing ambient light. The dimmers allow you to adjust light levels to create mood. If you will read, watch TV, do paperwork, or perform some other activity, you'll have to provide specific task lighting. In general, floor lamps that are 40 to 49 inches from the floor to the bottom of the shade provide generous light spread. Table lamps with shades are ideal because they direct light upward and downward with little glare. For reading, the bottom of the shade should be just below eye level. Each smaller area within the living room must have its own lighting dictated by activity. Lights might be dimmed when entertaining on a winter night as the fireplace is roaring. (See Chapter Three, "The Right Light," on page 56, for more information.)

# family room

The family room is often the home's real *living* room and perhaps the busiest room in the house. This space often has to pack in a lot—from TV viewing to play. Many considerations for living rooms and family rooms are the same, so see the section "Living Rooms," starting on page 179, for more information.

## Style and Color

Because this room is going to get a workout, select patterns, colors, and materials that are durable and will still look good over time. The family room is the place to be a little more personal, so display family photos or collections. There's no need to be formal. Some designers refer to the sought-after family room look as "casual elegance."

Special consideration should be given to great rooms—family rooms and kitchens contained in one open space. Coordinate them, but create visual separation, too. This can be achieved by arranging the family-room furniture to face away from the kitchen or by alternating materials. Use ceramic tile on the kitchen floor and hardwood in the family room, or use hardwood throughout the space, and cluster family-room furniture around area rugs.

When planning the two spaces, remember that the color and style of the kitchen cabinets should be similar or identical to cabinetry in the family room. High-gloss lacquer cabinets in the kitchen will look out of place with a colonial pine entertainment center nearby. Some custom cabinetmakers will design bookshelves, computer desks, and entertainment centers to match kitchen cabinets for a fully coordinated look, and even some semi-custom or standard cabinet lines offer coordinated pieces. You can also order matching panels that can be fitted to cover appliances, such as refrigerators, wine coolers, and dishwashers. (See Chapter Nine, "Kitchen Design," on page 206.)

The family room is the place to let your personality shine, though. Showcase a doll collection or a series of your favorite artist's prints. Frame some of your kids' artwork, or display your own handiwork by hanging a quilt on the wall.

ABOVE
**If there's only one fireplace in the house, having it in the family room is most desirable. A unique surround such as this one, fabricated from concrete, or mantel will make it distinctive.**

## Focal Point

The focal point of a family room might be a fireplace, an entertainment center, or a large view of the great outdoors. With all of the different activities that take place here and all of the furnishings that are required, it's important to have a focal point to anchor the room.

## Furnishings

Your shopping list might include a love seat, sofa, entertainment center, desk for computer, file cabinet, toy chest, game table, and so forth. Today's family rooms often include a snack center with a mini-refrigerator and sink. The furnishings in your family room depend on how you're going to be using the space.

Designers often advise their clients to select the best quality furnishings they can afford. Don't go for the least expensive sofa because you think, "the kids will ruin it anyway." Sturdy construction can always be reupholstered. Stay away from solid light colors that will show every bit of dirt. Use patterns which hide the wear. "If you want to have a relaxed room, you need to create a comfortable place, where you won't be uptight about hav-

### smart tip  FAMILY ROOMS

Probably the most common activity that takes place in your family room is TV viewing. To make your "home theater" experience ideal, select window treatments that open and close easily and can block out glare-causing sunlight. Leave a distance that is three times the size of the TV screen between the screen and opposite seating for optimal viewing.

ing the kids use it," says Melinda Sechrist. Select some lightweight pieces of furniture that can be easily moved—when suddenly more seating is needed around the television or you want to create mingling room when entertaining.

If the family room doubles as a playroom for kids, storage is essential. Select smaller bins that kids can handle rather than one large toy box that swallows up small items. Children are more likely to help pick up if it doesn't seem like an overwhelming task. A small bookshelf with clear bins to hold toys, baskets for stuffed animals, and shelves for games is a good idea.

## Lighting

Every activity that takes place in the family room has special lighting requirements, so start by making a list of those activities. A reading chair requires intense task lighting. Plan moderate task lighting over a game table. For the TV and computer, use low general lighting that does not create glare. Include bright supplementary lighting for doing extra-fine detail tasks, such as crocheting, needlework, or other crafting pastimes. Install dimmers on all of the lights. Follow the advice offered for living rooms, and consult Chapter Three, "The Right Light," on page 56.

LEFT
Comfortable seating pieces are a must in a room where family and friends will gather. Delicate materials are better-suited to a room that gets less use.

# dining room

Although today's fast-paced lifestyles often mean quick and easy meals, the dining room should be a place where people can sit down, relax, and enjoy a leisurely meal. If you use your dining room on a daily basis, you'll have to be practical and play it safe. But if you serve meals there only a handful of times during the year, you can be a little more daring.

## Style and Color

The dining room often opens to the living room, kitchen, or foyer, so the style and colors should coordinate with those spaces. The room can take on a more formal look if the family eats primarily in the kitchen. In fact, most interior designers and homeowners like to create a show-stopping dining room for entertaining and special occasions.

Dining rooms look great with a wonderful wallpaper that includes a color found on the adjoining room's walls. Stay away from overbearing patterns. Soft florals and stripes are good choices in traditional dining rooms, while faux finishes and tex-tured looks can perfectly complement contemporary or transitional decors. Wallpaper borders, used with an all-over wallcovering or alone, are also an option that you can use to introduce another pattern into the room.

Keep walls all the same color or wallpaper pattern for continuity. On the ceiling, use a bright white paint. If you're painting the walls a light neutral hue, however, why not add color to the ceiling? Pick up the burgundy or colonial blue on the upholstered chairs as an accent and for a formal touch, for instance. For drama, paint the walls a deep color and accent them with trimwork.

## The Focal Point

The focal point of a dining room is often the table itself or an interesting hutch, depending on the placement of the furniture and the orientation of the doorway. Add a centerpiece to the table for visual appeal. Anything from a vase of flowers to a seasonal display or dramatic sculpture will do it. A large window, painting, or mirror can also become a focal point. If a hutch is too large for your room, replace it with a buffet topped with a colorful painting or enlarged photograph from your last vacation. This, too, becomes a focal point.

RIGHT
**Today's lighter-weight metals make it possible to hang a chandelier such as this one without worrying whether it is too heavy for the ceiling.**

OPPOSITE
**Slipcovered wooden chairs keep the look light in this large dining room.**

## Furnishings

"How many will be in the room? How will it be used? If it's small, do you really need anything in the room other than table and chairs?" asks designer Barbara Schlattman. Space can be tight in a dining room, so select as big a table as you can comfortably fit. Leave a minimum of 32 to 36 inches between the table and the wall so that you can move easily out of the chair. The floor covering is especially important in a dining room where chairs are moved in and out and the table might be expanded to accommodate more people. Choose a floor covering that will allow you and your guests to move the chairs easily. If you use an area rug, a popular choice in dining rooms, make sure it will fit under the table when it's expanded to maximum size.

Most dining-room furniture is sold in sets. A set immediately gives you a coordinated look, but it isn't your only option. "It's much more interesting to buy the pieces separately. The chairs don't have to match the table, and the hutch doesn't have to match the table, either," says Barbara Schlattman. "Styles can mix—a traditional chair with a sleek table—or work with different woods."

## smart tip DINING ROOMS

Change the look of your dining room by slipcovering chairs. Short-skirted slipcovers give a more informal appearance; fabrics in graphic patterns, such as checks or floral prints, complement this style of slipcover best. Long-skirted covers are elegant additions to a formal dining room, particularly in solid color or tone-on-tone fabrics. Ties, buttons, or trim can add personality. Think about changing the slipcovers with the seasons. Use a heavy velvet for the fall and winter, and then switch to a lighter linen for spring or summer. Save slipcovers made of delicate fabrics, such as silk or taffetta, for special occasions.

A china closet is practical and aesthetically appealing. But rather than displaying your crystal and dinnerware, showcase objects that reveal a little of your personality. Or select a buffet, and use the wall space to group a collection of plates. For extra drama, use attention-grabbing lighting.

## Lighting

A chandelier or hanging fixture should hang above the center of the table. This may not be the center of the room, though, after arranging a hutch or other furniture. In a dining room with an 8-foot ceiling, install the fixture so that its bottom is 27 to 36 inches above the table. Raise the fixture 3 inches for every additional foot of ceiling height. A crystal chandelier looks great in a formal, elegant dining room, while a ceiling light and fan combination can add charm to a well-dressed transitional space. Display cases should have interior lighting. Wall sconces add decorative appeal and can draw attention to a buffet or painting. Make sure that lighting is sufficient for instances when the dining-room table doubles as workspace. (See Chapter Three, "The Right Light," on page 56.)

# kitchen

The kitchen represents a real design challenge. Large appliances, plenty of storage, work space, and possibly a casual eating area must come together in harmony. And in the kitchen, efficient function is crucial. "If it doesn't function, it doesn't matter how good it looks," notes Lori Jo Krengel, CKD, CBD, of Kitchens By Krengel in St. Paul, Minnesota. (See Chapter Nine, "Kitchen Design," on page 206.)

## Style and Color

You want the kitchen to coordinate with the rest of your rooms, but since it's essentially a work space, you've got some leeway here. If the kitchen is self-contained, meaning that it's not open to another room such as the family room, then it can comfort-

RIGHT

An L-shaped banquette saves space in this breakfast nook and provides storage underneath the seats. Chrome legs on the table and chairs add a Modern look that coordinates with the hardware. Pendants offer the right level of supplemental lighting at night.

ably depart from the main style of the house. There's nothing wrong with a relatively high-tech kitchen in a traditional-style home, as long as it doesn't clash outright with the integrity of the house. You might, for example, use white cabinetry here and another type elsewhere. But the door style might closely resemble that of the hutch in the dining room. Your accessories can also bring a taste of your main decor into the kitchen. For instance, if you are displaying a blue-and-white china collection in the family room, bring some pieces into the kitchen.

Cabinets are the dominant design element in the kitchen. If you're not sure what you want, play it safe with a traditional raised-panel door. That type of door style can take on a variety of looks, from contemporary to country, depending on the surroundings.

Light cabinet colors are best in small kitchens. If your heart is set on a dark wood stain, brighten up the space with a light countertop and backsplash, white or almond appliances, and ample lighting.

If you want a colorful kitchen, approach it as you would any other room: Get swatches and material samples from the manufacturers. Some terrific spots to add decorative color in the kitchen are a tiled backsplash or a ceramic tile floor, a solid-surfacing countertop inlaid with a stripe or custom pattern, or even a laminate floor that features a border. Mix countertop colors and materials. For example, use butcher block or granite on the work island and solid-surfacing material elsewhere. Cabinetry can be stained in colors, such as shades of red or blue. A cast-iron sink in a vibrant blue or green always looks dramatic or, if you're more daring, there are even ranges available in bright colors, such as royal blue and red. But you may want to play it safe with neutral colors on permanent fixtures in general.

TOP LEFT
Wood cabinets wear a mellow, medium-color stain that warms up this kitchen where stainless-steel appliances and a granite countertop are cool to the touch.

LEFT
Rustic floor tiles and pine cabinetry enhance the Old World look of this room. A large center island was designed to resemble an old country table.

## Focal Point

Cabinetry is the backdrop of a kitchen, but the focal point is often the window or the area around the range. Many designers like to dress the latter space up with a hand-painted mural or other interesting ceramic tiles. Sleek, shiny metal range hoods also help to emphasize this area.

In a great-room setup, where kitchen and family room become one, a fireplace might become the focal point. That's fine, but you'll also want to create some sort of separation between the spaces. An island or peninsula often doubles as a buffer.

## Furnishings

More and more kitchen designers are specifying freestanding furniture for their clients' kitchens. A hutch will provide sought-after storage space for dinnerware, glasses, or even pantry items. Glass-fronted cabinetry looks great, but the storage space inside needs to be neat and orderly.

Granite- and marble-top tables can act as a movable center island ideal for working with dough. Select a table and chairs that fit the style of the kitchen. Find interesting stools for an island that offers a casual eating area.

## Lighting

Professional designers always try to include as much natural light in a kitchen plan as possible. Task lighting, often under wall cabinets or above the island, is a must—although it's often tempting to eliminate the added expense. There should be a light over the sink and some type of general lighting. You may prefer hanging fixtures to all recessed lighting. You might also want to consider lighting inside cabinetry.

### smart tip KITCHENS

Don't choose trendy cabinetry for the kitchen—it can quickly look dated. Instead, add bold decorative touches with those things that are easy to change—novelty hardware, for instance. Backsplashes, countertops, sinks, and wallcoverings are also good choices. Replacing these items may require a little more effort, but the job can definitely be done without tremendous fuss.

# bedrooms

The master bedroom is your getaway space, so design it to please only yourself. Invest in a luxury touch here and there—beautiful bed linens or a four-poster bed, for example. In a busy world, everyone needs a pleasant day's-end retreat.

## Style and Color

The master bedroom generally conforms to the style chosen for the main rooms of the house. If possible, try not to allow the bedroom to become a multipurpose room. Don't give in to the idea that one corner could house a mini-office space perfectly—taking "work" into the bedroom is not a restful concept. If the master bedroom is shared, decide together whether or not to include a TV. To maintain a restful look in the room, choose cabinetry that conceals it.

You can draw your color scheme from the palette you've

chosen for one of the other spaces in the house, or you can pick favorite colors or those that look good on one or both of you. If you're a morning person and have the time to luxuriate in the bedroom until later, consider warm, invigorating colors. If you want your evening retreat to soothe away the cares of the day, pick from the cooler hues.

## Focal Point

The bed is usually the focal point of a bedroom, so dress it up with attractive bedding, including comfortable throw pillows. Often the headboard or space above it catches the eye as well. An ornate headboard will serve as a focal point, as will a canopy suspended from the ceiling and arranged with coordinating fabrics. A nicely framed painting or print—or perhaps a coordinating pair or groupings—over the bed can also look attractive.

A low dresser leaves the space above it as a possible focal point. Consider an ornately framed mirror, a series of interestingly shaped mirrors, or a mirror flanked by framed prints or a collection of items such as straw hats.

**OPPOSITE**
A faux-fur coverlet adds glamour to this bed. Accents of polished chrome and glass look contemporary and chic.

**TOP LEFT**
Traditional furnishings, including the scroll-back slipper chair, are all antique reproductions in this room.

**LEFT**
The wallcovering sets the theme here. Because the pattern is bold, the rest of the room's furnishings are subdued.

## Furnishings

There are some practical aspects to be addressed in a master bedroom, in which two people are often waking up and getting dressed at the same time. If space permits, separate storage for each one should be included: dresser and bureau, two closets, and twin night stands. A decorative screen can provide an interesting backdrop that will also create a small dressing area. A full-length mirror, whether freestanding or mounted on closet doors, is another important element.

If there's room, also include a comfortable chair along with a small table and a lamp. This quiet spot is great for reading, relaxing, or enjoying evening tea or morning coffee in the privacy of your retreat. Designers seldom purchase bedroom furniture in complete sets. Buy interesting individual pieces instead. Matched suites are passé.

Window treatments should be room-darkening to ensure that you're not awakened at first light: if you install lightweight curtains, use shades or blinds underneath for controlling light. For privacy, install two-way shades or half-curtains.

## Lighting

On each nightstand or above the bed there should be separate reading lamps for each party. For ambient lighting, an overhead light fixture is more decorative than recessed lamps. It should hang centrally. Consider an overhead ceiling fan/light combination, an asset on warm nights. Be sure to include proper task lights for applying makeup or other grooming habits. (See Chapter Three, "The Right Light," on page 56, for more guidance.)

RIGHT

In a guest room, every effort has been made to create a comfortable, restful environment, including a bedside table and a reading lamp.

## smart tip BEDROOMS

Whites, neutrals, or pale colors—blues, greens, or pinks— create a restful ambiance in the bedroom, making sleeping easier. Cheery colors, such as yellow, work for those who like rising with the sun (or those who need help waking up). All-over wallpaper patterns, particularly large-scale ones, can sometimes make a bedroom feel too enclosed, so use bold patterns sparingly.

# children's rooms

A good designer will interview both the child and the parents when designing a kid's room. From the child the designer will get personal preferences, and from the parents, he or she will hope to get an idea of how the room must function. "Too often, people focus on the look of the room, and function is an afterthought," says Michele Rohrer, Allied ASID, of Michelle's Interiors, in Grayslake, Illinois. "In a child's room, it's crucial to write down all of the functions of the room."

An older child uses it for doing homework, playing games, entertaining, and reading, in addition to sleeping. The room becomes the spot where friends come over to play. A baby's room will probably be the spot for diaper changing, lullaby singing, playing, and sleeping.

## Style and Color

"When selecting a palette for a child's room, expect it to meet his or her needs for about 5 to 7 years." As children develop, aquire more interests, and make friends, they—along with their tastes in favorite colors and decorating motifs—change. "A 6-year-old girl will not enjoy the same room or color scheme past the age of 12, nor can an infant room last past 6," notes Rohrer.

TOP RIGHT

An upholstered rocker is an important feature in this infant's room. Draperies can be closed for daytime napping.

RIGHT

A teenage girl's room expresses her individuality through colors and motifs that reflect her developing tastes.

# smart tip

## CHILDREN'S ROOMS

Keep safety in mind when planning a child's room. Make sure that there are covers on electrical outlets, guard rails on high windows, sturdy screens in front of radiators, and gates blocking any steps. Other suggestions include safety hinges for chests and nonskid backing for rugs.

Themes are suitable for children of any age, although the approach may change. Select more juvenile characters and patterns for a 3-year-old's bedroom than you would a 9-year-old's—but both can still feature a jungle or train motif. As in all rooms, trendy colors and styles date it. Use them sparingly and on elements that are easy to change. "Good design is always good," says Rohrer, "If something is trendy, like daisies from the '60s, we won't do it on a large scale. We'll use daisies on a pillow maybe."

## Furnishings

Furnishings should be selected according to how the space will function. A full-size bed is more practical in rooms where friends use the bed for seating. Children need their own space and their things nearby, from toys to a favorite cap. These years will pass by so quickly. Most designers encourage their clients to give in to some of their kids' whims. A child's room should be fun and lively.

Trundle beds and bunk beds are often used in kids' rooms to accommodate sleepovers. Flooring should be durable and comfortable. (See Chapter Four, "Style Underfoot," on page 82.) Area rugs are easier to remove for dry-cleaning, but they require using a nonskid mat underneath. School-age children need a desk or study area. Line a bookshelf with clear bins for easy-to-see storage. Under-bed storage keeps things out of view. Take advantage of closet space in small bedrooms by using built-in closet systems to maximize the space. "If a large closet exists, think about using it for clothing, and forego the dressers," says Rohrer. If the room is small, floor space can be used for other necessities.

## Lighting

Combine general overhead lighting with task lighting: a reading lamp over the headboard, a desk lamp, and perhaps a night light. Avoid floor lamps, which can be easily knocked over. (See Chapter Three, "The Right Light," on page 56, for more information.)

ABOVE
Vibrant color and energetic patterns and prints were selected by a young girl to create her own sweet retreat. In a room where so much is going on visually, clutter has to be held at bay. A set of shelves in the corner make way for a few photos; everything else remains out of sight in boxes and baskets.

OPPOSITE
If there's space for it, a double bed is more practical than one that is twin size, even when the room isn't shared. This one wears a vivacious coat of deeply saturated orange paint to match the chest.

# bathroom

In the bathroom, as in the kitchen, you can safely depart from the style of the rest of your house. It's a room, usuly a small one, that does a big job, but there's a place for form as well as function in today's bath. (See Chapter Ten, "Creating a Bathroom Design," on page 236.)

## Style and Color

The master bath and family bath are going to be used frequently, so it's especially important that you select a style and colors that everyone likes. In a master bath, coordinate the colors with those used in the bedroom, or you might draw the scheme for a bath from the hall. A powder room is the place to be more daring, but keep the basics of color theory in mind. "Look at the balance. You don't want a red, green, and purple bath. You have to follow the elements and principles of design, otherwise it will look like a hodge-podge," says designer Lori Jo Krengel.

In the bath, a neutral scheme can change with your whim simply by replacing the accessories. Shower curtains, rugs, towels, and even some fixtures are relatively easy and inexpensive to change. Small items, such as soap, can inject color.

RIGHT
An orange-red soaking tub, fabricated from colored concrete, counterbalances the all-neutral scheme in this room. Color is the sole "decoration" in the space, which is luxuriously minimal in style.

## smart tip BATHROOMS

No matter how big or small the room, details will pull the style together. Some of the best details that you can include are the smallest—drawer pulls from an antique store or shells in a glass jar or just left on the countertop. Add period flavor with crown molding, or dress up contemporary fixtures with polished stone fittings.

## Focal Point

"There's not necessarily a focal point in a bathroom," says Krengel. "You want an overall feel." You have to decide what that will be.

You can, however, create a focal point at the vanity or the tub. A clutter-free new countertop adorned with a decorative accent piece (from a basket of bathing goodies to a vase with fresh flowers) and backed with a striking yet practical mirrored medicine cabinet can grab attention. The same is true for a tub set in a custom-designed surround. Effective lighting above the tub or on the sides of the vanity can augment drama as well.

## Furnishings

There are certain elements that a full bath must include: toilet, tub or shower, lavatory, and storage.

BELOW
In another contemporary bathroom, the shape of the lav takes the look of art pottery. Intended as a double bowl, it features a pair of single-lever chrome faucets. The vanity has been mounted on the wall leaving a less-cluttered appearance. To the left is a separate area for the toilet. The inconspicuous pocket door can be closed for privacy.

Once you make your basic selections, start thinking about how you want to decorate. Permanent fixtures, except storage, should all be the same color for continuity. Add contrast with tile, paint, or patterned wall-coverings.

Storage is essential in a bathroom. If there is room, a vanity is useful and attractive. If you plan to install a pedestal sink, you'll have to find storage elsewhere. Many designers like to add freestanding pieces of furniture for extra drawer and cabinet space. This option is a practical one because it's easy to change. However, make sure that wooden pieces are protected against moisture with a sealant. Take advantage of wall space behind the toilet by adding a rack or cabinet there.

## Lighting

Minimally, in a bathroom that is less than 100 square feet, one fixture is sufficient. Add another fixture for each additional 50 square feet. However, you should also plan task lighting for grooming in the sink area. You might also consider adding a light in the shower ceiling or above the tub, but make sure that it is one specifically designed for a damp location and conforming to local building codes.

# working with professionals

If you have a design dilemma that you just can't solve your-self, consulting a professional is a good idea. These Smart Steps can help you find the right person and communicate your needs effectively.

## smart steps
## find the right one

### Step 1 NARROW DOWN YOUR NEEDS
To figure out the kind of professional you need, first get a clear picture of the level of help you require. Developing a color scheme, for example, requires less specific expertise than, say, space planning for a busy kitchen. If you don't like the colors a friend suggests, you simply don't have to use them. But you may not realize until it's too late that configuring a kitchen lay-out is too complicated a task for you. So be honest in your assessment of your skills to avoid problems.

### Step 2 LOCATE FREE HELP
Begin with free sources, and see whether you find answers that way. Home and decorating centers often employ designers to get potential customers through tough design decisions. If the advice you receive will mean large financial expenditures, ask the designer, casually, how much experience he or she has. In a freebie situation, it's usually not appropriate to ask for references, except in cases where the designer is not just giving advice on a single issue, but designing an entire room.

### Step 3 SEARCH THE WORLD WIDE WEB
If you have a home computer with internet access, you should know that many professional design organiza-tions have Web sites. Some offer troubleshooting tips or free design advice via e-mail. Web sites change over time and not all offer the same kind of resources, but there are a few worth looking into:

- *www.interiors.org*, the American Society of Interior Designers
- *www.nkba.org*, the National Kitchen and Bath Association
- *www.nari.org*, the National Association of the Remodeling Industry
- *www.nahb.com*, the National Association of Home Builders
- *www.aia.org*, the American Institute of Architects
- *www.aibd.org*, the American Institute of Building Design

Even if you don't get free advice on-line through these Web sites, you can locate design professionals in your area who may be able to help you.

### Step 4 FIND A PROFESSIONAL INTERIOR DESIGNER
If your project really can't go forward without sound professional advice and you've figured the cost into your budget, you can easily find someone to hire. If you've admired the work of a designer in someone else's home, simply ask for the reference. Sometimes retail establishments can recommend professionals they've worked with in the past. The good old Yellow Pages is always a source. Plus, if there is a designer showhouse in your area, visit it for ideas and to make contacts. A showhouse is a good way to see the work of any local talent.

### Step 5 LOOK AT PORTFOLIOS; CALL REFERENCES; CHECK CREDENTIALS
Make sure that the person with whom you choose to work is registered with a professional organization, such as the ones listed in Step Three. Interview candi-dates thoroughly about their business. A remodeling project can take a long time, so it is best to be friendly and comfortable with whomever your hire. Ask to examine the designer's portfolio to get a feeling of whether his or her style will suit you, or whether he or she has a wide enough range to meet your needs. Most importantly, don't neglect the final step of check-ing references. Pretty pictures of someone's dream project are easy to come by, but the whole story of a redesign or remodeling can be a nightmare. Call references, and if possible, visit sites and ask plenty of questions.

ABOVE
Some high-end furnishings are available to the trade only. That means you cannot purchase them directly but through
a qualified professional, such as a member of the American Society of Interior Designers (ASID).

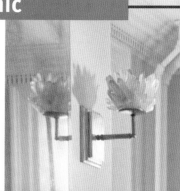

# design workbook
## NEW LOOK FOR A VINTAGE ROOM

### eclectic chic

Elements of classical architecture, such as the crown molding, contrast pleasingly with this living room's contemporary furnishings.

### fabric blend

Silk damask-covered pillows add an elegant accent to the less-formal style of the sofa, which has been upholstered in a linen-and-silk fabric.

### contemporary lighting

The unusual cut-crystal sconces, top left, mounted on both sides of an old frosted mirror, resemble shards of ice against the cool blue color on the wall.

### tabletop assemblage

An orderly tabletop grouping of art books and other objects, left, adds personality to the room. The glass-and-metal design has a modern sensibility.

# design workbook

## A NEW ENVIRONMENT

### call of nature

The artwork in this living room tells a lot about the homeowners, who prefer organic forms and natural materials.

### spice it up

Accent pillows in primary blue and red enliven and relieve the living room's otherwise all-neutral palette of earth tones.

### modern classic

The "Bertoia Diamond Chair," top left, is a mid-century-modern classic. Made of steel and wire, it was first introduced in 1952.

### subtle in stone

Slate tiles assert just enough strength to make the fireplace, left, an imposing, but not over-done, focal point.

# 9

# kitchen design

SET PRIORITIES  BASIC KITCHEN LAYOUTS  CHOOSING CABINETS
COUNTERTOP OPTIONS  SELECTING FEATURES  DESIGN WORKBOOK

O f all the rooms in a house, kitchens present unique decorating challenges because so much tends to happen in these spaces. In addition to preparing meals, most people use their kitchen as a gathering place, so the design has to be functional, comfortable, and inviting.

This one room has become so important, in fact, that many buyers consider the kitchen a deal maker—or breaker. If you are thinking about remodeling your kitchen for resale purposes, you may get as much back as you invest—maybe more, depending on where you live. If you are like most people, however, your motivations are much more personal.

Plain white cabinets and stainless-steel appliances put a fresh face on country style. A sky-blue backsplash adds subtle color.

A highly functional kitchen will not make you a master chef, but it will improve the quality of the time you spend there. Even the smallest remodeling job requires careful planning and forethought.

# set priorities

esign professionals interview their clients at length at the beginning of a project. If you will be your own designer, do the same thing. Likewise, you may even want to videotape your family (and yourself) in the kitchen during typical meal preparation or any other kitchen-based activities. If your parties often spill into the kitchen, for instance, videotape the next party, and pay attention to how difficult or easy it is to interact with guests while you're cooking or serving. Is there enough room for opening the refrigerator door when someone passes behind you? Is there ample space on the countertop to set up a small, informal buffet or bar?

Note the different situations that typically interrupt or assist your work flow and traffic patterns. Is the aisle you use to reach the oven the same as the one used to walk from the back door into the house? Observe how many times you have to walk across the room for something while you're cooking.

If you consult with a professional, don't be put off by questions. Any good designer has to get to know the habits, likes, and dislikes of the people who will live with the finished project. He wants to understand your basic requirements, as well as your wildest dreams, for the new kitchen.

A designer will also sketch the existing space to get an idea of what works and what doesn't. This rough drawing may include any adjacent areas that might be considered for expansion, such as a pantry or part of a hallway.

Once again, if you will be your own designer, do the same thing. Talk to everyone in the household. Ask what they think needs improvement, as well as any aspects of the space as it exists that they'd prefer to retain.

For the best results, approach the project in the same calm, analytical manner as a professional, one who understands design and can be objective about what has to happen to make the project a success.

# smart steps
## where to begin

### Step 1 CREATE A DESIGN NOTEBOOK

It's important to keep all of your ideas and records in one place. Buy a loose-leaf binder, and use it to organize everything from magazine clippings to photos of the old kitchen (extremely important when you choose

to resell the house); wish lists; notes and interviews with design professionals and family members; contracts; business cards; sample plans; shopping lists; color charts; tile, fabric, and wallpaper samples; and anything else related to the project. The file should be comprehensive, yet not too clumsy to cart around to showrooms, stores, or home centers.

### Step 2 ANALYZE THE EXISTING KITCHEN

Decide what you really want to gain by remodeling. You might begin by asking what's wrong with the existing kitchen? Maybe you and your partner enjoy cooking together, but the floor plan was designed to work for only one cook. Perhaps storage is inadequate or the appliances are old.

To be specific about your analysis, get out your notebook and record answers to questions such as, Is the size of the family likely to grow or shrink in the near future? If the kids are or will be in college soon, you might not need that large-capacity refrigerator. Likewise, if this is your first house and you expect to move up as your family size increases, it might be wise to refinish high-ticket items such as cabinets, and hang onto older appliances that are still working, spending only a modest amount of money, time, and energy on cosmetic changes in the kitchen. Other questions to consider include:

■ How many members of the household really cook? Note other ways each one uses the kitchen.
■ How convenient is it to work in the kitchen? Are people always bumping into each other? When cabinet or appliance doors are open, is the traffic pattern interrupted?
■ Is there enough storage? If you keep kitchen- or cooking-related items in other areas of the house such as the garage, it's time to analyze how to increase the storage capacity in the kitchen.
■ What is the condition of existing materials and appliances? How old are they? Are the appliances energy-efficient? Are the walls, floors, and counter-tops in good condition?

LEFT
If you don't use the microwave at mealtime, locate it outside the main food-preparation area.

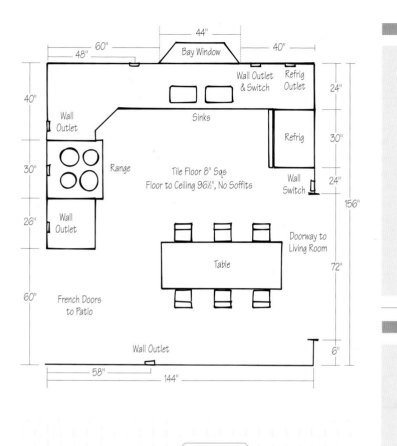

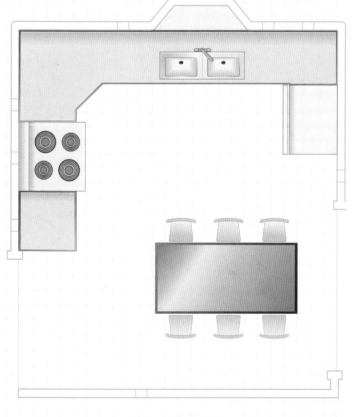

## Step 3 MAKE A WISH LIST

Besides the basic elements, you may want some special features in your new kitchen—a ceramic glass-top
range, modular refrigeration, interchangeable cooktop
components, or a warming drawer. Perhaps an elegant
slate or granite countertop or a gorgeous custom range
hood has caught your eye.

Create a list of all the accoutrements you would like
to include, whether or not you think you can afford
them. When you have a close-to-perfect plan, that's the
time to look for areas to trim if your budget is tight.
You might choose a countertop fabricated in an affordable stone look-alike, and use the dollars saved for
something you can't fake, such as an energy-efficient
window over the sink or a tiled backsplash.

## Step 4 SKETCH THE OLD FLOOR PLAN

Just like a professional designer, draw an existing floor
plan. Do a rough sketch first; then transfer your drawing to graph paper with grids marked at ¼-inch intervals. Draw it freehand or with a straightedge, but do it
to a scale of ½ inch is equal to 1 foot. This base plan,
or "base map," as it is called, should record the layout
of the space as it exists. Include measurements for
everything, from the width of every door to how far the
refrigerator protrudes into the room.

Start by taking measurements, beginning with the
length and width of the room. Then from one corner,
measure the location of windows, doors, and walls.
Record the swing of each door. Note each dimension in
feet and inches to the nearest ¼ inch.

Next draw the cabinetry and appliances, and indicate
their height. Measure the position and centerline of the
sink (showing how far the center of this fixture is from
the wall), but don't forget to list its overall length and
width. Also measure the height of the walls.

Include symbols for light fixtures, outlets, and heat
registers on the floor plan as well. Note load-bearing
walls, which cannot be moved without compromising

ABOVE LEFT
Take measurements of your existing kitchen, and record the
information on a preliminary sketch.

LEFT
Transfer the drawing to graph paper—a scale of ½ inch equals
1 foot is good—or computer design software.

structural integrity. If you are thinking about tearing out any wall and you don't know whether it is load-bearing, consult an architect or a structural engineer before you do anything.

It's a good idea to list your gripes about the old kitchen on the sketch. That way you can see at a glance what problem areas need to be changed.

Remember: this floor plan is only a guide. It doesn't have to be professionally drawn, only accurate in its rendition and measurements of the current space.

## smart tip  THE FRIDGE

In the old days, the refrigerator ruled. You put the bulky combination unit in a central place, if possible, then clustered your work zones around it to save steps. These days, thanks to the flexibility of modular cooking units that can be placed anywhere in the kitchen, you are no longer a slave to one immovable behemoth. Get creative and customize.

# basic kitchen layouts

Whether you are reconfiguring existing space or adding on, the floor plan plays a large role in how well the room will function. And while a kitchen addition to an outside wall of the house offers the best possibilities for unencumbered floor space, it is the costliest option. One way to save money is to restrict your addition to a "bumpout" of 3 feet or less. This doesn't necessarily require a new foundation, and it limits the need for a new roof. Consult an architect or builder, first, to make sure the existing structure is sound and can carry the additional load. Remember to inquire about local zoning ordinances before proceeding with your plans.

However you choose to proceed, any kitchen of any size requires a thoughtful arrangement of all its elements to make it both highly functional and efficient.

## The Work Triangle

Almost everybody has heard of the kitchen's classic *work triangle*. Essentially, it is an area that puts the three major work centers—the range, refrigerator, and sink—at the three points of a triangle. The spatial relationship among these sites and how they relate to other areas in the kitchen is what makes the room an efficient work space. The National Kitchen & Bath Association (NKBA) recommends that there be at least one work triangle in a kitchen. In fact, today's busy families—and multipurpose kitchens—often call for two or more work triangles. With traditional roles at home changing, so are attitudes about cooking. Two-cook families are more common than ever, and food preparation and cooking have themselves become excuses for social events where even the guests actively participate.

In the classic work triangle, the distance between any pair of the three task centers is no longer than 9 feet and no less than 4 feet.

To conserve walking distance from point to point without sacrificing adequate counter space, the sum of all three lines of the triangle should be no greater than 27 feet and no less than 12 feet. For a large kitchen, plan two or more work triangles. Although pairs may extend inside one another, sharing one side or "leg" of the triangle for maximum performance, do not overlap the sink and range areas. Another approach is to design smaller triangles set within the larger one.

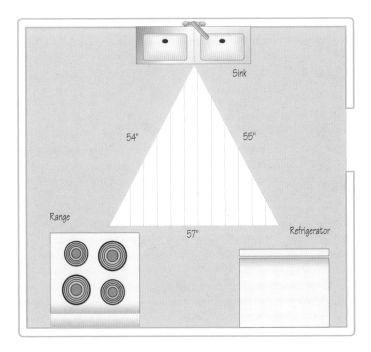

ABOVE
Designers use the work triangle to connect the primary work centers and define the optimal distances between them. It is a building block of kitchen design.

Because a goal of the work triangle is to keep normal kitchen traffic from interrupting the work flow, during your planning stage pay especially close attention to how everyone in the household comes and goes in the existing kitchen. You might even try this unusual but enlightening homespun experiment: dust the floor with a thin coating of cornmeal; then go about your normal food preparation and cleanup. You'll be able to track your movements from cabinets to appliances to the sink, and the rest of the family's moves around you—or whoever does the cooking. Once you see where the kitchen becomes most crowded, you'll be able to make the necessary changes. (And don't forget to sweep up the cornmeal.) Sometimes that's as simple as relocating an appliance—particularly a small one—to a less busy area. For ideas, take a look at the floor plan examples on the next few pages.

There is some debate today among professional kitchen designers concerning the traditional work triangle. Although most agree that it is still an important element, many see the triangular space evolving as cooking habits and lifestyles change. These designers feel that the more actual living done in the kitchen, the more expanded the basic triangle will have to become. And as kitchens grow larger—which appears to be the trend—they will embrace an increasing number of activities. This will result in the need for several autonomous triangles within the room. Whichever school of thought you believe, the bottom line still is and always will be: design for your sake, not for the sake of design.

As you consider a new layout, check that traffic moves easily from one place to another in the kitchen and from the kitchen to other rooms in the house, as well as outdoors. It is important that through-traffic doesn't interfere with the work triangle. Otherwise, carrying a hot pot from the range to the sink could put you on a collision course with youngsters heading for the back door.

Often you can correct a faulty traffic pattern simply by moving a door or removing a short section of wall. Another way to improve a kitchen's function is to experiment with basic layouts to see which suits your needs.

# Basic Layouts

There are five basic kitchen layouts: one-wall, galley (corridor), U-shaped, L-shaped, and G-shaped. Each has its challenges and advantages.

 **One-Wall.** This arrangement places all of the equipment, sink, and cabinetry along one wall. Since you cannot create a triangle in a one-wall kitchen, maximize accessibility by placing the sink between the refrigerator and the range. Although a one-wall kitchen is more typical in a small apartment, it may be found in a large, open-plan home. If you want to retain this arrangement but would like to close off the kitchen from other public areas of the house, install sliding doors or screens that can be opened or closed at will.

 **The Galley.** Also known as the corridor style, this compact layout locates the appliances, sink, and cabinets on two parallel walls in order to create a small pass-through kitchen. It's easy to create an efficient work triangle in this setup, but the layout really caters to one cook. Allow a 48-inch-wide aisle after all fixtures are placed so that cabinets and appliance doors can be opened easily while someone walks through. If space is really tight, you could make the aisle 36 inches wide, but appliance doors may collide with each other if more than one is open at a time.

BELOW
One-wall kitchens take up the least amount of space, but they are the least flexible of the basic kitchen shapes. To accommodate two cooks, place the sink as shown here.

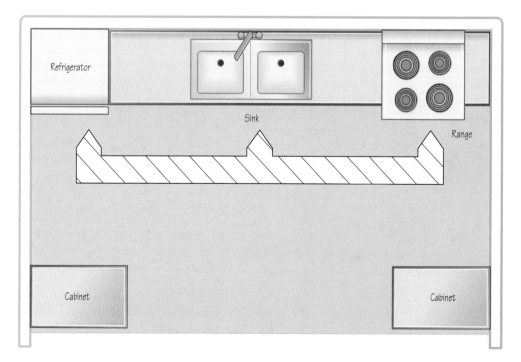

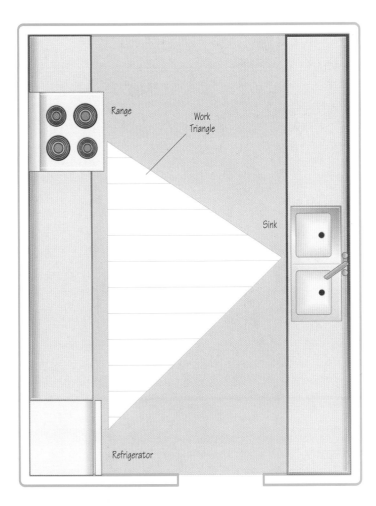

## smart tip  CORNERS

One of the trickiest parts of planning a run of cabinets and appliances comes when you arrive at a corner. There are ways to negotiate this with cabinetry. The two most popular and efficient ones are a blind base—a straight unit with a door on only one side that overlaps the beginning of the next run—or a corner base, which integrates two cabinets into a single L-shaped unit. With blind bases you usually need a filler so that doors will clear with one another.

Another tip: avoid installing a doorway at both ends of the galley or corridor. That way, you can keep people from walking through the work triangle while the cook is busy.

To ease as many traffic problems as possible, place the refrigerator near the end of the room—near the entrance into the kitchen. Another option is to install the primary refrigerator in the food-preparation area and a smaller, secondary refrigerator outside of the food-prep area.

■ **The L-shape.** This plan places the kitchen on two perpendicular walls. The L-shape usually consists of one long "leg" and a short one, and lends itself to an efficient work triangle without the problem of through traffic. If well designed, it is flexible enough for two cooks to work simultaneously without getting in each other's way.

Another advantage to this layout is the opportunity, if space allows, for incorporating an island into the floor plan. If you do, plan the clearances carefully. Walkways should be at least 36 inches wide. If the walkway is also a work aisle, increase the clearance to 42 inches. A 36-inch clearance is fine for counter seating, unless traffic goes behind it. In that case, clearance should be 65 inches.

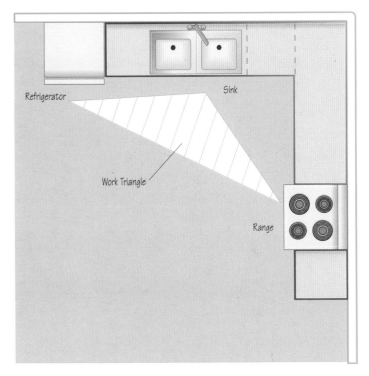

TOP LEFT
In galley kitchens, try to allow for a 48-inch-wide aisle. If that is impossible, plan for a narrower aisle, but maintain functionality by keeping the width above 36 inches.

LEFT
L-shaped kitchens provide more flexibility than the simpler shapes for locating the major work centers. If space allows, expand an L-shaped kitchen by placing a small island or even a table in the open area.

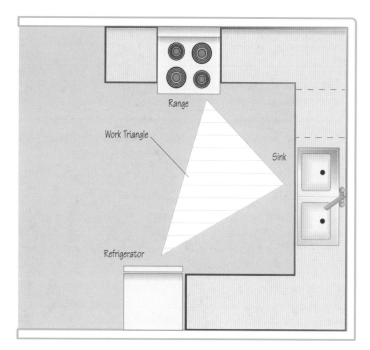

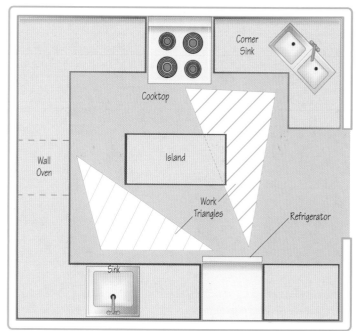

ABOVE
The U-shaped kitchen keeps unnecessary foot traffic out of the work area, and it provides the potential for uninterrupted counter space between the major work centers.

ABOVE
The G-shaped kitchen, which is a variation of the U-shaped layout, can accommodate two work triangles. Note that the refrigerator anchors the triangles shown above.

■ **The U-shape.** The U-shaped kitchen is the most efficient design. Cabinets, counters, and appliances are all arranged along three walls. The greatest benefit, perhaps, is the interrupted space for traffic flow.

A U-shaped layout incorporates a logical sequence of work centers with minimum distances between each. The sink is often located at the base of the U, with the refrigerator and range on the side walls opposite each other. The U shape takes a lot of space—at least 8 feet along the length and width of the kitchen. Corners may be a problem because they often create unusable space. However, consider angling cabinets into these otherwise "dead" areas. Upper cabinets with rolltop doors make roomy appliance garages, and bottom units fitted with carousel shelves or a lazy Susan actually make storage more handy than standard units.

Smaller U-shaped kitchens can be dark because of the sheer mass of all that cabinetry. You can counter this with a generous-size window, skylights, or under-cabinet task lighting, or by keeping surfaces a light color.

■ **The G-shape.** This is a hybrid of the U-shape with a shorter, fourth leg added in the form of a peninsula. While the G-shaped layout is great for more than one person working in the kitchen, it can feel confining.

This layout may feature a pair of sinks and a separate cooktop, as well as an oven range. One work triangle usually incorporates a sink, the cooktop, and the refrigerator, while the other houses the second sink, the oven, and overlapping the first triangle, the refrigerator. An island is usually placed in the corner of a G-shaped layout, within easy reaching distance to both work triangles.

The G-shaped kitchen often accommodates specialty appliances, such as warming drawers, modular refrigeration, or a built-in grill, to allow as much independence between the two work areas as possible.

## Islands and Peninsulas

In a roomy layout, you can shorten the distance between the three key work areas by adding an island or peninsula. A peninsula base and ceiling-hung cabinets offer convenient storage for tableware and linens. In an L- or U-shaped kitchen, an island can add visual interest by breaking up the space without confining it. It also provides an extra work surface, a spot for snacks or informal meals, as well as a place to set up a buffet.

An island or peninsula can also serve as an excellent location for a cooktop or second sink, if plumbing and ventilation hookups permit. It could also prove the ideal spot for a wine rack

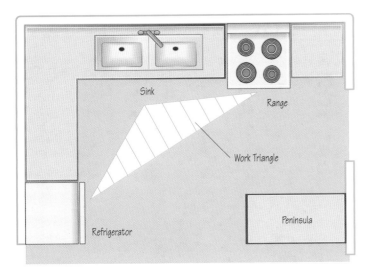

**ABOVE**
Adding a peninsula increases both storage and counter space. In the L-shaped layout shown above, the peninsula does not interfere with the work triangle.

**BELOW**
Use kitchen islands to solve a number of layout problems: to increase counter and storage space; to hold a sink or cooktop; or to create an eating counter. They can also divide space and direct traffic away from the cooking area.

**BOTTOM RIGHT**
Plan the size and location of tables and chairs. Allow for 12 to 15 square feet per person. To allow for a seated person to push back from the table, leave between 32 and 36 inches between the wall and the edge of the table.

## smart tip ISLAND DREAM

These days it seems just about every kitchen features an island. However, an island isn't always the right solution and, in fact, can present problems in a space that's just too small to accommodate it. Give up your dreams of an island if the space does not allow for the minimum clearances on all sides, which vary from 36 to 65 inches.

or cooler, a wet bar, warming drawers, modular refrigerator units, or additional general storage. For maximum efficiency, be sure the design provides a clearance of 48 inches from the island or peninsula to the wall cabinets.

## Eating Areas

There are specific minimum clearances you'll need to accommodate a table and chairs, which you mustn't forget to include in your design. Plan enough floor space for all of the furniture and for people to sit down, get up, and walk around it comfortably, without interfering with the work traffic.

**Seating Allowances.** If you feel as if you're a contortionist every time you get into or out of a chair at the table, you haven't done your space-planning homework. When you redesign, follow the guidelines here as you plan the layout, and you won't go wrong.

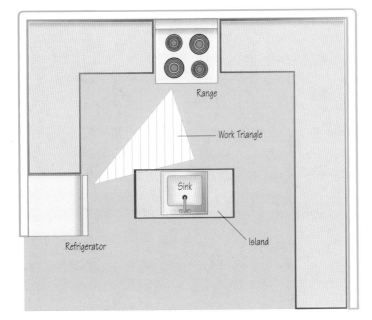

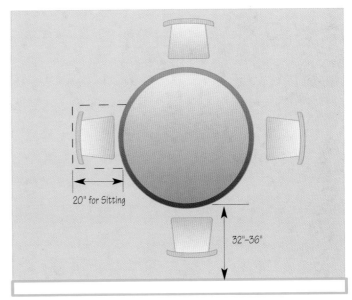

Even average-size people need a surprising amount of space to make a dining area accessible. Allow 12 to 15 square feet per person. That means a family of four will require at least 48 square feet in an eat-in kitchen. Assume that a 36-inch-diameter round table can seat four adults; a 48-inch-diameter one will accommodate six. Calculate 21 to 24 inches of table space per person for a square or rectangular table.

When planning space for your kitchen table, pay attention to the distance between it and the walls or cabinets. A seated adult occupies a depth of about 20 inches from the edge of the table but will need 12 to 16 additional inches of space to push back the chair and rise. This means you have to plan on 32 to 36 inches of clearance between the wall and the edge of the table. You can get away with a minimum of 28 inches if chairs are angled to the wall. However, plan on a 44-inch clearance to allow enough room on any serving side of any table, whatever its shape.

If you don't have enough room for a table, a booth (or a table with banquette) or bench seating may be the answer. A kitchen alcove or bay window offers a natural spot for either seating arrangement, or you can back it against an island, peninsula, or wall. Plan 21 inches of table space for each person with at least 15 inches of knee space underneath. This means that a family of four minimally needs a 42-inch-long table that measures 30 inches across. Because you slide in and out of a booth, the table may overhang the benches by 3 or 4 inches. Total floor space required for a four-person booth, therefore, measures only 5 feet across, compared with a minimum requirement of about 9 feet for a freestanding table with chairs.

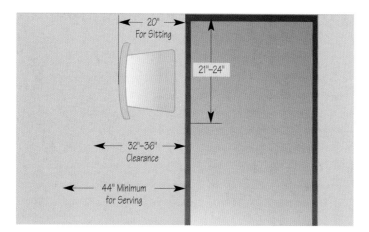

28" Minimum

20"
For Sitting

21"–24"

32"–36"
Clearance

44" Minimum
for Serving

**LEFT**
When placing a table in a small room, angle the chairs as shown. This arrangement allows you to place the table only 28 inches from the wall.

**BOTTOM LEFT**
Provide each person with 21 to 24 inches of table or counter space. Allow a 44-inch clearance for table-to-wall and serving clearances.

**BELOW**
Booths can provide seating in small kitchens. A booth that seats four need be only 5 feet across, compared with the recommended 9 feet for a table and chairs.

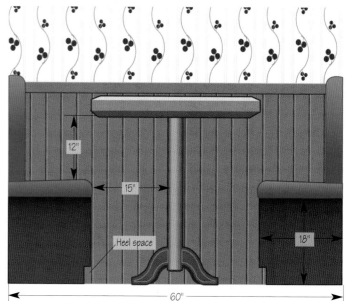

12"

15"

18"

Heel space

60"

Another popular option for in-kitchen dining is to let the island or peninsula serve double duty as an eating bar. Remember, each adult requires at least 21 inches of table space, so that means a 63-inch-long counter (a typical size) will accommodate three stools at most.

Seating depends on counter height. A 28- to 32-inch-high counter requires 18-inch-high chairs with 20 inches of knee space under the bar. If you make the island or peninsula the same height as the rest of the kitchen countertops (36 inches being the standard), you'll be able to accommodate 24-inch-high stools and 14 inches of knee space. Go up to bar height (42 to 45 inches), and you'll need 30-inch-high stools with footrests, also with 14 inches of knee space.

One more aspect of kitchen design to consider is storage—an element that needs to blend function with style. Once you conclude how you want your new kitchen space to function, you're in a position to tackle the next perplexing yet all-important challenge: selecting the proper cabinetry.

# choosing cabinets

Who can't relate to this scenario: you turn on the oven to preheat it, but wait, did you take out the large roasting pan first? How about the lasagna dish, muffin tins, pizza stone, and cookie sheets that are in there, too? Now where can you put everything that was in the oven while the casserole is baking, and the countertop is laden with the rest of tonight's dinner ingredients?

**ABOVE**
To break up the monotony of cabinets, install some alternative storage, such as these drawer-like baskets. Take advantage of the easy access by filling them with things you use often.

**RIGHT**
Shorter cabinets directly over the cooktop and sink open up the room, provide a safe distance between cabinetry and heat, and allow for decorative lighting in the form of fluorescent sconces.

The oven, it seems, has become the catch-all for the big, awkward stuff that you can't fit into kitchen cabinets but is just too ugly to display. Besides, the countertop is where you keep the toaster oven, food processor, coffeemaker, canisters, hand mixer, portable TV, notepad, coupon file, bills, hand lotion, car keys, and your vitamins! Wouldn't life be grand if there was a place for everything and everything was in its place? Good cabinetry outfitted with an assortment of organizing options can help you there. It can make your kitchen more efficient and a whole lot neater while establishing a style, or "look," for the room. Keep in mind, however, that cabinetry will also consume about 40 percent of your remodeling budget, according to the NKBA. So before making any expensive decisions—or costly mistakes—investigate all of the various cabinetry options that are available to you.

## Cabinet Construction

Basically, cabinets are constructed in one of two ways: *framed* or *frameless*. Framed cabinets have a traditional look, with a full frame across the face of the cabinet box that may show between closed doors. This secures adjacent cabinets and strengthens wider cabinet boxes with a center rail. Hinges on framed cabinets may or may not be visible around doors when they are closed. The door's face may be ornamented with raised or recessed panels, trimmed or framed panels, or a framed-glass panel with or without muntins (the narrow vertical and horizontal strips of wood that divide panes of glass).

Frameless cabinets—also known as European-style cabinets, although American manufacturers also make them—are built without a face frame and sport a clean, contemporary look. There's no trim or molding with this simple design. Close-fitting doors cover the entire front of the box; no ornamentation appears on the face of the doors; and hinges are typically hidden inside the cabinet box.

Choosing one type over another is generally a matter of taste, although framed units offer slightly less interior space. But the quality of construction is a factor that should always be taken into consideration. How do you judge it? Solid wood is too expensive for most of today's budgets, but it might be used on just the doors and frames. More typical is plywood box construction, which offers good structural support and solid wood on the doors and frames. To save money, cabinetmakers sometimes use strong plywood for support elements, such as the box and frame, and medium-density fiberboard for other parts, such as doors and drawer fronts. In yet another alternative, good-quality laminate cabinets can be made with high-quality, thick particleboard underneath the laminate finish.

There are other things to look for in cabinet construction. They include dovetail or mortise-and-tenon joinery and solidly mortised hinges. Also, make sure that the interior of every cabinet is well finished, with adjustable shelves that are a minimum $5/8$ inch thick to prevent bowing.

Unless you have the time and skill to build the cabinets yourself or can hire someone else to do it, you'll have to purchase them in one of four ways. *Knockdown* cabinetry (also known as RTA, ready to assemble) is shipped flat and, some-times, unfinished because you put the pieces together. Stock cabinetry comes in standard sizes but limited styles and colors; it is often available on the spot or can be delivered quickly. Like stock, *semi-custom* cabinetry comes in standard styles, but it is manufactured to fit a homeowner's specific size and finish needs. *Custom* cabinetry is not limited in terms of style or size because it is built to the designer's specifications.

**BOTTOM LEFT**
Color makes all the difference in a room. Here, a variety of creamy colors throughout the kitchen adds personality. Pretty green and blue cabinets are a nice change from plain white.

**BELOW**
An updated country style, cabinets with sleeker lines and elegant granite counters intermingle here with the usual down-home charm and informal mix of woods and hardware.

# Cabinet Accessories and Options

Most people would agree that no matter how much storage space they have, they need even more. The problem often isn't the amount, it's the inaccessible placement and inefficient configuration of the storage space. One of the greatest benefits today's designers and manufacturers offer is fitted and accessorized interiors that maximize even the smallest nook and cranny inside cabinets and drawers. These accommodations not only expand the use of space, but increase convenience and accessibility. Among them are the following:

▓ **Appliance Garages.** Appliance garages make use of dead space in a corner, but they can be installed anywhere in the vertical space between the wall-mounted cabinet and the countertop. A tambour (rolltop) door hides small appliances such as a food processor or anything else you want within reach but hidden from view. This form of minicabinet can be equipped with an electrical outlet and can even be divided into separate sections to store more than one item. Reserve part of the appliance garage for cookbook storage, or outfit it with small drawers for little items or spices. Customize an appliance garage any way you like.

▓ **Lazy Susans and Carousel Shelves.** These rotating shelves maximize dead corner storage and put items such as dishes or pots and pans within easy reach. A lazy Susan rotates 360 degrees, so just spin it to find what you're looking for. Carousel shelves, which attach to two right-angled doors, rotate 270 degrees; open the doors and the shelves, which are actually attached to the doors, put any item within hand reach. Pivoting shelves are a variation on the carousel design and may or may not be door-mounted. In addition, units may be built into taller cabinets, creating a pantry that can store a lot in a small amount of space.

▓ **Fold-Down Mixer Shelf.** This spring-loaded shelf swings up and out of a base cabinet for use, then folds down and back into the cabinet when the mixer is no longer needed, which reduces clutter by keeping the countertop clear of appliances.

▓ **Slide-Outs and Tilt-Outs.** Installed in base cabinets, slide-

ABOVE

These custom cabinets add unique options, such as pull-out storage for dish linens and angled cabinets that make use of small spaces.

out trays and racks store small appliances, linens, cans, or boxed items, while slide-out bins are good for holding onions, potatoes, grains, pet food, or potting soil—even garbage or recycling containers. A tilt-out tray is located in the often-wasted area just below the lip of the countertop in front of the sink and above base cabinet doors. It looks like a drawer but tilts open to provide a neat nook for sponges and scouring pads that look messy when left on the counter.

■ **Built-in Pantry Units.** These fold-out or slide-out units can be fitted into narrow areas that might otherwise remain wasted. Store dry or canned goods here. Fold-out units have door-mounted shelves and an in-cabinet shelf that pivots; slide-out units fit multiple shelves in a cabinet.

In addition to these options, check out everything that a cabinet manufacturer has to offer to make the most of a cabinet's storage capacity. Other items to look for include special racks for trays and cookie sheets, drawer inserts for organizing spices and utensils, watertight recycling bins, wine racks, fold-down recipe book rests, sliding pot racks, built-in canister drawers, and plate racks.

If you decide to make do with your existing cabinets, consider refitting the interiors with cabinet organizers. These plastic, plastic-coated wire, or enameled-steel racks and hangers are widely available at department stores and home centers.

Beware of the temptation to over-specialize your kitchen storage. Sizes and needs for certain items change, so be sure to allot at least 50 percent of your kitchen's storage to standard cabinets with one or more movable shelves.

# The Decorative Role of Cabinets

The look you create in your kitchen will be largely influenced by the cabinetry you select. Finding a style that suits you and how you will use your new kitchen is similar to shopping for furniture. In fact, don't be surprised to see many furniture details dressing up the cabinets on view in showrooms and home centers today.

Besides architectural elements such as fluted pilasters, corbels, moldings, and bull's-eye panels, look for details such as fretwork, rope motifs, gingerbread trim, balusters, composition ornamentation (it looks like carving), even footed cabinets that mimic freestanding furniture pieces. If your taste runs toward less-fussy design, you'll also find handsome door and drawer styles that feature minimal or no decoration. Woods and finishes are just as varied, and range from informal looks in birch, oak, ash, and maple to rich mahogany and cherry. Laminate finishes, though less popular than they were a decade ago, haven't completely disappeared from the marketplace, but an array of colors has replaced the once-ubiquitous almond and white finishes.

**CLOCKWISE FROM TOP**
Unique two-toned cabinetry adds interest in a country kitchen, top. The appliances are integrated with the same two-toned panels and the hardware echoes the geometric design. Cabinetry with the look of fine furniture integrates this kitchen almost seamlessly into an adjacent living space, bottom right. Personalize your kitchen with cabinets made from exotic wood and finished with a custom-mixed high-gloss laquer, bottom center. Glass-fronted bins are a colorful and convenient way to store pasta and dried beans, bottom left.

## Color

Color is coming on strong on wood cabinetry, too. Accents in one, two, or more hues are pairing with natural wood tones. White-painted cabinets take on a warmer glow with tinted shades of this always popular neutral. Special "vintage" finishes, such as translucent color glazes, continue to grow in popularity, as do distressed finishing techniques, such as wire brushing and rubbed-through color that add both another dimension and the appeal of handcraftmanship, even on mass-produced items. Contemporary kitchens, which historically favor an all-white palette, are warming up with earthier neutral shades, less sterile off-whites, and wood.

If you're shy about using color on such a high-ticket item as cabinetry, try it as an accent on molding, door trim, or island cabinetry. Just as matched furniture suites have become passé in other rooms of the house, the same is true for the kitchen, where mixing several looks can add sophistication and visual interest.

## Hardware

Another way to emphasize your kitchen's decorative style is with hardware. From exquisite reproductions in brass, pewter, wrought iron, or ceramic to handsome bronze, chrome, nickel, glass, steel, plastic, rubber, wood, or stone creations, a smorgasbord of shapes and designs is available. Some pieces are highly

polished; others are matte-finished, smooth, or hammered. Some are abstract or geometrical; others are simple, elegant shapes. Whimsical designs take on the forms of animals or teapots, vegetables or flowers. Even just one or two great-looking door or drawer pulls can be showstoppers in a kitchen that may otherwise be devoid of much personality. Like mixing cabinet finishes, a combination of two hardware styles—perhaps picked up from other materials in the room—makes a big design statement. As the famed architect Mies Van der Rohe once stated, "God is in the details," and the most perfect detail in your new kitchen may be the artistic hardware that you select.

Besides looks, consider the function of a pull or knob. You have to be able to grip it easily and comfortably. If your fingers or hands get stiff easily, or if you have arthritis, select C- or U-shaped pulls. If you like a knob, try it out in the showroom to make sure it isn't slippery or awkward when you grab it. Knobs and pulls can be inexpensive if you can stick to unfinished ones that you can paint in an accent color picked up from the tile or wallpaper. If you don't plan to buy new cabinets, changing the hardware on old ones can redefine their style. The right knob or pull can suggest any one of a number of vintage looks or decorative styles from Colonial to Victorian to Arts and Crafts to Postmodern.

**CLOCKWISE FROM TOP LEFT**
Satin-finish hardware looks great against paint with a soft metallic sheen, while the center of each handle reflects the granite countertop, top left. Unique braided handles personalize plain cabinetry, top right. Notice how the homeowner matched this pattern in the adjacent accessories. Adding natural-wood accents, such as these drawer handles, helps balance the traditional and modern styles that are both in play in this kitchen, below.

**OPPOSITE**
This cabinet color was chosen to echo one of the colors in the granite countertop and backsplash.

# countertop options

Selecting countertop material is not as simple as it once was because there are infinitely more choices in color, pattern, and texture thanks to new materials and applications. The trend is to use more than one, specifying types based on the functions at hand. For example, you might use a solid-surfacing material in one part of the kitchen, a marble insert at the bake center, and stainless steel next to the cooktop. Or you could pair one countertop material with the cabinetry that runs along the wall, and choose another for the island counter.

In addition to enhancing the function of your work surfaces, the countertop materials that you choose can underpin your decorating theme. Wood is a natural choice for a country-style kitchen, for example, whereas concrete looks handsome in a contemporary setting. The concrete can be poured or prefabri-

cated into a mold on site. You can add color to it or create a one-of-a-kind inlaid design with stones, shards of glass, china, tile, shells, or just about anything else you can think of adding.

There are no hard-and-fast rules about any material you choose, but one important factor that should play a role in your selection is maintenance. Some materials demand greater care than others. Marble, for instance, must be sealed periodically because it can absorb liquids that will mar its looks. If you don't have time for the upkeep, can you live with the battle scars of everyday use?

Here's a rundown on choices for countertop material. After you've read about the attributes of each, you can decide which ones may be right for your application. Also, consider each type as a possibility for a matching or entirely different backsplash.

LEFT
Create an unusual countertop using natural slate tiles in various colorations. The cabinet color brings out the reddish-purple hues in the slate.

ABOVE
Natural stone is a popular countertop choice because of its durability and its rustic, textured appeal. This earthy, heavily veined countertop balances the contemporary elements of the kitchen.

## Solid-Surfacing Material

An extremely durable, easily maintained synthetic material, solid surfacing is made of polyester or acrylic. It's expensive, costing almost as much per linear foot as luxurious granite or marble, but it wears long and well. The material is completely impervious to water, and you can repair any dents or abrasions that may occur with a light sanding.

## Stone

Marble and granite are probably the most expensive materials you can choose for a countertop. Though it is stone, marble is actually a soft, porous material that can be gouged and stained easily. Considered chic today, a granite countertop is a handsome status symbol. Like marble, it has a cool surface that pastry makers favor, but it is less absorbent. This makes it less likely to stain than marble.

BELOW
A standard laminate countertop has seams that are visible along the edges. Black seams don't interfere with this dark color scheme. The forest-green countertop complements the cherry-colored wood of the cabinets.

## Ceramic Tile

Ceramic tile is a perennial favorite. Impervious to water, it's perfect for installation at the sink. Tile is also durable and doesn't scratch, burn, or stain. Aside from its practical attributes, ceramic tile offers the greatest opportunity for adding color, pattern, and texture to your kitchen. Custom designs bring personality into the room. Hand-painted, imported, and antique versions are very pricey, but you can combine inexpensive standard tiles with raised or silk-screened patterns to create unique designs and murals.

## Plastic Laminate

Made of several layers of melamine, paper, and plastic resin bonded under heat and pressure, then glued to particleboard or plywood, plastic laminate is inexpensive, relatively easy to install, and available in a vast array of colors and patterns. Plastic laminate resists stains, water, and mild abrasion very well, but it can be chipped or scratched by sharp knives, and it will scorch if you put a hot pot down on it. There is no repair option available except replacement. More expensive solid-core laminates eliminate unsightly black edges at the joints because the color goes all the way through the material.

Two other stone materials, limestone and concrete, are finding their way onto countertops in the hands of creative designers. Limestone is available as tiles, as is concrete, but the latter can be poured and molded, too. Becoming even more creative, designers are adding color to concrete and creating inlaid designs as well.

## Wood

Wood is unrivaled for its natural warmth and beauty. But it expands and contracts, depending on environmental conditions, and may warp if exposed to water. To protect a wood countertop, apply a film finish using varnish. Other alternatives include applying lacquer or oil periodically. Teak is an excellent choice for a wood countertop. Another option is butcher-block, which is actually a laminated-wood product. Eastern hard-rock sugar maple is the most durable wood for a butcher-block application.

## Stainless Steel

Many of today's kitchens feature lots of metal, but they don't appear antiseptic or cold. That's largely because designers balance the look by introducing vibrant colors and other materials, such as ceramic tile or wood, into the room. Stainless steel used for a countertop, whether it is for the entire counter or just a section of it, can look quite sophisticated, especially with a wood trim. Stainless steel is vulnerable to scrapes, stains, and corrosion, so shop for a product with high chromium and nickel content, which won't show dings and dents as easily.

# selecting fixtures

What could be more basic to the modern kitchen than a sink and faucet? Yet in today's world, there's practically nothing basic about them. Style comes in all price ranges, but high-performance technology is accompanied by an equally high price tag. There are designs and finishes to suit any contemporary or traditional taste. And far from being just necessary items in a kitchen, sinks and faucets have evolved into highly decorative elements. Here's what's on today's bountiful market.

# Sinks

These receptacles come in all sizes, shapes, and colors and are typically fabricated from enameled cast iron, stainless steel, a composite material (solid surfacing, acrylic, or a mixture of natural quartz or granite with resins), or solid stone. They may be hand-painted or decorated with silk-screened designs, contoured, beveled, brushed to a matte finish, or polished to a mirror finish. The trend is to include the largest sink that you can accommodate within the confines of your space. Deep bowls make it easier to deal with awkward oversized items, such as large roasting pans and tall pots used for cooking pasta and soups. A good example is the farm-style (or exposed-apron) sink that, at one time, would have been regarded as déclassé but is reemerging in glamorous solid colors or with decorative patterns. Shallow-basin sinks are also available. These are useful when there is no other place to install the dishwasher but underneath the sink.

Two- and three-bowl sink configurations are also gaining wide popularity. This arrangement allows you to separate clean dishes from dirty ones as well as from waste materials. Some sinks come with a colander and cutting board. Typically, a waste-disposal unit is installed with one of the bowls, usually the larger one. Just peel your potatoes, then whisk the skins down the disposer. Lay the cutting board over the top of the bowl for chopping, and afterwards, push the potato slices into the colander for easy rinsing.

CLOCKWISE FROM OPPOSITE TOP
Stainless steel makes a lot of sense as countertop material next to the stove or cooktop because it can handle hot pots, top left. A center-set gooseneck faucet serves beautifully on this marble-topped island, top right. This widespread installation is suited to a double-bowl sink, left. Richly stained wood countertops add warmth to this cool, black-and-white kitchen, far left. Lever-style handles are easy for anyone, of any age or ability, to use.

RIGHT
If you cook lots of pasta or soups, a pot-filler faucet that is installed on the wall just above the cooktop is a practical idea.

Some designers recommend installing sinks in two separate areas. The primary sink often anchors the main food preparation and cleanup areas, while a smaller secondary sink serves outside of the major work zone. A second sink is a must when two or more people cook together routinely, but it is also handy if you do crafts in the kitchen or entertain often.

Like every other kitchen product, there are numerous choices of sinks from which you will have to make a final selection, so it won't always be easy. In terms of durability, any one of the materials mentioned above will hold up well for years, if not decades, with the right care. Enameled cast-iron sinks tend to discolor, but can be cleaned easily with a nonabrasive cleanser. Stainless steel and stone should be cleaned the same way. However, composite sinks are scratch resistant, with the exception of inexpensive acrylic models, so you can use an abrasive agent on them. Expect a quality sink to last as long as 30 years. In terms of installation, there are five types of sinks to consider for the kitchen.

▧ **Undermounted.** If you want a smooth look, an undermounted sink may be for you. The bowl is attached underneath the countertop.

▧ **Integral.** As the word "integral" implies, the sink and countertop are fabricated from the same material—stone, faux stone, or solid surfacing. There are no visible seams or joints in which food can accumulate.

▧ **Self-rimming or flush-mounted.** A self-rimmed sink has a rolled edge that is mounted on the countertop.

▧ **Rimmed.** Unlike a self-rimming sink, this type requires a flat metal strip to seal the sink to the countertop.

▧ **Tile-in.** Used with a tiled countertop, the sink rim is flush with the tiled surface. Grout seals the sink to the surrounding countertop area.

## Faucets

Faucets are no longer just conduits for water. From sleek European-inspired designs to graceful gooseneck shapes, today's selections add beauty as well as function to a kitchen. An excellent example is the pot-filler faucet, which is mounted to the wall over the cooktop. Some versions have a pull-out spout; others come with a double- or triple-jointed arm that can be bent to reach up and down, or swiveled back and forth, allowing the cook to pull the faucet over to a pot on the farthest burner. Anyone who has ever had to lug a heavy pot of water from the tap to a burner will appreciate this convenience. Just remember: you'll need additional hot- and cold-water plumbing if you install one of these faucets over your range or cooktop.

State-of-the-art technology in faucets gives you not only much more control over water use, but better performance and a more extensive choice for finishes as well. Some speciality features to look for include pullout faucet heads, retractable sprayers, hot- and cold-water dispensing, single-lever control, anti-scald and flow-control devices, a lowered lead content in brass components, and built-in water purifiers to enhance taste.

For a quality faucet, inquire about its parts when you shop. The best are those made of solid brass or a brass-base material. Both are corrosion-resistant. Avoid plastic components—they won't hold up. Ask about the faucet's valving, too. Buy a model that has a washerless cartridge; it will cost more, but it will last longer.

Besides selecting a spout type (standard, arched, gooseneck, or pullout), you may choose between single or double levers. Pullouts come with a built-in sprayer, if you want one. The others will require installing a separate sprayer. Until recently, a pressure-balanced faucet (one equipped with a device that equalizes the hot and cold water coming out of a faucet to prevent scalding) came only with single-lever model. Now it is available with faucets that have separate hot- and cold-water valves. You may mix your spout with one of many types of handle styles: wrist blades, levers, scrolls, geometric shapes, and cross handles.

Chrome, brass, enamel-coated or baked-on colors, pewter, and nickel are typical faucets finishes. Make a fashion statement by mixing finishes or pair a matte, brushed, or antiqued look with one that is highly polished. Some finishes, such as chrome or enamel, are easier to care for than others—brass, for instance, which may require polishing. In terms of installation, there are three types of faucets from which you'll have to choose.

■ **Center set.** There are two separate valves, one for hot, the other for cold water, and a spout in a center set faucet. But all three pieces appear connected in one unit.

■ **Widespread.** A spout with two separate valves that appear to be three distinct pieces is a widespread faucet.

■ **Single lever.** This faucet has a spout and single lever contained in one piece for one-hand operation.

When you design your sink and faucet area, don't be sidetracked by the good looks of a product. Think about whether it works for your application. Today, good looks come in all types. Instead, compare the size of your biggest pots and racks to see whether the sink you're considering will accommodate them. If it won't and you can't install something deeper, pair the sink with a pullout or gooseneck faucet. Always make sure it directs the flow of the water into the center of the bowl and slightly to one side. A spout that is proportionally too tall for the depth of the sink will splash water; one that is too short won't allow water to reach to the sink's corners. If you plan a double- or triple-bowl configuration, the spout should deliver enough water to each of the bowls.

Thoughtful planning isn't only applied to the kitchen—it works for the bath as well, which is discussed in the next chapter.

LEFT
A countertop with an integral double-bowl sink has been formed from concrete. This antiqued-bronze, single-lever faucet can be operated with one hand, which makes it great for multitasking.

ABOVE
These stylish high-arc faucets in a satin-nickel finish coordinate beautifully with stainless-steel sinks and come with helpful extras, such as a spray attachment and a soap dispenser.

# design workbook
## STREAMLINE YOUR DESIGN

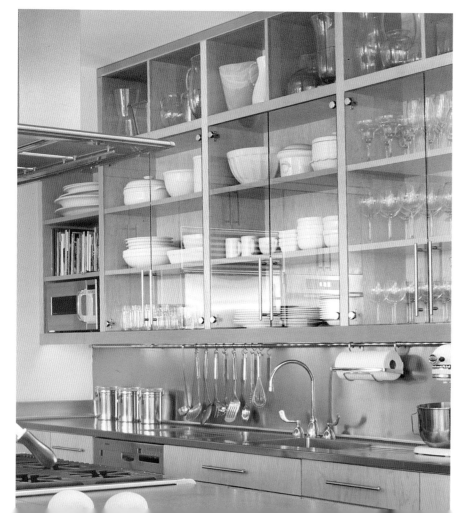

## update the look

Sleek lines, light wood, glass-front cabinets, and smooth stainless-steel countertops and appliances are all consistent with the elements of modern design.

## set priorities

Organization is a top priority in this kitchen. Clear-glass doors, bottom left, require a disciplined approach to storage to remain attractive.

## keep it convenient

Convenience also ranks highly. Pull-out wire bins provide easy access to often-used items, and a sink near the cooktop saves burdened steps. (See also top left.)

## clear the counters

Counter space is maximized by hanging items on the backsplash, left. Each item is organized at its point of use— utensils by the cooktop, towels by the sink, and so on.

# design workbook

## DO WHAT SUITS YOU

### decide on a design

Natural materials and earthy colors reveal the Tuscan inspiration for this design. Stone counter-tops, pendant lighting, and modern fixtures update the look.

### fashion meets function

An island with a stylish sink and built-in micro-wave serves as both a snack bar and an extra workspace. Task lighting overhead is both beautiful and functional.

### make it work for you

Sturdy farmhouse-like cabinets and furniture create plenty of closed storage space, top left. They are delib-erately mismatched and made to look like individual fur-niture pieces.

### transition seamlessly

The dining area, left, glows with the same color scheme and textures of the kitchen. A wrought-iron chandelier per-fectly tops off this rustic Old World design.

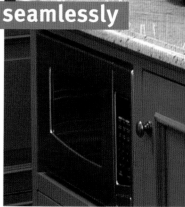

# 10

# bathroom design

Many professionals believe that bathrooms may be the most difficult rooms in the house to design properly. The space is often small, yet it must be able to accommodate a variety of large fixtures. In addition, many homeowners tend to focus, at least initially, on the way the bathroom looks. They fall in love with the whirlpool tub that is really too large for the space or exquisite materials that demand too much effort to maintain. Design your bath to be functional as well as beautiful.

Even if you are designing a modest bath, you can greatly increase its performance and your ultimate comfort by thoughtfully planning out every square inch of floor and wall space. In fact, small spaces require more attention to details than larger spaces. Whatever the size of your investment, you should get the most out of it.

Limestone tiles are installed throughout this spacious bathroom. The large squares are separated by bands of limestone in a contrasting tone.

238

# set priorities

ABOVE
Classical elements, such as arches and pillars, and timeless materials, such as stone, tile, and wood, will retain their appeal for decades to come.

I f you will be working with a design professional, expect to be interviewed at the beginning of the planning stage. He or she will want to get to know you and whoever else will use the new bathroom. Your designer isn't being nosy. He or she simply wants to understand your likes and habits, as well as your basic requirements and greatest expectations with respect to the new bath. The designer will also make a sketch of the existing space to get an idea of what works and what doesn't. The rough drawing may include any adjacent areas that might be considered for expansion, such as a closet, part of a hallway, or a small room.

If you will be acting as your own designer, do the same. You can't assume that you instinctively know what has to be done to transform the old bathroom into a fabulous new space just because you live there. That's acting on emotion. For the best result, approach the project in the same analytical manner as a professional who understands design and can be objective about what has to happen. To learn how to sketch a floor plan as if you were a professional, see the Smart Steps in Chapter Nine, on page 210.

# basic layouts

If the existing floor plan works for you, all you have to think about is updating old fixtures, installing new tile, and perhaps replacing the cabinetry. Even so, you may want to play around with the idea of modifying the layout on paper. You may be surprised to discover, in fact, that a few minor changes in the floor plan can enhance your original arrangement. Just keep in mind: moving plumbing fixtures in an existing bath may significantly raise costs.

## smart steps
## where to begin

### Step 1 MAKE A NEW BASE DRAWING

As in the base drawing you made in the last chapter for the old kitchen, use a ½-inch scale. (If you haven't made a base drawing, see the Smart Steps in Chapter Nine, on page 210.) If you are using a ¼-inch grid, each square represents a 6-inch square of real floor space. Begin by drawing the outer walls, and then add the windows and doors. Remember to sketch in any spaces surrounding the bathroom that you may annex.

### Step 2 MAKE TEMPLATES OF THE FIXTURES

Creating paper templates of fixtures and cabinets is an easy way to experiment with different layouts. You can draw the fixtures to scale on graph paper, or copy the templates in the Appendix of this book. Then cut them out so you can move them around your plan. If you have collected pictures and spec sheets (printed product information from the manufacturer), use the dimensions given. When cutting out templates, include both the fixtures and the required front and side clearances—that way you won't get caught short. Usually, plumbing codes require a minimum clearance for each fixture. Fixture clearances are shown in the drawings on this and the next two pages. The top number of each pair indicates the minimum required by code or function. The bottom dimension allows more room between fixtures. For an efficient but convenient layout, aim for somewhere between the two numbers when you draw your plan.

### Step 3 PLACE THE FIXTURES

You will use some fixtures more often than others: first the lavatory, next the toilet, then the tub or shower. An efficient plan places the lav closest to the door, followed by the toilet, and finally the tub, which is located the farthest away. If there is any leeway in your plan, place the toilet so that it will not be visible when the door is open. Even in a small bathroom, the direction of the door swing can help shield the toilet from view.

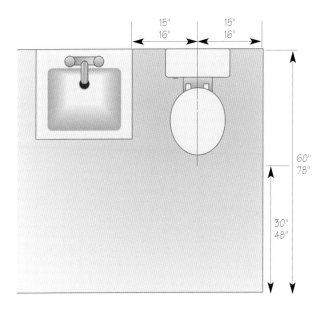

**ABOVE AND BELOW**
Here are the recommended clearances for sinks, toilets, and bidets. The bottom number is best, but the top will do in tight spaces.

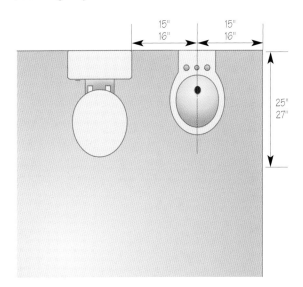

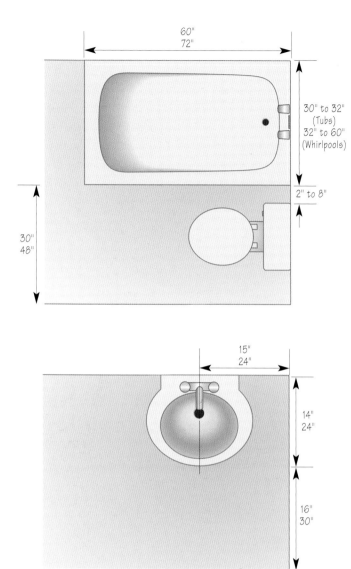

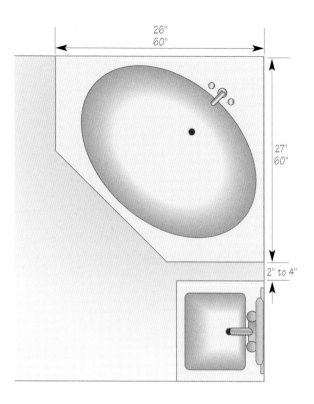

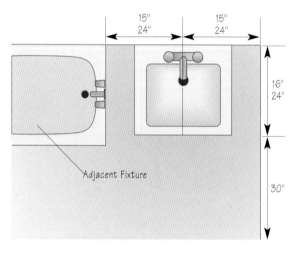

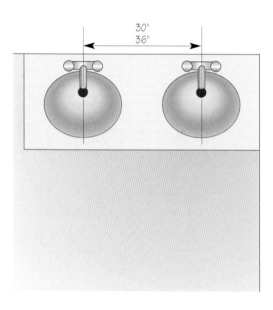

**CLOCKWISE FROM ABOVE**

When measuring for clearances around lavatories, take the measurement from the center of the fixture, which is usually the drain. In these drawings of lavs, the bottom number is the preferred clearance, but the top number will do in small rooms. Note the recommended clearances in front of the lavs. Both rectangular and corner tubs should have about 48 inches of open floor space in front of them for safety.

**Tub/Shower.** Another easy way to place fixtures on your plan is to start with the largest ones. If you know you want a whirlpool bath and separate dual shower, pencil them in first. (Hint: position the length of the tub perpendicular to the joists to distribute the weight safely. If you don't, you'll incur the costs of adding structural support to the floor.) To make the tub the focal point of the room, put it opposite the door or within a direct line of view from the door. If there will be a separate tub and shower, locate them near each other so that they can share plumbing lines and the same sight lines. This also makes it easier to plan the space around them.

**Lavatory.** After placing the big items, locate your lavatory. Do you want two lavs or just one? Do you want two lavatories near each other or located on opposite sides of the room? Will two people use the room at once? Answer these questions before you pencil in the location.

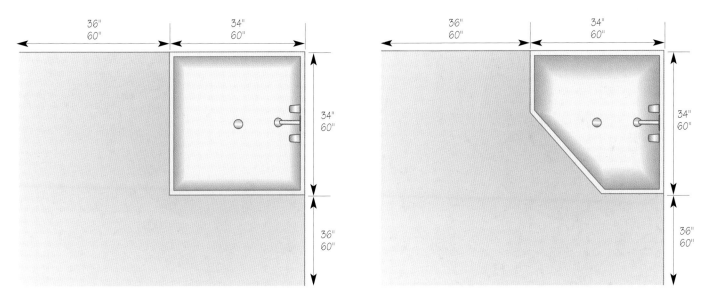

ABOVE LEFT AND RIGHT
Showers may vary in size but the recommended clearances in front of them do not. If possible, allow 60 inches of clearance, but never anything less than 36 inches.

BELOW LEFT AND RIGHT
Location is everything. The toilet is visible from the hall in the drawing bottom left. To solve the problem, flop the toilet and lavatory and change the swing of the door.

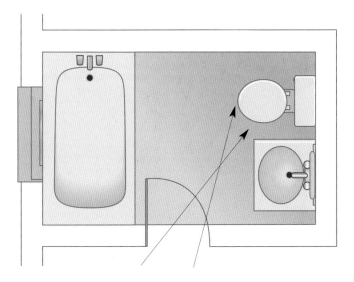
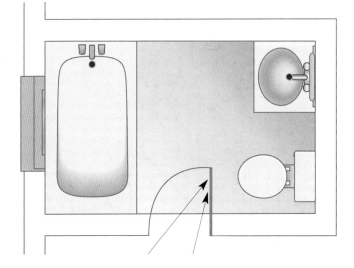

If you are placing two lavatories side by side, leave enough maneuvering space and elbow room. One smart way to do this is to install storage between them. Some families install two lavatories at different heights. Not only is this more comfortable and ergonomic, it defines space as adult-designated or child-designated in a bathroom shared by all.

**Toilet.** Once you have the lavatories in place, go ahead and locate the toilet and bidet, if you have one. (A bidet resembles a toilet but is actually a fixture used for personal hygiene.) The bidet is another item you will want to keep away from the bathroom door and out of its sight line.

**Extras.** With the main elements penciled in, start adding the extras—the windows, doors, skylights, greenhouse, gym, sauna, and whatever other amenities you are considering. You can play with the design as long as you like, trying different ideas and placements, but make sure you take practical matters, such as pipes and codes, into consideration.

**Customize.** Although there are recommended guidelines for comfort and convenience, only you will be able to determine what will be most comfortable for you. If you happen to be 7 feet tall, you can probably forget about the height clearances and raise them! Likewise, if you are a small person, lower the counters. Don't worry about being able to resell your home later; another person of your height may appreciate the comfort of a higher or lower surface. If the need arises, installing a new vanity with standard-height countertop is not easy, but it's not a major project either.

# types of bathrooms

The most-common-size American bathroom measures 60 x 84 inches or 60 x 96 inches. The most common complaint about it is the lack of space. The arrangement may have suited families 50 years ago, but times and habits have changed. If it's the only bathroom in the house, making it work better becomes even more important.

When planning the layout, try angling a sink or shower unit in a corner to free up some floor space. Unlike a traditional door, which swings into the room and takes up wall space when it is open, a pocket door slides into the wall. Another smart way to add function to a small bathroom is to remove the drywall and install shelves between the studs.

You can also make a small bathroom feel roomier by bringing in natural light with a skylight or roof window or by replacing one small standard window with several small casement units that can be installed high on the wall to maintain privacy.

LEFT
**The classic lines of the bathtub combined with the black and white mosaic floor tiles and dark wood furniture give this new space its traditional appeal.**

LEFT
An above-counter, or vessel-style, lav is
an artful element in a powder room or a
master bath—and it doesn't encroach
upon under-counter storage space.

nothing more than a lavatory and a toilet. You can find small-scale fixtures specifically designed for the powder room, from the tiniest lavs to unusually narrow toilets. In general, however, maintain a clearance that meets code on each side of the toilet, and include comfortable reaching room for the toilet-paper dispenser. Most powder rooms measure at least 36 inches wide by 54 to 60 inches long, depending on the layout of the space.

Keep a small powder room as light and open as possible. Plan to install good lighting because the powder room is often used for touching up makeup. (For more about properly lighting your bathroom, see Chapter Three, "The Right Light," on page 56.)

A carefully thought-out floor plan makes a difference in this usually small space. Make sure the door swings out against a wall, not inward, or use a pocket door for easy access. If it must be accessible for someone in a wheelchair, include a minimum 5-foot-diameter circle of space in the center of the room, which is just large enough for a wheelchair to turn around.

In the powder room, the vanity is often the focal point. The room offers the best opportunity to showcase a decorative piece, such as a hand-painted pedestal sink or a custom-made vanity. Because the powder room is often for guests and is normally located on the ground floor near the living area, take extra care to ensure privacy. If possible, the best location is in a hallway, away from the living room, kitchen, and dining area. This room can also handle stronger wall colors—either dark or bright ones—as well as larger, bolder wallpaper patterns because it is a short-stay room.

If you are adding a second or possibly a third bathroom to your house, here are a few other ideas for your consideration—and inspiration.

# The Powder Room

The guest bath. The half bath. It has a lot of names, and it may be the most efficient room in the house, providing just what you need often in tight quarters. A powder room normally includes

# The Family Bath

Compartmentalizing is the best way to start planning the family bath. But remember, when you separate the bathroom into smaller, distinct areas, you run the risk of making the room feel cramped. Try to alleviate this with extra natural light, good artificial lighting, and translucent partitions made of glass blocks or etched glass. Anything that divides with privacy while also allowing light to enter will help ease the closed-in feeling.

If separating the fixtures is not possible, include a sink in the dressing area within the master bedroom to provide a second place for applying makeup or shaving. Investigate building a back-to-back bath in lieu of one large shared room. Another popular option is to locate the bathing fixtures, both the tub and separate shower, in the center of the room; install the bidet, a toilet, and sink on either side in their own separate areas. To make the arrangement work, keep each side of the room accessible to the door.

**ABOVE**
Separating the lav and grooming areas with a wall and pocket door allows two people to use the bathroom while retaining privacy.

**LEFT**
A great setup for both master and family baths, this layout consists of two lavs and a grooming table.

**RIGHT**
These cabinets are recessed into the wall, creating plenty of out-of-sight space for bulky items, such as rolls of toilet tissue.

# The Master Bath

The concept of the master bath has come of age in the past decade. It is one of the most popular rooms to remodel and gives one of the highest returns on investment upon resale. It's where you can create that sought-after getaway—the home version of a European spa.

Some popular amenities to include in your plan are a sauna, greenhouse, exercise studio, fireplace, audio and video systems, faucets and sprayers with full massaging options, steam room, whirlpool tub, and dressing table. You are only limited by size and imagination—and some local codes.

Extras can be tempting but may require special planning. For example, you may need additional support in the floor, as well as supplemental heating and ventilation. You would not want to slip into a tub and have it fall two floors to the middle of the living room. Unfortunately, this really does happen when the weight of an oversized contemporary tub is installed on top of a 50-year-old floor. Older houses simply weren't built to accommodate the volume of water some people now use when bathing.

Some of the best floor plans for the modern adult bath also include a separate room for the toilet and bidet, a detached tub and shower, and dual sinks on opposite sides of the room with adjacent dressing rooms and walk-in closets. Modern couples want to share a master bed and bath, but they also want to have privacy and the ease of getting ready in the morning without tripping over their mates. The only way to do this harmoniously is to mingle the parts of the room that invite sharing and separate those elements that are always private.

TOP RIGHT
**Large mirrors, well-placed lighting, and a vanity with plenty of storage ensure that this bath will function well for two or more people.**

RIGHT
**Making clever use of the space between wall studs, the designer of this bath created shelves on both sides of the vanity.**

# shopping for bath products

The products you select to outfit your new bathroom will affect both your design and your budget. If you choose top-of-the-line products, expect a top-of-the-line bill. Factors that influence the cost of new fixtures, cabinetry, countertops, and flooring include updated technology and type of finish. The smarter the device, the more you'll pay for it. Likewise, the fancier the finish, the higher the price tag. But cost does not always reflect quality, nor does it equate necessarily with satisfaction. And quality and personal satisfaction are the most important factors to consider when making any product selection.

So, how can you make smart choices about items such as tubs and showers, tile, and cabinets? How can you tell whether a product is reliable and will endure the daily abuse of water and moisture? Are there basic differences that make one faucet or a particular toilet better than another? To find out, you can do a little research. Shop around. Visit bath designer showrooms, read books, and don't be afraid to ask questions. Otherwise, you can take your chances on buying an item that might not suit your needs. If you're not the gambling type, however, here are some steps you can take to select products and materials for your new bath with confidence.

## smart steps
### where to begin

### Step 1 SEPARATE THE PRODUCT FROM THE HYPE

A high price does not always mean high quality. Find out what is different about a toilet that costs $100, for example, and one that sells for $300 or even $1,000. This way you can decide whether the higher price is worth it. A knowledgeable salesperson will be able to tell you. If not, contact the manufacturer. Many have

toll-free numbers and Web sites set up to handle consumer questions. Sometimes the price hike is because of a feature you can't see. For example, a faucet with replaceable parts costs much more than a new faucet with parts that cannot be replaced. How much do you want to gamble that the faucet you buy won't break?

### Step 2 WEIGH YOUR OPTIONS

Analyze the benefits and the risks that come with each product. Once you have that information, a decision will be easier. If you are sprucing up an old bath or adding

A colored concrete surround and deck accommodates this white porcelain tub. A stylish high-arc faucet, sleek handles, and a hand-held sprayer enhance the Modern look.

A bathtub with a nostalgic "French telephone" faucet features a practical hand sprayer and porcelain handles, which integrate the fittings all the more flawlessly with the vintage-style tub.

a new one in a house you expect to sell soon, you might install a less-expensive countertop material, for example. But if you are making a major investment in a remodeling project that you plan to live with for a long time, you might be happier in the long run with something that may cost more but gives you greater satisfaction and will be more reliable for years to come.

## Step 3 SEEK RELIABLE ADVICE

Ask the manufacturer about the expected life of the product or its efficiency. Don't take advice from a store clerk unless he or she is an experienced remodeling professional. Talk to your contractor, who may be familiar with the product or can pass along critical feedback from other clients who may have purchased the same item or something similar to it.

## Step 4 DON'T MAKE A CHOICE BASED ON STYLE OR COLOR

It doesn't work for cars, and it won't work for building materials. Sure, style and color are important, but it's just as easy to find a first-rate fixture that looks great in your new bathroom as it is to find one that looks fabulous but performs poorly. Opt for quality.

## Step 5 BE WARY OF SOME HANDMADE PRODUCTS FOR THE BATH

You may be tempted by a handsome unglazed sink from a chic pottery shop. Certainly, it will add a unique cachet to your design, but an unglazed sink may not meet local code. Don't buy on impulse before checking out the building codes in your area. If there's any doubt in your mind, ask if you can leave a refundable deposit on the item, and then speak with your contractor, who should be familiar with the rules and can save you from a costly mistake.

## Step 6 PRORATE COSTS

You may be dismayed by the initial sticker price, but when you divide the cost of the product or material by its anticipated longevity (how many years you expect it to last), you may be amazed at how reasonable it really is. Of course, this won't alleviate an immediate cash-flow problem, but it will ease some of the sticker shock. An expensive product that will last for 20 years may be a better choice than a cheaper one that may have to be replaced in five years. Again, weigh that decision against how long you plan to stay in the house. Are the extra benefits worth it?

## Step 7 INQUIRE ABOUT GUARANTEES AND SERVICES

Some offers are definitely better than others. Look at the warranties that come from the manufacturer, as well as those offered by the place of purchase. A store may offer immediate replacement of the entire unit. While this may sound great, it isn't if you have to pay for labor or schedule time off from work for the removal and reinstallation of a fixture. Find out whether there is a better way. If all that is wrong with a faucet is a faulty washer, you may not want to yank out the entire unit. It should be your call. Find a place that offers a warranty based on the problems with the product. And always get written copies of all warranties from the store or your contractor.

# fixtures

Thirty years ago, items like tubs, toilets, and sinks were standard fare, not to mention boring. Who could have imagined they would generate the excitement they do today? As bathrooms have been elevated to symbolize status in American homes over the last couple of decades, second in prestige only to kitchens, even the most pragmatic items have become elements of design. But in addition to appearance, the workings of bathroom fixtures have become technologically more glamorous as well.

## Tubs

The possibilities are nearly endless: soakers, whirlpools, classic claw-footed models, tubs for two, spas for four, contoured shapes, ovals, squares, or rounded tubs, streamlined or sculptured models, tubs with neck rests and arm rests, freestanding tubs, tubs set into platforms, and tubs you step down into. It's your soak, so have it your way.

Ask yourself: How do I like to bathe? Do I prefer a long, lingering soak or an. invigorating hydromassage? A popular trend is the sunk-in whirlpool tub, which comes with an array of therapeutic and relaxing options in the form of neck jets, back jets, side jets, multiple jets, or single jets that are installed in the walls behind the tub. Other options include on-off control panels that can be reached from inside the tub (as opposed to a wall timer) and an automatic turnoff that prevents motor burnout.

Generally, tubs are made of one of the three following materials:

■ *Fiberglass* is a lightweight and moldable material. A fiberglass tub is the least expensive type you can buy. But it's prone to scratching and wear after about a dozen years. Some come with an acrylic finish, which holds up against wear longer.

## Step 8 DO A REALITY CHECK

Look at your situation, and choose the best products and materials for the way you live. Don't get swept away by bells and whistles that can blow your budget. Your bottom line isn't bottomless, so compare each extra-cost feature to your real needs and lifestyle. A sumptuous shower with 18 massaging hydrojets may be your fantasy, but if your morning routine is a race against the clock to get to work on time, invest the extra money elsewhere. Besides, multiple shower outlets, as well as large tubs, may require larger water-supply lines, and that might not be an option.

## Step 9 LEAVE NOTHING TO CHANCE

Investigate every option and detail for the new bathroom. Don't find yourself bemoaning what you should have done when it's too late. After you sign the final check is not the time to realize you could have installed an in-line heater to keep bath water consistently warm or a steam unit in the shower. Discover everything that's out there—before getting started on the remodeling. Don't miss any of the fun stuff, and you won't have any regrets or extra charges for changes made after work has begun.

Although the trend in recent years has been to increase the size of the bathroom, most are still relatively small compared with other rooms in the house. Yet this room remains the most expensive per square foot to renovate. This behooves you to invest wisely.

■ *Solid acrylic* is a mid-price range product that is more durable than fiberglass and less prone to scratching because the color is solid all the way through. Whirlpool tubs are usually made of acrylic because it can be shaped easily. It's also lightweight, an important feature for large tubs that can put damaging stress on structural elements under the floor.

■ An enamel-coated *cast-iron* tub will endure as long as your house stands. It's heavyweight, though, and not recommended for a large soaking tub, even if the floor has been reinforced.

The most common size for a tub that backs up against a wall is 32 x 60 inches, but you can find models in widths of 24 to 42 inches. If someone in the family is tall, no problem: You can purchase a standard tub that's up to 72 inches long.

## Showers

Spectacular spray options and spa features make showering as sybaritic as the most luxuriously appointed bath. Shower units separate from bathtubs can be prefabricated from molded fiberglass or acrylic. They come in widths of 32, 36, and 48 inches, with a standard depth of 36 inches and a height of 73 inches. Custom-built showers are typically constructed of solid-surfacing, ceramic tile, or stone. Top-of-the-line features include massaging hydrotherapy sprays, steam units, a foot whirlpool, built-in seating and storage, even a CD player. Amazing technology lets you enjoy a full body massage on a miserly amount of water. Although by law, new showerheads may not deliver more than 2.5 gallons of water per minute, you can install as many as you wish.

The only thing limiting your shower is your imagination and your budget. If you want it, it's out there. Unless you're interested in a strictly no-frills unit, think

about installing more than one showerhead and mixing and matching devices from any or all of the following three basic spray categories.

■ A *fixed-spray* showerhead is mounted on the wall or ceiling, and it may or may not come with a massage option. New versions include a device that propels water into the air to give you a hydromassage. Other nifty models, called rain bars, let you close your eyes and pretend you're in a rain forest where gentle mists pamper you with a soft rinse. Or you can opt for a cascade of water that is delivered by a waterfall spout.

**RIGHT**
The elegance created by a mixture of tile in this bathroom extends into the large walk-in shower.

▓ A *handheld spray* is convenient for directing water where you want it. It stores in a wall-mounted slide bar and can be adjusted up and down to accommodate the tallest or shortest bather. Combine a handheld spray with a stationary showerhead, and add a massager with as many as eight settings and a body brush, and you've created a custom shower environment that rivals any first-class away-from-home spa.

▓ *Jet sprays* are housed behind the shower walls, just as those used in whirlpool tubs are. One manufacturer offers as many as 16 with its shower unit. Jet sprays can be programmed to various settings. Get a therapeutic hydromassage to relax stiff neck muscles or a sore back, for example. If you like, select a full body massage at whatever intensity is comfortable for you.

## Toilets

Believe it or not, you do have choices when selecting a toilet for your new bathroom. Vitreous china is still the material of preference, but there's a wide range of colors and style options to suit contemporary or traditional tastes. If you like something sleek, select a European-inspired elongated bowl. Though toilet sizes vary somewhat among manufacturers, an elongated bowl will extend about 2 inches more into the room than a standard version. The typical height of a toilet seat is 15 inches, but some come as high as 18 inches, which can be more comfortable for tall or older persons.

Another option is whether your new toilet will be a one-piece, low-profile model or a two-piece unit. There are style variations within both types, including rounded bowls, long square shapes, and vintage looks. Nostalgia lovers will be happy to know that Victorian-style high-tank toilets are still manufactured. Scaled-down toilets are available, too, for condos and apartments short on space or for tiny powder rooms, such as those tucked into a stairwell or made out of an old hallway closet.

If you are still fighting in your household about whether the seat should be kept up or down, give peace a chance. Look into these new gender-friendly features: a lid that automatically lowers when the toilet is flushed or a toilet that shines a red light in the bowl when the seat is up and a green light when the lid is down.

If that isn't enough, consider a residential urinal. One type fits into the wall; another sits on the floor next to the toilet.

LEFT

**Toilet handles come in a variety of new styles and materials. Choosing one that blends with the other elements in your bath will help pull together the design.**

Besides style and type, you should be concerned about the flushing mechanism. Although appearance factors can affect cost (low-profile, one-piece, and elongated bowls being at least twice the price of standard two-piece models), the flushing mechanism may have an even bigger impact on the price tag. New toilets must conform to the government's low-flush standard, which mandates that no more than 1.6 gallons of water be used per flush. (Older model toilets used 3.5 gallons and really old models used a whopping 5 gallons per flush.) There have been many complaints about the effectiveness of low-flush toilets, especially the early models. But the technology is improving steadily.

There are three basic types of flushing mechanisms, listed in order of their cost, starting with the least expensive.

■ A *gravity-fed* mechanism is the standard device used by two-piece toilets. Press down the lever, and the force of the water that is released from the tank and into the bowl flushes waste down the drain and out through the pipes.

■ A *pressure-assisted* type uses household water pressure to compress the air in a chamber in the toilet tank. Flushing releases the compressed air, forcing the water into the trap almost instantly.

■ There is also a *vacuum-flush* toilet. In this type, two internal chambers create a vacuum that is released when you flush. The force created by the vacuum forces water into the bowl and through the trap.

A toilet and matching bidet feature architectural design details that blend in with similar motifs in a traditional-style home. The hardware matches throughout, further unifying the room.

# Bidets

A standard fixture in European bathrooms for decades, bidets have been slow to catch on in the American market. They are gaining in popularity, however, particularly in new construction and high-end remodeling, where they are becoming status symbols in master suites. Typically, a bidet is selected to match the toilet, and the fixtures are installed side by side.

# Lavatories

You may find it practically impossible to select one lavatory over another because they come in so many sizes, shapes, styles, and colors. Sensuous curves, sculpted bowls, and beautiful, durable finishes can make this vessel a work of art—and an important element in your overall design. Today's lavatories can be made of vitreous china, cast iron, enameled steel, fiberglass, acrylic (solid-surfacing material), stone, faux stone, or metal. Its finish may be hand painted, contoured, beveled, brushed, or polished. A sink can be a freestanding pedestal, or it can be mounted to the wall or be part of a vanity top.

Vanity sinks, in pairs or as a single lav, are designed to be installed in one of four ways:

▪ A *self-rimming* sink is surface-mounted. The bowl drops into the counter while the rim rests on and forms a seal with the countertop surface. This rim can be decoratively carved or hand painted.

▪ An *under-mounted* sink gives a tailored look. In this instance, the bowl is attached underneath the countertop for a clean, uncluttered appearance.

▪ An *integral* sink is fabricated with a countertop from the same material—stone, faux stone, or solid-surfacing. The look is sleek, seamless, and sculptural.

▪ Unlike a self-rimming sink, a *rimmed model* requires a metal strip to form the seal between the top of the sink and the countertop.

**ABOVE**
A console vanity with a concrete top and integral sink creates a cool, contemporary look. It leaves plenty of open space underneath for neatly wrapped towels and decoration.

There are attractive, shapely lavs in every price range. Colored lavatories are usually a bit pricier, as are delicate hand-painted designs. If you will do anything at the sink besides washing your hands and face and brushing your teeth, consider choices in design and size carefully before you buy.

Something that is too shallow, for example, may not be practical for rinsing hair or hand washables. A pedestal sink may be pretty, but if you apply makeup, style your hair, or shave, this type may not provide surface storage for related grooming items. Hand-painted designs may look beautiful, but they may require special care to avoid wear, as well as more gentle cleaning—not the right option for an active family. Think before acting.

## Faucets and Other Fittings

Like showers, faucets are no longer just conduits for water. Today's faucet technology gives you much more control over your water. You can program an instrument for a pulsating effect or select the gentler rhythm of a babbling brook or a cascading waterfall; preset water temperature so that the water never gets hotter than you like; or protect young children, as well as disabled or elderly family members, from scalding.

For quality, inquire about the materials used for the faucet's innards. The best choices are solid brass or a brass-base metal, which are corrosion-resistant. Avoid plastic—it won't hold up. Inquire about the faucet's valving, too. Many faucets come with a washerless ceramic or nylon cartridge that lasts longer and is less prone to leaks. Ceramic is the better choice. Select finishes depending on your taste and other elements in the room that you may wish to coordinate with the fittings. Finishes include chrome, polished brass, enamel-coated colors, pewter, nickel, gold, and gold-plated. Handles may match the faucet or come in crystal, marble, or other materials.

LEFT
**This artfully detailed gooseneck faucet with cross handles fits perfectly into a corner above the lav. A satin finish complements the muted tile backsplash.**

Make a fashion statement by mixing finishes or selecting a design with inlaid stones or gems. Think of faucets as jewelry for your bathroom, and accessorize accordingly. There are three basic types of faucets for your consideration:

■ A *center-set* faucet has two separate valves (one for hot, another for cold) and a spout that are connected in one unit.

■ The *widespread* type features a spout with separate hot- and cold-water valves. All of the parts appear to be completely separate pieces.

■ The *single-lever* type has a spout and a single lever in one piece for one-hand control.

Whatever your decorating motif, you can find faucets to coordinate with the look you wish to achieve. Reproduction styles in brushed-metal finishes look good in traditional decors, as do graceful gooseneck spouts. Sleek geometrical shapes with enameled or high-gloss finishes enhance contemporary designs. And don't forget baubles. Stone, faux stone, or faux gem inserts on handles provide rich-looking details in strong architecturally inspired designs.

While you're admiring all the handsome faucet styles on today's market, remember function. Cross handles are charming, but they can be difficult to grasp for the elderly, disabled persons, or the very young. Levers and wrist blades make more sense in these cases. If you like the simplicity of a single-lever faucet, install one with a hot-limit valve so that kids can't scald themselves.

## Grab Bars and Towel Bars

The first thing to remember is that grab bars and towel bars are not interchangeable items. A grab bar must be installed so that it securely attaches to wall studs or blocking behind a shower or bathtub or at the toilet. (If you are remodeling your bathroom, reinforce the walls at grab bar locations.) For quality, shop for grab bars made of solid brass. For style, coordinate them with other hardware, such as the towel bars, faucets, shower heads, and cabinet pulls and handles.

Like faucets, towel bars can be likened to jewelry for the bath. Don't skimp on this detail: look for ones with matching toilet paper holders and door and wall hooks. Shop for quality brass or chrome construction with a finish that won't rust or tarnish when exposed to moisture.

# storage for the bath

U ndoubtedly, an important aspect of your new bath's design is storage. Besides toiletries, grooming aids, extra linens, a hamper, and cleaning supplies, you may want to store gym equipment, books, magazines, and CDs, particularly if the room will be a place you can retreat to for adult quiet time after a day at work or with the kids. To store all these items, you'll need to be creative and utilize as much space as possible.

## smart tip  STORAGE

A linen closet inside the bathroom is an amenity some homeowners think they can't afford if the space is small. If that's your dilemma, a little rethinking and reshuffling may yield the necessary room you thought you didn't have. First, reconsider the size of the bathroom fixtures you've been planning for your design. Would a smaller tub, shower unit, or vanity relieve the crunch? Second, think about building the closet into an adjoining room, if possible. Your designer may have other ideas, too.

You can't go wrong if you make good use of even the smallest pocket of space, like the toe-kick area at the bottom of the vanity, where you can install extra drawers or a slide-out step for kids who can't reach the sink yet. If there's a low-profile toilet next to the vanity, extend the countertop over the toilet. Ask your builder to suspend a drawer from underneath the extension. Don't forget to include a built-in shelf inside the shower or tub enclosure to hold soaps and shampoos. Use the wall space; install open shelves for extra towels, bars of soap, bubble bath, and the like. Better yet, think about opening up a wall between two studs and using the dead space for recessed shelving. One caution: don't cut the studs in case it is a load-bearing wall.

**LEFT**
Unify the bathroom by choosing the same finish for all of the fittings, such as towel and grab bars and faucets.

**ABOVE**
Bathroom furniture doesn't have to look like it was made for the bathroom. Frosted-glass cabinet doors are a trendy addition.

No matter what the size of the bathroom, it should contain a reasonable amount of storage. To get it, you'll have to thoroughly analyze the space and prioritize what items you must have handy, as well as any extras you'd like. Believe it or not, even a tiny 5- x 7-foot bathroom can accommodate spare rolls of toilet paper, additional bars of soap, a blow dryer, and curling iron, as well as a stack of clean towels, as long as you think storage issues through at the design stage of the project.

If you are working with a professional, he or she will have more than a few storage tricks to offer if you are specific about what you need. Be prepared by asking yourself some storage questions about your new bath. Is a vanity sufficient? Will it be for one or two persons? Do you require a medicine cabinet? How about a linen closet? Extra shelves? Drawers?

When you are acting on your own, think about how you intend to use the new bath. Make a list of everything you want

at hand. Scale back if necessary, but start big. For example, if your children will bathe in this room, include storage for bath toys—ideally, someplace other than along the ledge of the tub. If you'll shave, groom your hair, or apply makeup at the vanity, pencil in a place—not the countertop—to keep essentials away from the sink and protected against exposure to water. If you're tired of toting dirty clothes downstairs to the basement or ground-floor laundry room, see whether your plan can accommodate a compact washer/dryer. If you're always dashing to the hallway linen closet for towels, add shelves or, if there is space, a closet in the bathroom. These are just a few of the storage-related issues that could affect your project.

In any event, it's likely that you'll want at least a vanity and a medicine cabinet in your new bath. Like fixtures and fittings, they make important statements about how the new space will look, as well as how it will function.

# Vanities

Today there are many creative ways to approach the vanity. One is to treat the vanity as a decorative receptacle for a drop-in sink with just a countertop and legs and no attached cabinetry. If you can sacrifice the storage a cabinet provides, this option will add drama to your design, especially if the countertop is outfitted with handsome tile, stone, or colored concrete. But if you're limited by space and have to make the most of every inch, a vanity cabinet, which features drawers and shelves, is the wisest choice. Cabinets are available in three ways:

■ *Stock vanities* are factory-made in a range of standard heights, sizes, and finishes. They are usually—but not always—the most economical type. Styles are limited.

■ *Semi-custom vanities* are factory-made and outfitted with custom options upon your order. Usually midrange in price, semi-custom vanities include extras, such as pullout bins, spin-out trays, special door styles, or custom finishes.

■ *Custom vanities* are built-to-order to your bathroom's specifications. The cabinets can be designed by your architect, interior designer, or designer/builder. This is typically—but not always—the most expensive option.

A popular vanity trend is to retrofit a piece of fine wood furniture, such as an antique chest, with a lav, reproduction fittings, and an elegant countertop. But the wood surface has to be sealed with a protective coating that resists water and mildew. If you don't have the right piece of old furniture but want the same look, check out the new cabinet styles offered by manufacturers today. Look at designs created for the kitchen, as well as the bath. Some are interchangeable and display furniture details. Fluted pilasters, elegant moldings, and filigree patterns adorn many models that

**This handsome custom vanity keeps towels, toiletries, and bathroom appliances all neatly organized and out of sight.**

**Richly stained, wall-hung cabinets maintain the streamlined style of this lavish powder room.**

also come with beautiful hardware and finishes engineered to hold up to humidity and mildew. They wipe clean easily, too, so you don't have to worry about upkeep. Some are available with faux stone or wood laminate countertops, or granite or marble surfaces.

Whether you select a vanity style that is traditional or contemporary, with a plastic laminate, metal, or wood finish, give the vanity cabinet as much consideration as you would if it were meant for the kitchen. Top-of-the-line solid-wood construction may be too expensive for most budgets. However, a sturdy plywood frame combined with dovetail and mortise-and-tenon joinery is excellent, too. Make sure the interiors are well finished, however, and shelves are not flimsy.

There are basically two construction styles for stock and semi-custom cabinetry: framed and frameless. Both styles are available from any American manufacturer.

■ *Framed cabinets* feature a full frame across the face of the unit. Hinges may or may not be visible around doors and drawers.

■ *Frameless cabinets,* often called European-style cabinets, are built without a face frame and therefore have a sleek appearance. Because the doors are mounted on the face of the box or are set into it, hinges are typically hidden inside.

## Medicine Cabinets

You can find attractive medicine cabinets that can be wall-mounted or recessed into a nonload-bearing wall between the studs. From ultra-contemporary visions in glass and lights to designs that make bold architectural statements, there's a wide selection of stock units to match any decor or cabinet style.

When shopping for a medicine cabinet, look for one that offers room for everything from toothbrushes to shaving cream and bandages. Choose one that spans the width of your vanity or beyond it, if wall space allows. In other words, buy the largest one you can find! Look for deep shelves that accommodate objects larger than a small pill bottle. Built-in lighting, swing-out mirrors, and three-way mirrored doors are some of the other extras you may want in a medicine cabinet. In addition, some units come with a lock or a separate compartment that can be locked to keep potentially dangerous substances out of the hands of young children.

# serviceable surfaces

Even in well-ventilated bathrooms, steam and moisture can take their toll. So it's important to select materials for the walls, floor, and countertop that can hold up to water. Plastic laminate and vinyl are good choices that come in different price ranges, depending on quality. Generally they are the most affordable. Ceramic tile, solid-surfacing material, and concrete fall into the middle to high end of the spectrum. Natural stone, such as slate, granite, and marble, are at the high end of the price scale.

## Laminate

Consider laminate for your bathroom countertops. When installed on counters, plastic laminate resists moisture superbly and is easy to maintain. Laminate is made of melamine, paper, and plastic resin bonded under heat and pressure, then glued to particleboard or plywood. It comes in so many colors, patterns, and textures that finding one to coordinate with other elements in your design—fixtures, tile, wallcovering—is easy. Want a countertop made of slate or marble, but can't afford the real thing? Does buttery leather, cool glass, or warm wood appeal to you? A faux version in laminate may be the answer. Besides giving you a price break, plastic laminate offers a practical alternative to some natural materials that would be too delicate for such an installation. In that sense, it is versatile and practical. Plastic-laminate countertop material comes in various grades. It is generally affordable, so don't skimp by purchasing the cheapest one you can find. To get your money's worth, select the highest quality, which won't chip easily and stays looking good longer. At the very top of the line is "color-through" laminate. As opposed to laminate with color on the surface only, this type will not show a brown seam line at the edge.

With regard to flooring, the latest laminate products boast easy care, as well as moisture and stain resistance. Manufacturers now offer literally dozens of designs that are dead ringers for real wood or stone. These come in either tongue-and-groove planks or as tiles. Like sheet laminate used for countertops, laminate flooring is more economical than the natural materials it portrays, and in more cases, it installs right over old flooring.

## Ceramic Tile

Besides its practical attributes, such as imperviousness to water, durability, and easy maintenance, ceramic tile offers the greatest opportunity to bring style and personality to your bathroom. Use it to add color, pattern, and texture to the wall, floor, or countertop. Enclose a tub or shower with it. Tile is versatile. It comes in a variety of shapes, sizes, and finishes. Use decorative tiles with hand-painted finishes or raised-relief designs to create a mural or mosaic. You're only limited by your imagination. Hand-painted tile is expensive, but it allows you to do something truly unique. If cost is a factor, accent standard tiles with a few hand-painted designs. Or achieve a similar look at less cost by using mass-produced tiles with silk-screened designs. Visit a tile showroom in your area or the design department of a nearby home center to get ideas. Mix and match embossed tiles, accent and trim strips, edges, and a contrasting colored grout (the compound that fills the joints). For long-lasting wear and easy maintenance, always apply a grout sealer in areas exposed to water, such as the countertop or tub surround.

Consider the finish when you're shopping for tile. There are two kinds: glazed and unglazed. Unglazed tiles are not sealed and always come in a matte finish. If you want to use them in the bathroom, you will have to apply a sealant. Glazed tiles are coated with a sealant that makes them impervious to water. This glaze can be matte finish or one that is highly polished. Highly glazed tile, however, can be a hazard on the floor. Instead, opt for a soft-glazed tile intended for floor installation. When shopping, inquire about the manufacturer's slip-resistance rating for the tile you are considering. It's also a good idea to make sure any tile selected for a countertop installation can handle the spills and knocks that occur typically around the sink and on the countertop surface.

## Solid-Surfacing Material

An extremely durable, easily maintained synthetic made of polyester or acrylic, solid-surfacing material is used to fabricate countertops, sinks, shower enclosures, and floors. It's not cheap, costing almost as much per linear foot as granite or marble, but it wears long and well. It is completely impervious to water, and any dents or abrasions that may occur over time are repaired easily with a light sanding. At first, solid surfacing was available only in shades of white or pastel colors, but now its color palette has greatly expanded and includes faux-stone finishes, too.

## Stone and Concrete

Granite, marble, and slate are probably the most expensive materials you can choose for a countertop. They are all extremely durable and rich looking. Two other stone materials, limestone and concrete, are finding their way into the creative hands of designers today, too. Unlike granite, marble, and slate, limestone has more of a primitive, textured appeal. Concrete offers flexibility, but it cracks easily. It can be colored, shaped, carved, and inlaid with objects, such as pieces of tile, glass, or shells, for a sophisticated effect.

As countertop material, any one of these materials introduces a dramatic element to the room. The only thing you have to worry about is sealing your natural countertop properly against moisture.

These materials are also heavy, so beware if you plan to use them to fabricate a tub or shower. Check with your builder or a structural engineer to find out whether you'll need additional support under the floor to carry the extra weight.

When considering any one of these options for flooring, however, remember that they are cold underfoot and unforgiving—anything you drop that is delicate will break. Stone may pose a safety hazard on the floor, too, because it gets slick when wet. A fall on a stone floor can cause serious injury. Older persons and children are at particular risk. If you choose one of these materials, use slip-resistant carpeting over it. Also, the task of installing a stone or concrete floor is not easy. Leave the laying, cutting, and fitting stone or pouring concrete to a professional.

LEFT
A colored-concrete soaking tub with a sloped back support coordinates with the room's stone and wood surfaces.

## Wood

Wood has typically been taboo in the bathroom because of its susceptibility to water damage, mildew, and warping. However, if you seal it properly with one of today's sophisticated, high-tech finishes you can use it safely. This should come as good news to homeowners who like the incomparable warmth offered by real wood. On walls or countertops, wood requires a urethane finish. Some kinds of wood, such as teak, hold up better than other softer, porous types, such as pine.

# what's your style?

Before locking yourself into one rigid style when choosing products for your bath, remember the first rule of thumb about decorating: please yourself. While you may want to emulate a certain look, don't become a slave to it and squash your creative spirit. The key is to build a room around a theme or a mood while carefully incorporating your personality. A favorite color is a good starting point, as is a repeated motif or an attractive pattern.

When considering style, everyone needs a little inspiration. Think about rooms you have admired and what attracted you. Was it a painted finish? A pretty fabric? Elegant cabinetry? How did the room make you feel? Restful? Energetic? Cheerful?

You can also take a cue from the rest of your home. Look at the style of the architecture. Is it contemporary? Colonial? Even if the architecture is nondescript, you can introduce a period flavor with reproduction fixtures, wallcoverings, molding, and accessories. You can build on these preferences in the new bathroom or depart from them entirely. Find one transitional element, such as the floor treatment or a wallcovering, to create a visual bridge from room to room.

Whatever you do, your approach to decorating the new bath should be deliberate. Let it evolve over time; don't rush your choices. Remember to let your own preferences guide you in the end.

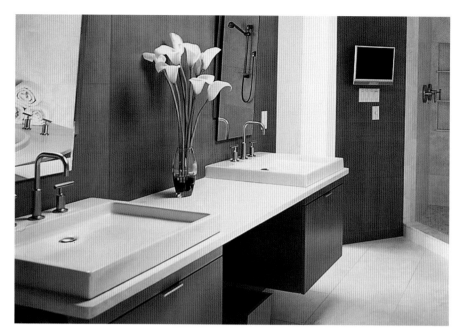

# design workbook
## NATURALLY BEAUTIFUL

### follow your bliss

A neutral color scheme, simple lines, a skylight, and natural accessories enhance this bathroom's earthy inspiration. (See also bottom left.)

### streamlined storage

A wall-hung double vanity, which seems to float, reveals the floor underneath. It's one way to make a large element less obtrusive. (See also top left.)

### have a seat

The large walk-in shower features a built-in bench and a recessed niche for keeping soaps and shampoos handy. A fixed showerhead provides a rain-like stream.

### relax in style

A deep soaking tub, left, with a sun- or moonlit view of the outdoors, provides a restful retreat. Using the same style fittings throughout unifies the room's design.

# design workbook
## MODERN SENSIBILITY

## with design in mind

This deep soaking tub is within easy reach of a warm, dry towel. Both the tub and the windows above it blend elements of modern and classic design.

## storage with style

A double-bowl vanity, left, outfitted with handsome hardware, features plenty of storage for two in drawers and cabinets. Built-in shelves handle the excess.

## finishing touches

This bath is especially unified by its matching hardware. The drawer handles echo the design and finish of the faucets, as well as that of the towel warmer.

## shower power

This walk-in shower, left, includes a convenient built-in toiletry niche, and both adjustable and fixed showerheads. Glass walls add a feeling of unencumbered space.

# 11
# outdoor living areas

DECORATING SUNROOMS AND PORCHES
PATIOS, DECKS, AND GAZEBOS  TIPS ON LANDSCAPING
DESIGN WORKBOOK

Today, the line between interior and exterior living spaces is blurring thanks to new all-weather fabrics, materials, and furnishings, sophisticated outdoor kitchen appliances, and heating and cooling devices. With so much living and entertaining happening outdoors, it's important to give more consideration to the style and comfort of these outdoor rooms. Is the space in front or on the side of the house in full view of passersby? How does it look from inside the house? Consider the scale of furnishings. Indoor/outdoor furniture comes in a variety of sizes and styles: some sleek and space-saving, some designed to visually fill up an area. Plan outside furnishings so that they augment a good view instead of blocking it. Once you have a style in mind, develop a plan that defines the function of the space. Here are some ideas.

This luxurious balcony setup embodies the ideal outdoor living space. A cozy conversation area, it extends the design and feel of the interior.

# decorating sunrooms and porches

A ttached outdoor spaces that provide total or partial shelter should be considered an extension of the home's interior design. In most cases these areas embrace an entrance or serve to join two interior areas—a breezeway, for example. Traffic patterns figure importantly in overall furniture arrangements, as does the selection of furniture, durable fabrics, and other elements.

## smart steps
### where to begin

### Step 1 DOCUMENT YOUR IDEAS

Keep a folder full of your inspirations and any ideas you may have. Photograph the area you want to decorate from both inside the house and facing toward it from the outside. Keep clippings of similar spaces and furnishings, shades, and lighting that you like from magazines and product brochures; collect paint color chips and samples of fabric and flooring, too. Don't forget plantings, including window boxes and potted plants, and anything else influencing the design. Consider all the seasons during which the space is used. Will you want to add curtains to a sunroom for insulation come winter so that you can continue to use it longer into the cold weather? Will blinds or curtains add to a porch's comfort by blocking spring and fall winds?

### Step 2 MAKE A FLOOR PLAN

Use the same steps for developing a grid and cutting out representative furniture pieces as recommended for inside rooms. (See Chapter One, "Design Basics," on page 12.) Add special features unique to your space, such as notations indicating good and bad views. You will want to arrange furniture to take advantage of a good view or to face away from an ugly one.

Indicate the sun's exposure throughout the day, and note whether it should influence furniture placement. For example, you may need shades for the southern side of a porch, or you may want to group furniture to face fabulous sunsets in the west.

### Step 3 MAKE FURNITURE TEMPLATES

Make templates of the furniture you plan to use, as well as of other elements, that require clearance space, such as planters, window boxes, or blinds. You can

LEFT
This spacious sunroom is divided into two sections to make the most of its length. The breakfast area was placed in the sunniest spot.

ABOVE
Using the same mixture of materials throughout this large, open plan unifies the space. The cozy loveseat has the best view in the house for sunsets.

also use the furniture templates in the Appendix on page 284. Group them on the floor plan; try different configurations to see which is best.

## Step 4 FACTOR IN TRAFFIC PATTERNS

Indicate pathways to and from the house. Take into account the swing of each door because you cannot place furniture in those spaces. For sliding glass doors, indicate which side is the entrance.

Arrange furniture so that conversational areas are not interrupted by traffic to and from the house. For instance, a common problem is a porch with a central door and a stepped entrance directly opposite the door. Rather than arranging furniture in one big grouping, create smaller areas at each end of the porch.

Suggestions include a table with chairs on one side and a conversational grouping on the other. A table just outside the door can double as a buffet table. Plot any other traffic aisles, and make sure that you have not blocked any necessary passages.

# Furnish with Care

Furniture for outdoor use spans the designs made popular through the centuries. You can select benches similar to those used in Versailles, Adirondack chairs, antebellum wrought iron inspired by Victorian New Orleans, and myriad other choices. A word of caution: just as decorative birdhouses won't last outdoors, some furniture with outdoor looks may not stand up to weather. Check warranties, and read directions on the furniture for care and maintenance. Then match your choices to the possible weather exposure of the furniture itself. It may be made of one or more materials.

**Wood.** Naturally weather-resistant woods, such as cypress, teak, or redwood, require little upkeep and don't need staining or preservative coatings. Treated wood is decay resistant and may have a greenish-brown color; it can be painted, stained, or left natural and protected with a clear water-resistant finish. Other wood should be treated with a moisture-resistant preservative, either clear or pigmented.

**Wicker and Rattan.** Check that the frame is weather resistant, such as aluminum with a baked-on finish. If the location is protected, some bamboo frames are porch-suitable. Synthetic wicker and special finishes on natural wicker materials offer various levels of resistance to sun and rain.

**Iron.** Its weight makes iron a good choice for windy areas, but it is heavy and difficult to rearrange. Either cast or wrought iron will rust unless treated with special rust-retarding paint and touched up or repainted over the years.

**Aluminum.** From budget tubular furniture to wrought or cast frames, aluminum is rustproof and lightweight. Pieces designed to look like ironwork often have a baked-on enamel or textured finish. Look for finishing details such as smooth seams on welded parts. Cast-aluminum pieces and those of thick, heavy-gauge alloys are top of the line.

**Plastic and Fiberglass Furniture.** Buy the best quality you can afford, because inexpensive polymer pieces that break easily will decorate the dump for decades to come. Warranties are a guide, but test pieces by sitting on them and rocking around. Tubular parts made of PVC (polyvinyl chloride) can sometimes be disassembled for storage, depending upon how they are joined. Resin pieces are molded into a variety of shapes. Both come in a range of colored plastics; some are not able to withstand direct sunlight without discoloring.

LEFT
Asian decor, filled as it is with elements of nature—bamboo, colorful flowers, earthenware, and natural stones—makes this sunroom the perfect transition between the interior and the exterior areas of this home.

# Filling It Out

Pillows, upholstery, slipcovers, shades and blinds, lighting, flooring, and rugs all make a sunroom or a porch lush and comfortable. What you can use depends on how rigorous the weather is on the furnishings. In a relatively moisture-free hot climate, for instance, sun resistance is the quality you want to look for, but mildew resistance is not essential. In other areas, both sun and moisture (caused by dew at night) can damage the goods. Select products specifically resistant to mold and mildew and ultraviolet rays. Choices abound for products that work well in a protected outdoor environment. Here's some guidance on which are suitable for the outdoors.

**Shades and Blinds.** Simple matchstick or rattan rollups can protect furnishings from some rain and sun. Other treatments might include fabulous see-through screens and blinds that block ultraviolet rays while allowing breezes to waft

ABOVE
The furniture on the patio echoes the style and color scheme of the interior living space. An arbor cover creates just the right amount of shade for relaxing outside.

through the space. Shower curtains or simply made fabric curtains are decorative solutions that add privacy as well as beauty. (Bed sheets are an inexpensive alternative to fabric.) Remember, however, if the fabric isn't sun resistant, the curtains will fade over time.

**Flooring and Rugs.** Tile, slate, concrete, and weatherproof painted wood are floor choices that require minimal care. Soften the look and the feeling underfoot with natural-fiber rugs, such as sisal or hemp, which by nature resist moisture damage; this type of floor covering works best in sheltered outdoor spaces. Another possibility is indoor-outdoor carpeting, which can be left outside all year long.

**Fabrics.** Cushions and pillows with fillings that allow water to drain through them take very little care. Add to this a wide range of new fabrics—acrylics, woven vinyl-coated polyester, laminated cotton that feels like uncoated fabric—and almost anything is possible. Look for these fabrics at tent, awning, or fabric stores, as well as the porch and patio sections of department stores and pool-supply stores. Don't overlook clear plastic to protect some fabrics, and go ahead and use conventional fabrics that catch your fancy if the area is protected. Store pillows when the weather turns foul. Fabrics treated for stain resistance are more expensive but wear better.

CLOCKWISE FROM TOP
Tall wooden shutters close to protect this indoor living space from the elements when necessary, top. When open, the balcony acts as an extension of the interior. The small amount of coverage on this patio is enough to protect the hardwearing wicker furniture, below. Wood and iron furniture stand up to all kinds of weather with a little care, left. While the cushions on the chairs are made for the outdoors, it's still wise to store them in bad weather.

**Lighting.** Outdoor ground-fault circuit interrupters (GFCIs), built-in lighting, and fans make all the difference for nighttime use of porches and sunrooms. Avoid conventional indoor lighting unless your space is attached to the house. And be kind to your neighbors: be sure lighting does not encroach on their space. (The same goes for any noise you create, such as from a television, radio, or stereo system.) Don't over-light, but do provide adequate transitional lighting from inside to outside, allowing eyes to adjust.

# patios, decks, and gazebos

Freestanding outdoor spaces, such as gazebos or other garden structures, differ from sheltered areas in several ways. Generally, they are not seen from the front of the house and are usually integrated with the landscape. Gazebos or small garden pavillions provide an opportunity to let loose a little and give in to the fanciful side of your nature.

First, consider how you will use your outdoor room. Will it be for dining, barbecues, or full-scale cooking? As a place for the kids to muck about in a wading pool and sandbox? As a quiet spot to read and relax? For warm-weather parties? Or will it be all of these things? Also consider how much privacy you want.

Decks, patios, and terraces usually exist next to a wall of the house or adjoin a porch. Attached areas call for making the most efficient use of existing doors, windows, and steps. A deck or patio might also be a short walk from the protection of the dwelling or alongside a pool, pond, or playground area. In that case, you have the luxury of developing your own entrances and traffic patterns.

As with porches and sunrooms, make a plan before you start work on your patio or deck. Use the Smart Steps for porches and sunrooms as a guide in developing ideas. (See page 268.) Creating workable traffic patterns is important, as you will sometimes be carrying trays full of food, entertainment equipment, and games and toys through the space. You have to organize furnishings so that access is easy, trips to and from the house are no longer than necessary, and you can maneuver easily through the space. Stubbed toes can ruin a relaxing afternoon.

ABOVE
An impressive pergola frames the elevated view, creates a division of space, and slightly shades the patio.

BELOW
This intricate gazebo provides a whimsical retreat at the end of a deck. Elaborate landscaping adds to the effect.

LEFT
This twig garden seat looks as if Nature itself created it out of the brush. Surrounded by trees and colorful flowers and outfitted with eclectic outdoor furnishings, it provides a private retreat.

OPPOSITE
Under a large open porch, the owners created a cozy patio area with a large stone fireplace and built-in seating that rivals many interior living rooms.

In most instances, you will want to make the patio or deck as large as possible so that it can function as a combination outdoor family room, cooking and dining area, and even a play area for kids. If space is restricted, you might consider creating an intimate area, with a small table and a pair of bistro chairs, that serves as a breakfast nook or even as a place to do paperwork in the sun.

To figure out traffic patterns, think about how you will enter this outdoor room. Will it be mostly from the house? Is the approach a path from the house or porch? Are there other areas, such as garden beds, potting sheds, bird baths, or lawn seating, that should determine exits from the patio or deck? It can be irritating to have to circumvent a deck rail or hedge to get to a frequently used destination, such as the potting shed or the barbecue grill. Figuring out potential trouble spots in advance will save you time and aggravation.

Most open spaces look best when they are defined by either hedges or fencing. Low plantings provide definition without impeding the view. Choices are nearly endless, ranging from clipped boxwood and privet hedges to low-growing junipers to a flower border of perennials or annuals. Consider what colors and fragrances you would like to have. (To learn about arranging your garden, see "Landscaping Tips" on page 278.)

For even greater privacy—or to formalize the boundaries of a deck or patio—opt for fencing. Height depends upon your sit-

uation. A low slatted fence is a good choice for containing small children without blocking the view or interfering with the flow of air. Taller options that also allow air to flow and only partially block the view include lattice panels and alternating-board fences. Deck railing and fencing are often designed with built-in seating, consisting of attached uprights, rails, and benches that may contain storage underneath.

Lighting defines spaces at night. It is also a safety factor. Both on-deck and in-ground systems with low voltage can be easily installed by a do-it-yourselfer. Other systems can be intricate and costly and may require a licensed electrician. Features may include fixtures for highlighting plantings or other yard features and timed sequencing that turns on and off automatically or when triggered by motion.

# The Family Room/ Conversation Area

A deck or patio is used most often as a fair-weather family room. Comfortable seating comes first, arranged for conversation as it would be in an indoor room. Add to this an area for snacking and outdoor recreation. Consider the activities of your household, how and whom you entertain, what your hobbies are, the age of your family members, and other factors that define your needs. Remember that this is an outdoor room: the more components that can remain in place in inclement weather, the easier for you.

Decide up front whether you need shaded areas, as well as those exposed to the sun. Where you position your space in relation to the shade provided by your house, trees, or other buildings will determine how much sun it gets. Awnings, umbrellas, pergolas, and even built-in trellises are good choices for sun protection on decks and patios.

When the same space is used for large parties, it is likely that most of the furniture will be pushed to the perimeters and more furniture will be added so that guests can mingle. Replot your traffic patterns and do a walk-through before the party to make sure everything is convenient for you and your guests.

# smart steps
## where to begin

### ■ Step 1 PROVIDE STORAGE

Make your own bin with a lift-up top large enough to contain the pillows and other non-waterproof accessories you like to have on hand, or purchase a ready-made unit designed for this purpose. A bin can keep things dry during rainstorms, but don't count on it to replace permanent storage during winter. It may not be weather resistant enough to protect outdoor furnishings. Keep ease of winter storage in mind when you are deciding on furniture, cushions, umbrellas, extra folding tables, and the like.

### ■ Step 2 INVEST IN COVERUPS

Vinyl slipcovers and protective cloths are available to place over large-sized pieces of cushioned furniture, and you will not have to move the cushions. They are not expensive and are easy to store.

## The Kitchen/Dining Area

Some people set up complete, permanent cooking centers as the focus of their outdoor spaces. Others content themselves with a simple grill. In either case, practical planning makes outdoor cooking efficient and more enjoyable, whether it is for the family or a host of guests.

Decide exactly what features you want in the cooking area. Aside from the grill, do you want an elaborate setup with a sink or a refrigerator? Perhaps a dishwasher? If so, these appliances need to be protected from the elements; place the cooking center in a sheltered location. If you prefer to keep it simple with just a grill, this option still requires some decision making. Do you want a charcoal, liquid propane (LP), or natural-gas grill? Charcoal grills are the least expensive; natural gas ones are the most expensive. The number of burners and features, such as a push-button ignition, increase the cost, too. You can also choose from a num-

ber of accessories, such as rotisseries, side burners, smoke ovens, and warming racks.

Then choose a site for the cooking area. It can be placed either nearby or far away from the house. Both locations have their advantages. A cooking area that is near the house benefits from easy access to the indoor kitchen, but one that is positioned away from the house keeps heat and smoke from diners. Remember, elaborate outdoor kitchens need gas, electric, and plumbing lines; it is easier and less expensive to run lines when the cooking area is near the house.

In general, when arranging any outdoor cooking area, make sure that all accoutrements—including serving platters, a spatula, a knife, and a pair of tongs—are readily at hand for the cook by providing plenty of surfaces and shelving. You need to accommodate both raw food and the finished product; a roll-around cart may suffice. Keep the pathway clear from the kitchen to the cooking area. A fire extinguisher nearby is an excellent safety precaution.

Any countertop material should be able to withstand varying weather conditions. Rain, snow, and bright sunlight will fade, pit, and rot some surfaces, so choose carefully. Tile, concrete, or natural materials, such as stone or slate, are good options. (Seal porous stone to prevent grease stains.) Avoid using a laminate countertop, unless it's in a well-protected area—an enclosed porch, for instance— because exposure to the weather may cause the subsurface to deteriorate. Solid surfacing is more durable, but may also need to be in a sheltered location. Think twice about using teak or other decay-resistant woods for a countertop, as they stain easily and may harbor bacteria.

Decay-resistant wood, such as redwood, cedar, teak, or mahogany, is the right choice for cabinetry, however. Other types of wood should be sealed and stained or painted. Oriented-strand board (OSB), which is made of bonded wood fiber, is also weatherproof enough for outdoor cabinetry.

CLOCKWISE FROM OPPOSITE TOP
Bentwood chairs and table, a glass table top, and outdoor cushions can stand up to crosscutting rain that might find its way into this covered patio, opposite top. Sometimes an umbrella is all the shade you need for meals outside, top left. A stone bench fits unobtrusively into a handsome wall surrounding a patio, left. A grill, built into the stone surround, has stone slabs on either side to act as counterspace for meal preparation, opposite bottom.

# landscaping tips

N o outdoor living space is completely successful until it is integrated with the surrounding landscape. Just as there are principles for designing interior spaces, there are also guidelines for exterior ones. If you are choosing a site for a gazebo or a patio, it is one of the most important landscape design decisions you'll make. If the structure already exists, you can enhance it by assessing and changing the landscape. For instance, you may want to plan a garden around a gazebo, planting shrubs and flowers to highlight the beauty of the site. Or you may want to treat the gazebo as a secluded retreat. Achieving either goal takes careful planning of the site and surrounding plantings.

## smart steps
### where to begin

### Step 1 EVALUATE THE SITE

The landscape design should provide a framework for your outdoor living space. The views, lines, property configuration, and traffic patterns need to work together. Spend some time getting acquainted with your site and noting any special features. What are the site's assets? Are there beautiful views? Are there natural features, such as trees or streams? Consider the size and shape of your lot, the style of the house itself, as well as your own lifestyle needs and preferences.

### Step 2 BALANCE THE ELEMENTS

This is the process of arranging various site elements so that they are resolved and balanced. A visually heavy or large object can be balanced by a visually lighter or smaller object on the site if the smaller object is darker in color value, is unusually or irregularly shaped, has a contrasting texture, or is more elaborately detailed. All of these strategies will help to draw attention to the smaller object and thereby visually balance it with the larger object. For example, let's say you have a large clump of pine trees on one side of your yard. To visually balance the trees you might plant smaller, more colorful ornamental trees on the other side of the yard, or you might use a man-made object such as a gazebo.

### Step 3 CREATE A COHESIVE DESIGN

Harmony can be achieved by selecting and using elements that share a common trait or characteristic. By using elements that are similar in size, shape, color, material, texture, or detail, you can create a cohesive feeling and relation among the various elements on the site. An example of this might be using a shape, such as a square. Imagine having a square concrete patio scored in a square (or diamond) pattern with a square table covered in a checkered tablecloth. The results can be extremely pleasing and harmonious.

### Step 4 ADD INTEREST

While both balance and harmony are used to achieve unity, too much unity can be, well, boring. That's where variety and contrast come in handy. By varying the size, shape, color, material, texture, and detail, you can introduce a note of interest or a focal point into the total composition. For instance, placing a round wooden planter onto the square-patterned patio discussed in Step Three will provide a pleasing contrast of both shape and material. The contrasting object (the round wooden planter) will draw attention to itself and provide visual relief and interest to the total setting.

**FAR LEFT**
Stone stairs, decorated with small natural stones and tufts of plant life, are integrated seamlessly into the surrounding landscape.

**LEFT**
Two chairs tucked in a small clearing create a private retreat. The encircling plants leave a space for the sun to bathe the chairs.

**BELOW**
These antique carved faces were salvaged from an old stone fountain and add interest to a plain wall surrounding a garden.

## Step 5 ESTABLISH VISUAL RHYTHM

In design terms, rhythm—or how elements are spaced relative to similar elements—can create another type of unity in a composition. Rhythm helps to establish a visually satisfying progression or sequence to a site design. For example, you can create a regular rhythm on a walkway if you place a band of decorative brick at 4-foot intervals. On the other hand, a song composed of only one sequence of notes is boring. Vary such things as the interval, color, size, shape, texture, or material of the elements.

## Step 6 EMPHASIZE AN ELEMENT

This point assumes that within your site some of the elements have more significance than the rest and that these special elements should be emphasized. This is probably starting to sound familiar to you by now, but a special element is given its due emphasis by making it larger; by giving it a different shape (round versus square); by using a singular color, texture, or material; by shifting or rotating its orientation; by centering it within a circle or at the end of walkway; or by lighting it at night. However, if you emphasize too much, you may end up with a visually confusing design.

## Step 7 LET SIMPLICITY BE YOUR GUIDE

Simplicity is one of the hardest things to achieve in a design because there is a tendency to use all available tools and elements. The most elegant site designs are those that begin and end with simplicity as their guiding design principle. The Zen rock gardens of Japan are a good example.

# design workbook
## MAKE THE MOST OF YOUR SPACE

### inside out

This spacious patio brings the living room, dining room, and kitchen outside to create an outdoor living space as visually appealing as its indoor counterpart.

### embrace materialism

The fabrics used for the cushions coordinate with those in the adjacent indoor family room, and they are coated for sun and water protection. (See also top left.)

### the updated campfire

A stylish built-in fireplace replaces the campfires of old, left. A decorative accessory balances the wall with its size and opposite shape, and matches the glow of the fire.

### catch some rays

Two lounge chairs, far left, can be wheeled around to the brightest spot for some sunbathing or to the conversation area. The chair backs are adjustable for comfort.

# design workbook

## ENJOY MORE OUTDOORS

### be at home anywhere

Relaxing in this lush outdoor living space is like being in your own living or dining room but with copious natural light and fresh air. What could be better?

### integrate your design

This patio is surrounded by and accented with landscaping and potted plants. This not only beautifies the patio but integrates it with the rest of the backyard.

### keep it cozy

A wood-burning fireplace, top left, extends the family's enjoyment outdoors well into the evening and into the fall.

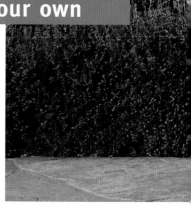

### make it your own

With a tall counter-tile backsplash, adjacent windows, cabinetry, and decorative touches, this grilling area is not only fully functional but also personalized, left.

# appendix

## WINDOW AND DOOR TEMPLATES

Windows

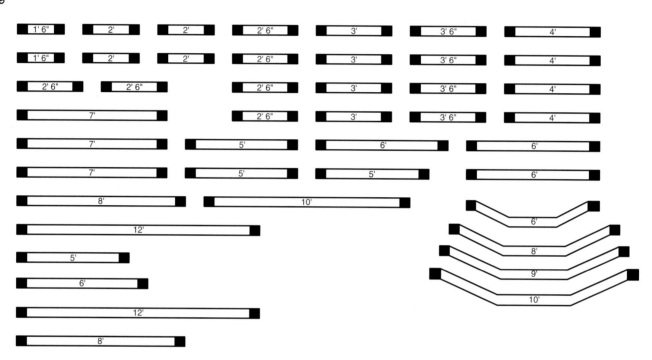

Doors

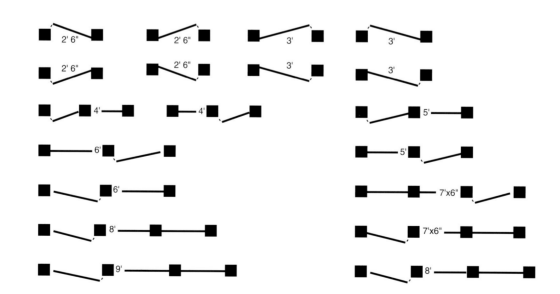

# FURNITURE TEMPLATES

## Sofas, Love Seats, and Sofa Beds

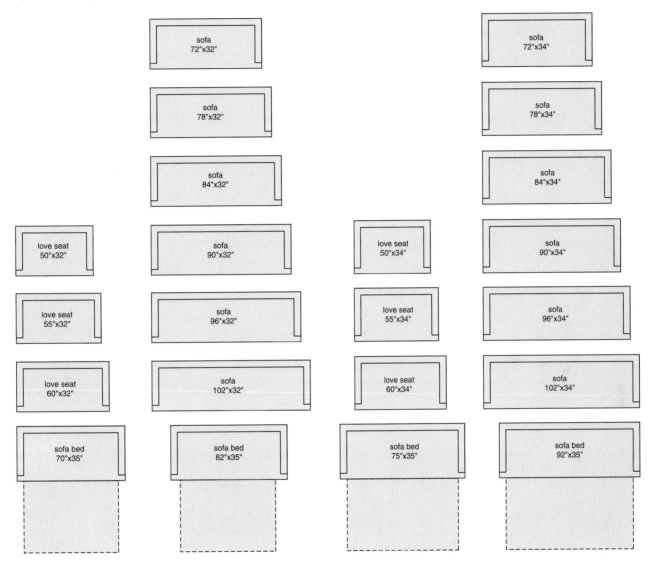

## Beds

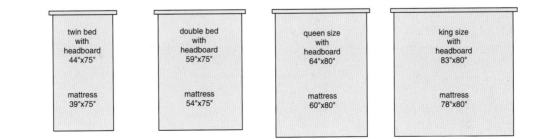

# FURNITURE TEMPLATES

## Chairs and Ottomans

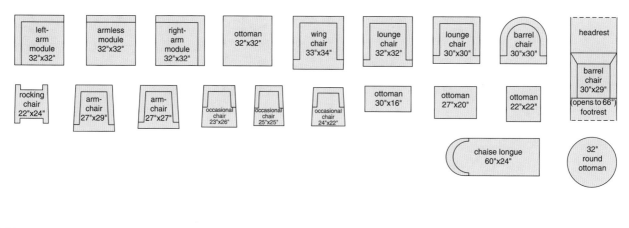

## End Tables

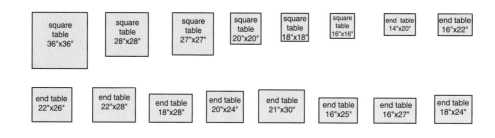

## Coffee Tables and Desks

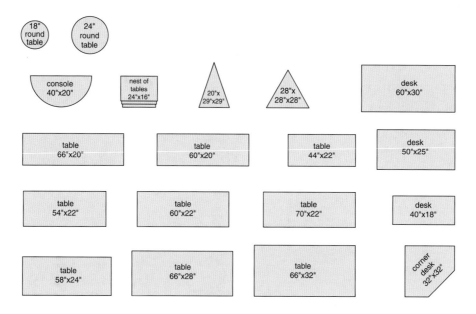

# FURNITURE TEMPLATES

Accessories

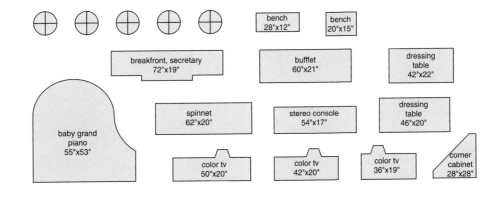

bench
28"x12"

bench
20"x15"

breakfront, secretary
72"x19"

bufffet
60"x21"

dressing
table
42"x22"

baby grand
piano
55"x53"

spinnet
62"x20"

stereo console
54"x17"

dressing
table
46"x20"

color tv
50"x20"

color tv
42"x20"

color tv
36"x19"

corner
cabinet
28"x28"

# KITCHEN TEMPLATES

Dining and Café Tables

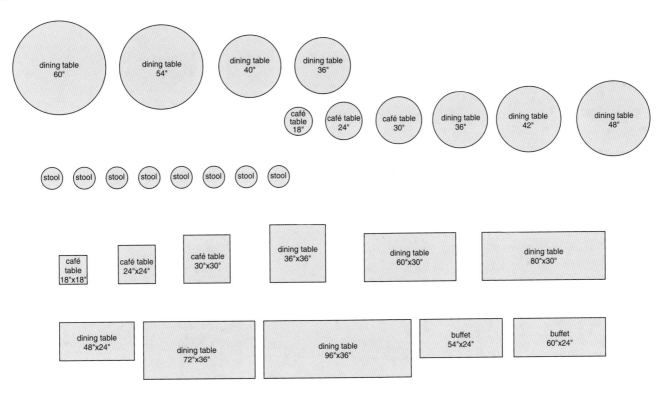

dining table
60"

dining table
54"

dining table
40"

dining table
36"

café
table
18"

café table
24"

café table
30"

dining table
36"

dining table
42"

dining table
48"

stool stool stool stool stool stool stool stool

café
table
18"x18"

café table
24"x24"

café table
30"x30"

dining table
36"x36"

dining table
60"x30"

dining table
80"x30"

dining table
48"x24"

dining table
72"x36"

dining table
96"x36"

buffet
54"x24"

buffet
60"x24"

# KITCHEN TEMPLATES

## Countertops

## Base Cabinets

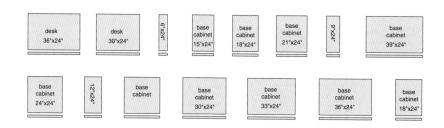

## Islands and Appliances

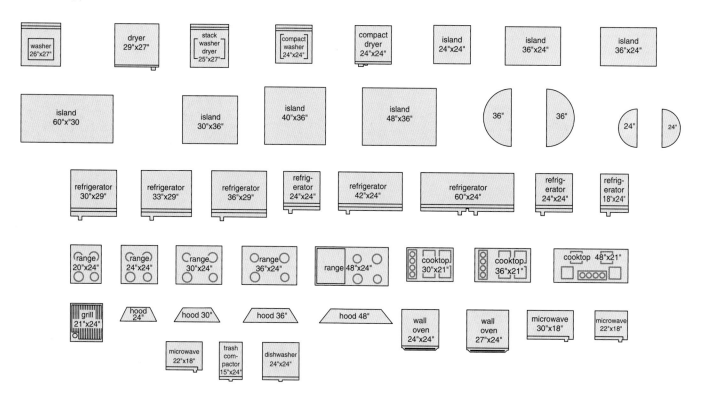

# KITCHEN TEMPLATES

Sinks

Pantries

# BATHROOM TEMPLATES

Lavatories

Toilets

Tubs and Shower

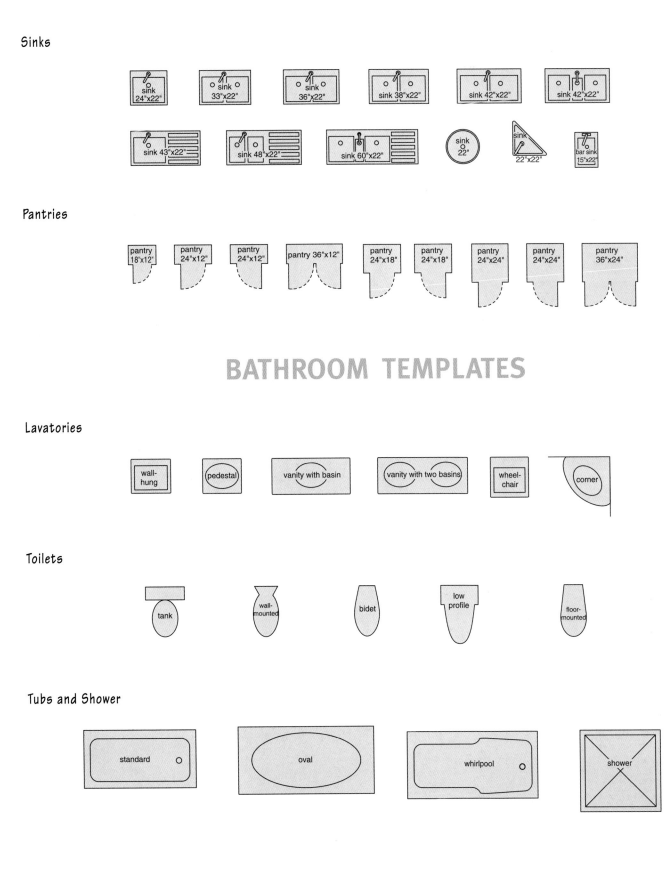

# BATHROOM SYMBOLS

Hardware

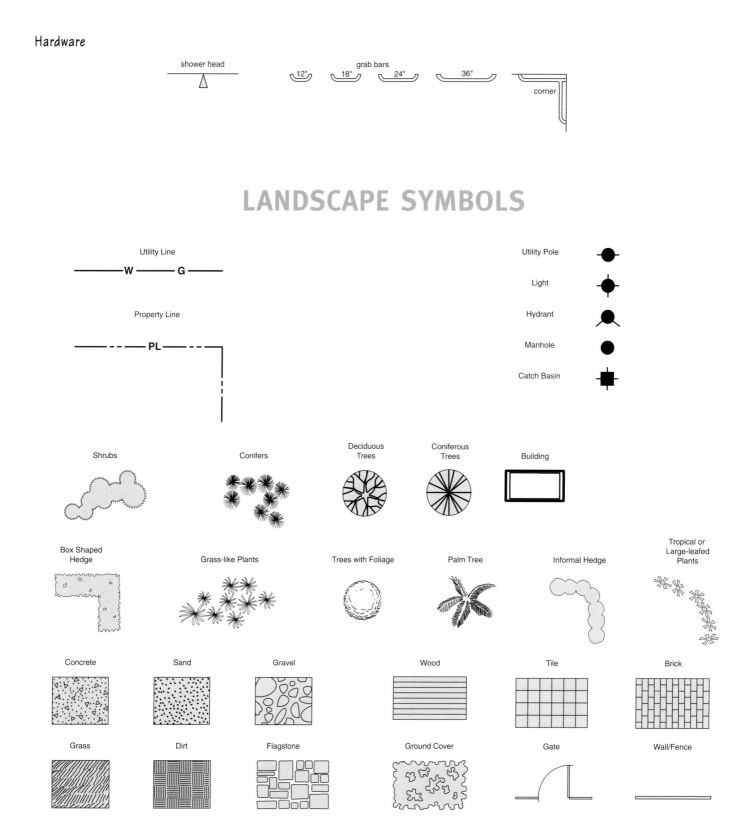

shower head

grab bars

12"  18"  24"  36"

corner

# LANDSCAPE SYMBOLS

Utility Line

— W — G —

Property Line

— PL —

Utility Pole

Light

Hydrant

Manhole

Catch Basin

Shrubs

Conifers

Deciduous Trees

Coniferous Trees

Building

Box Shaped Hedge

Grass-like Plants

Trees with Foliage

Palm Tree

Informal Hedge

Tropical or Large-leafed Plants

Concrete

Sand

Gravel

Wood

Tile

Brick

Grass

Dirt

Flagstone

Ground Cover

Gate

Wall/Fence

Scale: 1 square=1 foot

# resource guide

The following list of manufacturers and associations is meant to be a general guide to additional industry and product-related sources. It is not intended as a listing of products and manufacturers represented by the photographs in this book.

**American Furniture Manufacturers Association (AFMA)**
317 West High Ave.
High Point, NC 27261
Phone: 336-884-5000
www.afma4u.org
*A trade organization that provides information on American-made furniture.*

**American Institute for Conservation of Historic and Artistic Works**
1717 K St. NW
Washington, DC 20006
Phone: 202-452-9545
www.aic.stanford.edu
*Provides information on restoring and maintaining antiques.*

**American Society of Interior Designers (ASID)**
608 Massachusetts Ave. NE
Washington, DC 20002
Phone: 202-546-3480
www.interiors.org
*Provides a referral service for consumers.*

**Baker Furniture**
1661 Monroe Ave. NW
Grand Rapids, MI 49505
Phone: 800-592-2537
www.bakerfurniture.com
*Manufactures furniture.*

**Bernhardt Furniture Company**
P. O. Box 51, Dept. B-F
Asheville, NC 28802
Phone: 877-205-5793
www.bernhardt.com
*Manufactures furniture.*

**Brewster Wallcovering Company**
67 Pacella Park Dr.
Randolph, MA 02368
Phone: 800-366-1700
www.brewp.com
*Manufactures wallcovering.*

**Broyhill Furniture Industries, Inc.**
One Broyhill Park
Lenoir, NC 28633
Phone: 800-327-6944
www.broyhillfurn.com
*Manufactures furniture.*

**Congoleum Corporation**
Dept. C
P. O. Box 3127
Mercerville, NJ 08619
Phone: 800-274-3266
www.congoleum.com
*Manufactures flooring.*

**Graber Window Fashions**
Spring Industries
P. O. Box 70
Fort Mill, SC 29716
Phone: 800-221-6352
www.springs.com
*Manufacturers window treatments.*

**Eisenhart Wallcoverings Company**
400 Pine St.
Hanover, PA 17331
Phone: 800-931-9255
www.eisenhartwallcoverings.com
*Manufactures wallcovering.*

**Harden Furniture, Inc.**
8550 Mill Pond Way
McConnellsville, NY 13401
Phone: 315-245-1000
www.harden.com
*Manufactures furniture.*

**Hickory Chair Company**
P. O. Box 2147
Hickory, NC 28603
Phone: 828-328-1801 x 7295
www.hickorychair.com
*Manufactures furniture.*

**Lane Home Furnishings**
P. O. Box 1627
Tupelo, MS 38802
Phone: 662-566-7211
www.lanefurniture.com
*Manufactures furniture.*

**Lexington Home Brands**
P. O. Box 1008
Lexington, NC 27293
Phone: 800-539-4636
www.lexington.com
*Manufactures furniture.*

**Mannington, Inc.**
75 Mannington Mills Rd.
Salem, NJ 08079
Phone: 856-935-3000
www.mannington.com
*Manufactures flooring.*

**National Kitchen & Bath Association (NKBA)**
687 Willow Grove St.
Hackettstown, NJ 07840
Phone: 800-652-2776
www.nkba.org
*A trade organization that offers consumers information.*

**National Paint and Coatings Association (NPCA)**
1500 Rhode Island Ave. NW
Washington, DC 20005
Phone: 202-462-6272
www.paint.org
*A nonprofit trade association offering consumer information.*

**Paint Quality Institute**
www.paintquality.com
*Provides information on paint selection and painting.*

**Seabrook Wallcoverings**
1325 Farmville Rd.
Memphis, TN 38122
Phone: 901-320-3500
www.seabrookwallcoverings.com
*Manufactures wallcovering.*

**Thibaut Wallcoverings**
480 Frelinghuysen Ave.
Newark, NJ 07114
Phone: 973-643-3777
*Manufacturers wallcovering and fabric.*

**Thomasville Furniture Industries, Inc.**
P. O. Box 339
Thomasville, NC 27361-0339
Phone: 800-225-0265
www.thomasville.com
*Manufactures living room, bedroom, and office furniture.*

**Woodard, Inc.**
300 W. Washington, Ste. 500
Chicago, IL 60606
Phone: 312-423-5648
www.woodard-furniture.com
*Manufactures outdoor furniture.*

**York Wallcoverings**
750 Linden Ave.
York, PA 17404
Phone: 717-846-4456
www.yorkwall.com
*Manufactures wallcovering.*

# glossary OF HOME DECORATING

**Accent Lighting:** A type of directional lighting that highlights an area or object to emphasize that aspect of a room's character.

**Accessible Designs:** Designs that accommodate persons with physical disabilities.

**Adaptable Designs:** Designs that can be easily changed to accommodate a person with disabilities.

**Analogous Scheme:** See *Harmonious Color Scheme*.

**Ambient Lighting:** General illumination that surrounds a room and is not directional.

**Art Deco:** A decorative style that was based on geometric forms. It was popular during the 1920s and 1930s.

**Art Nouveau:** A late-nineteenth-century decorative style that was based on natural forms. It was the first style to reject historical references and create its own design vocabulary, which was ornamental and included stylized curved details.

**Arts and Crafts:** An architectural and decorative style that began in England during the late nineteenth century, where it was known as the Aesthetic Movement. Lead by William Morris, the movement rejected industrialization and encouraged fine craftsmanship and simplicity in design.

**Backlighting:** Illumination coming from a source behind or at the side of an object.

**Backsplash:** The vertical part at the rear and sides of a countertop that protects the adjacent wall.

**Box Pleat:** A double pleat, underneath which the edges fold toward each other.

**Broadloom:** A wide loom for weaving carpeting that is 54 inches wide or more.

**Built-in:** Any element, such as a bookcase or cabinetry, that is built into a wall or an existing frame.

**Cabriole:** A double-curve or reverse S-shaped furniture leg that leads down to an elaborate foot (usually a ball-and-claw type).

**Candlepower:** The luminous intensity of a beam of light (total luminous flux) in a particular direction, measured in units called candelas.

**Casegoods:** A piece of furniture used for storage, including cabinets, dressers, and desks.

**Clearance:** The amount of space between two fixtures, the centerlines of two fixtures, or a fixture and an obstacle, such as a wall.

**Code:** A locally or nationally enforced mandate regarding structural design, materials, plumbing, or electrical systems that state what you can or cannot do when you build or remodel.

**Color Wheel:** A diagram, usually circular, showing the range and relationships of pigment and dye colors.

**Complementary Colors:** Hues directly opposite each other on the color wheel. As the strongest contrasts, complements tend to intensify each other.

**Contemporary:** Any modern design (after 1920) that does not contain traditional elements.

**Dimmer Switch:** A switch that can vary the intensity of the light it controls.

**Faux Finish:** A decorative paint technique that imitates a pattern found in nature.

**Federal:** An architectural and decorative style popular in America during the early nineteenth century, featuring delicate ornamentation, often depicting swags and urns, and symmetrically arranged rooms.

**Fittings:** The plumbing devices that bring water to the fixtures, such as faucets.

**Fluorescent Lighting:** A glass tube coated on the interior with phosphor, a chemical compound that emits light when activated by ultraviolet energy. Air in the tube is replaced with a combination of argon gas and a small amount of mercury.

**Focal Point:** The dominant element in a room or design, usually the first to catch your eye.

**Foot-candle:** A unit that is used to measure brightness. A foot-candle is equal to one lumen per square foot of lighted surface.

**Framed Cabinet:** A cabinet with a full frame across the face of the cabinet box.

**Frameless Cabinet:** A cabinet without a face frame. It may also be called a "European-style" cabinet.

**Frieze:** A horizontal band at the top of the wall or just below the cornice.

**Full-Spectrum Light:** Light that contains the full range of wavelengths that can be found in daylight, including invisible radiation (ultraviolet and infrared) at each end of the visible spectrum.

**Georgian:** An architectural and decorative style popular in America during the late eighteenth century, with rooms characterized by the use of paneling and other woodwork, and bold colors.

**Gothic Revival:** An architectural and decorative style popular during the mid-nineteenth century. It romanticized the design vocabulary of the medieval period, using elements such as pointed arches and trefoils (three-leaf motifs).

**Greek Revival:** An architectural and decorative style that drew inspiration from ancient Greek designs. It is characterized by the use of pediments and columns.

**Harmonious Color Scheme:** Also called analogous, a combination focused on neighboring hues on the color wheel. The shared underlying color generally gives such schemes a coherent flow.

**Hue:** Another term for specific points on the pure, clear range of the color wheel.

**Incandescent Lighting:** A bulb (lamp) that converts electric power into light by passing electric current through a filament of tungsten wire.

**Indirect Lighting:** A more subdued type of lighting that is not head-on, but rather reflected against another surface such as a ceiling.

**Inlay:** A decoration, usually consisting of stained wood, metal, or mother-of-pearl, that is set into the surface of an object in a pattern and finished flush.

**Lumen:** The measurement of a source's light output—the quantity of visible light.

**Molding:** An architectural band used to trim a line where materials join or create a linear decoration. It is typically made of wood, plaster, or a polymer.

**Neoclassic:** Any revival of the ancient styles of Greece and Rome, particularly during the late eighteenth and early nineteenth centuries.

**Panel:** A flat, rectangular piece of material that forms part of a wall, door, or cabinet. Typically made of wood, it is usually framed by a border and either raised or recessed.

**Pattern Matching:** To align a repeating pattern when joining together two pieces of fabric or wallpaper.

**Pediment:** A triangular piece found over doors, windows, and occasionally mantles. It also refers to a low-pitched gable on the front of a building.

**Peninsula:** A countertop, with or without a base cabinet, that is connected at one end to a wall or another counter and extends outward, providing access on three sides.

**Primary Color:** Red, blue, or yellow that can't be produced in pigments by mixing other colors. Primaries plus black and white, in turn, combine to make all the other hues.

**Secondary Color:** A mix of two primaries. The secondary colors are orange, green, and purple.

**Task Lighting:** Directional lighting that concentrates in specific areas for tasks, such as preparing food, applying makeup, reading, or doing crafts.

**Tone:** Degree of lightness or darkness of a color.

**Track Lighting:** Lighting that utilizes a fixed band that supplies a current to movable light fixtures.

**Trompe L'oeil:** French for "fool the eye"; a painted mural in which realistic images and the illusion of three-dimensional space are created.

**Tufting:** The fabric of an upholstered piece or a mattress that is drawn tightly to secure the padding, creating regularly spaced indentations.

# index

# photo credits

page 1: Beth Singer page 2: Eric Roth page 6: Eric Roth, architect: Chris Walsh & Co. Architects page 8: Karyn R. Millet page 10: Eric Roth page 11: Karyn R. Millet page 12: Tria Giovan page 13: Tria Giovan page 14: *top right* Eric Roth, design: Benjamin Nutter; *bottom right* Anne Gummerson; *left* Tria Giovan pages 16–17: *both* Julian Wass, design: Diamond Baratta Design page 18: Karyn R. Millet, design: Bonesteel Trout Hall page 19: Mark Lohman page 21: Joseph De Leo pages 22–23: *all* Mark Lohman pages 24–25: *all* Eric Roth, design: John DeBastiani Interior Design page 26: Tria Giovan page 27: Mark Lohman page 28: *both* Jessie Walker, design: Donna Aylesworth page 29: Jessie Walker, design: Kim Elias of Truffles pages 30-31: *all* Mark Lohman pages 32–33: *all* Karyn R. Millet, design: Sheldon Harte page 34: Thomas McConnell page 36: Eric Roth, design: Susan Sargent Design pages 38–41: *both* Bob Greenspan, stylist: Susan Andrews pages 42–43: *both* Karyn R. Millet, design: Bonesteel Trout Hall page 44: Ngoc Minh Ngo, design: Rob Southern page 45: *left* Ngoc Minh Ngo, design: Abigail Turin; *right* Julian Wass, design: Miles Redd page 46: *both* Tony Giammarino/Giammarino & Dworkin, design: Susan Eckis page 48: *top* Bob Greenspan, stylist: Susan Andrews; *bottom right* Eric Roth; *bottom left* Eric Roth, design: Susan Sargent Design page 49: Eric Roth, design: Peter Niemitz Design page 50: Bob Greenspan, stylist: Susan Andrews page 51: Eric Roth, design: Peter Niemitz Design pages 52–53: *all* Mark Lohman pages 54–55: Ngoc Minh Ngo, design: Thomas Paul page 56: Casey Dunn page 58: Todd Caverly page 59: Beth Singer pages 60–61: *all* Joseph De Leo, design: Jonathan Taylor Design

page 62: *left* Mark Lohman; *right* Greg Hursley page 63: *top* Mark Lohman; *bottom* Casey Dunn page 65: Joseph De Leo, architect: Andrew Mann page 66: Karyn R. Millet, design: Sheldon Harte page 67: *both* Mark Lohman page 68: Mark Samu page 69: *top* Jessie Walker, design: Lee Youngsberg; *bottom* Bob Greenspan, stylist: Susan Andrews page 70: courtesy of Seagull Lighting page 71: Casey Dunn page 72: Tony Giammarino/Giammarino & Dworkin, design: Fran Decker page 73: Tony Giammarino/Giammarino & Dworkin, design: Todd Yoggy page 74: Mark Samu page 75: Mark Lohman pages 76–77: *all* Greg Hursley pages 78–79: Thomas McConnell pages 80–81: Mark Lohman page 82: Ngoc Minh Ngo, design: Jonathan Adler page 84: courtesy of Teragren page 85: courtesy of Robbins/Armstrong pages 86–87: *both* courtesy of Bruce pages 88–89: *all* courtesy of Armstrong pages 90–91: *both* Mark Lohman page 92: www.davidduncanlivingston.com page 93: Mark Lohman page 94: Ngoc Minh Ngo, design: Denise Canter page 95: Mark Lohman page 96: Anne Gummerson, design: Darryl Savage, DHS Design page 97: Anne Gummerson, design: Brennan + Company Architects page 98: *top* courtesy of Mannington; *bottom* Mark Samu page 99: Robert Perron page 100: *top* courtesy of Island Stone; *bottom right* www.davidduncanlivingston.com; *bottom left* courtesy of Mannington page 101: www.davidduncanlivingston.com page 102: Eric Roth pages 104–105: *both* www.davidduncanlivingston.com page 106: *both* Eric Roth, design: Chris Walsh & Company Architects page 107: *both* www.davidduncanlivingston.com page 108: *top & bottom right* www.davidduncanlivingston.com; *bottom left* Tony Giammarino/Giammarino

& Dworkin page 109: *left* Beth Singer; *right* Tony Giammarino/Giammarino & Dworkin page 110: melabee m miller, faux painter: Dan Mulligan page 111: *top* melabee m miller, design: Laurie Fritz ASID; *bottom both* Don Wong/CH page 112: Mark Samu page 113: Mark Lohman pages 114–115: *both* Mark Lohman page 116: courtesy of Thibaut page 117: *top* Karyn R. Millet, design: Michael Foster; *bottom* Mark Lohman page 118: *left* www.davidduncanlivingston.com; *right* Tony Giammarino/Giammarino & Dworkin page 119: *left* Tony Giammarino/Giammarino & Dworkin; *right* Ngoc Minh Ngo, design: Richard Keith Langham page 120: *top* Mark Lohman; *bottom* www.davidduncanlivingston.com page 121: *left* www.davidduncanlivingston.com; *right* Tony Giammarino/Giammarino & Dworkin page 122: www.davidduncanlivingston.com page 123: *top* Beth Singer; *bottom* Mark Lohman page 125: Beth Singer page 126: *left* Tony Giammarino/Giammarino & Dworkin; *right* Eric Roth, design: CJ Designs page 127: *left* www.davidduncanlivingston.com; *right* Tony Giammarino/Giammarino & Dworkin page 128: *all* www.davidduncanlivingston.com page 129: Mark Lohman pages 130–131: *all* Mark Lohman page 132: www.davidduncanlivingston.com page 134: *top* Tony Giammarino/Giammarino & Dworkin, design & hand painting: B. Scherr; *bottom* www.davidduncanlivingston.com page 135: Deborah Sherman page 136: Eric Roth, architect: Benjamin Nutter Associates page 137: Karyn R. Millet, design: Elizabeth Dinkel page 138: www.davidduncanlivingston.com page 139: *top* Eric Roth; *bottom* Beth Singer page 140: Eric Roth page 141: *both* Tony Giammarino/Giammarino & Dworkin, design: www.WendyUmanoff.com page

142: *top* Karyn R. Millet; *bottom both* Karyn R. Millet, design: Michael Foster **pages 143:** Eric Roth, design: Peter Niemitz Design **page 144:** Eric Roth, design: Molly Skok Design **page 145:** Eric Roth, design: Peter Niemitz Design **page 147:** Tony Giammarino/Giammarino & Dworkin **pages 148–151:** *all* www.davidduncanlivingston.com **page 152:** Bob Greenspan, stylist: Susan Andrews **page 154:** Karyn R. Millet, design: Bonesteel Trout Hall **page 155:** Karyn R. Millet **pages 156–157:** Karyn R. Millet, design: Bonesteel Trout Hall **page 158:** *top* Karyn R. Millet, design: Elizabeth Dinkel; *bottom* Deborah Sherman **page 159:** Anne Gummerson **pages 160:** Eric Roth, design: Susan Curren Interior Design **page 161:** Eric Roth **page 162:** Eric Roth, design: Kathleen Sullivan Elliott Interior Design **page 163:** *left* Eric Roth, design: Hamilburg Interiors; *right* Eric Roth **page 165:** Ngoc Minh Ngo **page 166:** Deborah Sherman **page 167:** Karyn R. Millet, design: Elizabeth Dinkel **page 168:** Bob Greenspan, stylist: Susan Andrews **page 169:** Joseph De Leo **page 170:** Eric Roth **page 171:** Bjorg Magnea **pages 172–175:** *all* Olson Photography, LLC **page 176:** Karyn R. Millet **page 178:** *both* Karyn R. Millet **page 179:** Deborah Sherman **pages 180–181:** *all* Karyn R. Millet, design: Elizabeth Dinkel **pages 182–183:** *both* Anne Gummerson **pages 184–185:** *all* Joseph De Leo **pages 186–187:** *both* Bob Greenspan, stylist: Susan Andrews **pages 188–189:** *both* Karyn R. Millet, design: Bonesteel Trout Hall **page 190:** Karyn R. Millet **page 191:** *top* Anne Gummerson, architect: Hammond-Wilson Architect; *bottom* Deborah Sherman **page 192:** Eric Roth **page 193:** *top* Eric Roth; *bottom both* Karyn R. Millet, design: Elizabeth Dinkel **page 194:** Eric Roth **page 195:** *top* Karyn R.

Millet, design: Elizabeth Dinkel; *bottom* Julian Wass **page 197:** *both* Eric Roth **pages 198–199:** *both* Deborah Sherman **page 201:** Beth Singer **pages 202–205:** *all* Eric Roth **page 206:** Tria Giovan **page 208:** www.davidduncanlivingston.com **page 209:** Bob Greenspan, stylist: Susan Andrews **page 217:** Mark Lohman, design: Kyser Interiors **page 218:** Mark Samu, design: Paula Yedyank **page 219:** Mark Samu, courtesy of Hearst Magazines **page 220:** *left* Mark Lohman, design: Janet Lohman Interior Design; *right* Mark Samu, design: Jean Stoffer **page 221:** Mark Lohman, design: Cheryl Hamilton-Gray **pages 222–223:** *top* Anne Gummerson, design: Gina Fitzsimmons, Fitzsimmons Design Associates; *bottom right* www.davidduncanlivingston.com; *bottom center* Tony Giammarino/Giammarino & Dworkin; *left* Mark Samu, design: Ken Kelly **page 224:** Mark Samu, design: Ken Kelly **page 225:** *top both* Mark Samu, design: Jean Stoffer; *bottom* Mark Samu **pages 226–227:** *left* www.davidduncanlivingston.com; *center* Mark Samu; *right* courtesy of Formica **page 228:** *top* www.davidduncanlivingston.com; *bottom* Mark Samu, design: Sam Scofield AIA **page 229:** *top* www.davidduncanlivingston.com; *bottom* Mark Samu, design: Lucianna Samu **page 230:** Tria Giovan **page 231:** *top* Mark Samu, builder: Access Builders; *bottom* courtesy of Sonoma **pages 232–233:** *all* Tria Giovan **pages 234–235:** *all* Mark Samu, design: Jean Stoffer **page 236:** Paul Bardagjy, architect: Nik Holland **page 238:** Mark Lohman **page 242:** Mark Lohman **page 243:** Beth Singer, design: Jeffrey King Interiors & Richard Ross Interiors, archtitect: Bryce McCalpin & Palazzola Architects, builder: Ray Wallick **page 244:** *top right & bottom right*

www.davidduncanlivingston.com; *bottom left* Mark Samu, courtesy of Hearst Magazines **page 245:** *top* www.davidduncanlivingston.com; *bottom* Mark Samu, courtesy of Hearst Magazines **page 246:** www.davidduncanlivingston.com **page 247:** Minh + Wass **page 248:** Mark Samu, design: Lee Najman **page 249:** Mark Samu, design: The Tile Studio **page 250:** courtesy of Moen **page 251:** courtesy of Kohler **page 252:** *left* courtesy of DEX Studios; *right* Mark Samu, design: Sherrill Canet **page 254:** Minh + Wass, tile & design: Bisazza Mosaica **page 255:** Mark Samu, design: Lucianna Samu **page 256:** Mark Samu, courtesy of Hearst magazines **page 257:** photo & design: Brukoff Design Associates **page 258:** Mark Samu **page 259:** www.davidduncanlivingston.com **page 260:** Tria Giovan **page 261:** *left* Mark Samu, design: Lucianna Samu; *right* Mark Samu, builder: Bonaccio Construction **pages 262–263:** Nancy Elizabeth Hill, design: Diane Burgoyne Interiors **pages 264–265:** Mark Lohman, design: Harte Brownlee & Assoc. **page 266:** Mark Lohman **pages 268–271:** *all* www.davidduncanlivingston.com **page 272:** *top* www.davidduncanlivingston.com; *bottom left* Julian Wass; *bottom right* Mark Lohman **page 273:** *top* www.davidduncanlivingston.com; *bottom* Tony Giammarino/Giammarino & Dworkin **page 274:** Tony Giammarino/Giammarino & Dworkin, design: Reggie Case **page 275:** www.davidduncanlivingston.com **page 276:** *both* www.davidduncanlivingston.com **page 277:** *top* Tony Giammarino/Giammarino & Dworkin, design: Maureen Klein; *bottom* www.davidduncanlivingston.com **pages 278–279:** www.davidduncanlivingston.com **pages 280–281:** *all* Karyn R. Millet **page 282–283:** Julian Wass

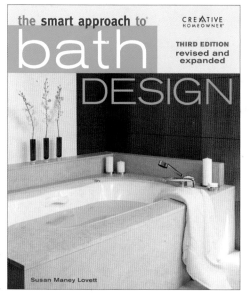

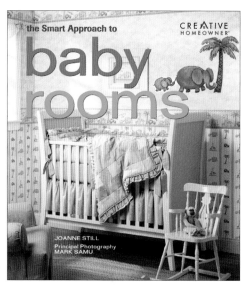